International ESG Perspectives

Karolina Łudzińska

International ESG Perspectives

Polish, European and Global Contexts

palgrave
macmillan

Karolina Łudzińska
Faculty of Management
University of Warsaw
Warsaw, Poland

ISBN 978-3-032-11665-9 ISBN 978-3-032-11666-6 (eBook)
https://doi.org/10.1007/978-3-032-11666-6

Translation from the Polish language edition: "Od społecznej odpowiedzialności do ESG w zarządzaniu" by Karolina Łudzińska, © Copyright by Wydawnictwa Uniwersytetu Warszawskiego, Sekcja Wydawnicza Wydziału Zarządzania Uniwersytetu Warszawskiego, Warszawa 2024. Published by University of Warsaw Press. All Rights Reserved.

The original submitted manuscript has been translated into English. The translation was done using artificial intelligence. A subsequent revision was performed by the author(s) to further refine the work and to ensure that the translation is appropriate concerning content and scientific correctness. It may, however, read stylistically different from a conventional translation.

This Palgrave Macmillan imprint is published by the registered company Springer Nature Switzerland AG.
The registered company address is: Gewerbestrasse 11, 6330 Cham, Switzerland

Acknowledgments This monograph serves to expand upon and complement the issues that have been presented in the book entitled "Od społecznej odpowiedzialności do ESG w zarządzaniu. Wybrane aspekty" (Łudzińska, 2024), authored by the same researcher and published in Polish by University of Warsaw Press. The author is indebted to the University of Warsaw for its invaluable support in the development of the preceding work, which established the conceptual foundations for the present study.

Competing Interests The author has no competing interests to declare that are relevant to the content of this manuscript.

About this Book

The monograph *International ESG Perspectives: Polish, European and Global Contexts* provides a comprehensive and timely analysis of how ESG principles are reshaping organisational and financial practices in Poland, with attention to broader European and global developments. The publication focuses specifically on the evolving ESG agenda, its institutionalisation, and the implications of new EU regulations such as the CSRD and CSDDD directives. Utilising a qualitative and comparative approach, the book undertakes a comprehensive examination of ESG integration within Polish companies, the emergence of ESG financial instruments, the evolution of ESG indices on the Warsaw Stock Exchange, and the development of socially responsible investment strategies. The study addresses critical challenges, including inconsistencies in ESG ratings, rising regulatory complexity, and growing backlash, particularly in the United States, while highlighting the European Union's dual role as both an adopter and co-shaper of ESG standards. The publication not only surveys regulatory and market transformations, but also offers an original conceptual model framing ESG as a process of continuous improvement. Conducted between 2021 and 2025, the project combines a narrative literature review, comparative analysis, and synthesis of legal, financial, and institutional sources. The result is a multidimensional and context-sensitive account of ESG implementation, tailored to local specificities while informed by international experience. This book serves as a useful reference for researchers, practitioners, and policymakers navigating the increasingly complex landscape of sustainable management, corporate governance and finance.

Contents

About the Author

Karolina Łudzińska is a scholar with an interdisciplinary academic background, holding degrees in Pedagogy and Business Culture from the University of Warsaw, and a PhD in Economics from the Warsaw School of Economics. She is currently an Assistant Professor at the Faculty of Management, University of Warsaw, where she also serves as the Faculty's Equality Plenipotentiary. Her research focuses on Corporate Social Responsibility (CSR), Environmental, Social, and Governance (ESG), sustainability, shared value creation, stakeholder management, and executive education. She is an active member of the Academy of Management and the European Academy of Management. Dr. Łudzińska teaches in both Polish and English across undergraduate and graduate programmes. Her courses include Principles of Management, CSR, Business Ethics, Sustainable Development Management, and Sustainable Value Chains, delivered also within the Erasmus program, and Sustainable Supply Chains in the Food Sector, taught as part of the international Master in Food Systems program.

List of Figures

List of Tables

CHAPTER 1

Introduction

Despite the considerable progress witnessed in the past decade in terms of global economic growth and technological development, particularly with regard to the widespread adoption of artificial intelligence, these developments have occurred alongside significant environmental and social challenges. The prevailing economic development model has been shown to have certain inherent limitations, as evidenced by a number of factors, including ecosystem degradation, climate change, growing social inequalities, deepening divisions and political-economic tensions. Consequently, there has been an increase in the expectations placed upon businesses by legislators, regulators, management theorists and practitioners, business owners and shareholders, employees, consumers and the general public.

According to the World Bank (2024), the global population living in extreme poverty, defined as individuals with an income of less than $2.15 per day, is estimated to be approximately 700 million. Concurrently, cyclical studies conducted by Credit Suisse indicate that global wealth accumulated at the conclusion of 2020, reaching a novel zenith of $418.3 trillion (representing an augmentation of 7.4% in nominal terms when compared with the preceding year) (Credit Suisse, 2021). At the same time, 2.9 billion individuals, constituting 55% of the global adult population, possessed assets amounting to less than $10,000. As demonstrated in the international studies conducted by the World Inequality Lab (2023), similar patterns emerge. These studies were conducted by 100 researchers over the years

K. Łudzińska, *International ESG Perspectives*,
https://doi.org/10.1007/978-3-032-11666-6_1

2018–2022, under the direction of an international group of economists, including Chancel, Piketty, Saez and Zucman. As demonstrated in the research, in 2021, the economic elite, representing 10% of the global population, possessed a considerable proportion of 52% of the world's income (World Inequality Lab, 2023). The data indicate that the poorest half of the global population received a mere 8.5% of this income. This finding suggests that the annual income of a statistical representative of the wealthiest echelon of the population (the top 10%) was approximately $122,100, whereas an individual from the poorest half of the population earned a mere $3920 per annum (World Inequality Lab, 2023).

Humanity is also confronted with profound ecological challenges that threaten the stability of natural systems. In the year 2025, seven out of nine planetary boundaries were found to have been breached, by Planetary Health Check (2025). These boundaries include climate change, biosphere integrity, land system change, freshwater, biogeochemical flows, novel entities and ocean acidification. The WWF organisation has expressed concern over the findings of its Living Planet Index (LPI), which encompasses over 38,000 populations of mammals, birds, reptiles, amphibians and fish. The organisation has reported a 69% decrease in the LPI in 2022 compared to 1970, indicating a substantial decline in the size of vertebrate species populations on Earth, amounting to nearly two-thirds of the total population (Westveer et al., 2022). Moreover, the planet's natural resources are being depleted. As analyses indicate, in order to meet present needs, it would be necessary to have not one, but at least 1.6 planets (World Wildlife Fund, n.d.). It is evident that the present generation is living on ecological credit and perpetually depleting its own natural capital, thereby significantly impeding the ability of future generations to live. The recent synthetic UN report on climate change, published in 2023, is similarly not optimistic (IPCC, 2023). The emission of greenhouse gases is causing progressive warming and climate change on Earth. The report indicates that in order to limit climate change, a substantial and ongoing reduction in emissions is necessary. In the period between 2011 and 2020, the average global temperature increased by 1.1°C compared to the 1850–1900 period. Since 1970, the global surface temperature of the Earth has increased at a rate unprecedented in the last 200 years. Furthermore, the adverse effects of climate change, caused by human activity, are projected to intensify.

Despite the challenges outlined above, corporate engagement in social and environmental initiatives remained largely voluntary and non-binding until recently. Nevertheless, recent years have witnessed considerable changes in this domain. From a European and Polish perspective, two key regulatory developments now define the scope of corporate social and environmental responsibility as well as reporting obligations: the Corporate Sustainability Reporting Directive (CSRD) (European Parliament & Council, 2022) and the Corporate Sustainability Due Diligence Directive (CSDDD or CS3D) (European Parliament & Council, 2024). The first of these, the CSRD, introduces a requirement for leading companies in the European Union to report on their sustainability-related activities with effect from 1st January 2025. This directive stipulates that non-financial reports must be prepared in accordance with the new, uniform European Sustainability Reporting Standards (ESRS) (European Commission, 2023). The second of these, the CSDDD, addresses the company's impacts across its value chains and establishes an obligation to implement due diligence procedures concerning human rights and environmental issues. Originally scheduled to take effect on 1 January 2027, this requirement has recently been postponed by two years (European Commission, 2025).

The aforementioned documents have become pivotal components of the EU's strategy for sustainable development, incorporating key environmental, social and corporate governance aspects into corporate activities. Drawing upon these findings, as well as earlier EU directives and regulations and the achievements of research, practices and management methods in the field of corporate social responsibility (CSR), a coherent perspective is currently being formulated for the implementation of the Environmental, Social and Governance concept in organisational practice.

The concept of Environmental, Social and Governance (ESG) was initially formulated in 2004, as detailed in a report entitled *Who Cares Wins. Connecting Financial Markets to a Changing World*, a project developed by a consortium of 20 financial institutions in response to the initiative of the UN Secretary-General, Kofi Annan (UN, 2004). The impetus for the conceptualisation of the ESG framework stemmed from the need expressed by financial market participants to develop universal criteria that would enable investors, analysts and other stakeholders to evaluate companies in terms of their potential investment attractiveness. This evaluation would encompass not only financial aspects but also non-financial dimensions. Since then, the integration of environmental, social and corporate governance factors has gained importance as one of the most widely used indicators of social, ecological and responsible management and investing worldwide.

The development of universal, coherent ESG assessment frameworks is an ongoing endeavour with a wide range of institutions, companies and organisations involved. The International Monetary Fund (IMF) has indicated that ESG issues have the potential to exert a significant influence on the profitability of companies. The IMF has recommended that lawmakers and regulators collaborate on the development of consistent guidelines for assessing companies' ESG performance and disclosing non-financial information. The purpose of this collaboration is twofold: firstly, to promote transparency and accountability, and secondly, to incorporate environmental aspects into business and investment decisions (International Monetary Fund, 2019). The IMF also emphasises the importance of developing a comprehensive approach to ESG, to fill growing data gaps through standardisation of ESG terminology and support for consistent ESG reporting by companies, which will facilitate the process of collecting and assessing ESG data for stakeholders. In a similar vein, the Organisation for Economic Cooperation and Development (OECD) has advocated for the establishment of global guidelines, while the World Economic Forum has announced its collaboration with prominent consulting firms to develop universal ESG monitoring standards (Boffo, 2020).

Concurrently, ESG assessments have evolved into an integral element of investment decision-making, with investors and regulators adopting them as a primary instrument for evaluating the social, environmental and governance performance of companies (Wan et al., 2024). Preliminary research findings suggest that ESG assessments are an effective and objective means of measuring companies' ESG performance. This provides investors and regulators with comparable and comprehensive information, thereby supporting the elimination of information asymmetry (Cappucci, 2018). However, market practice has begun to reveal inconsistencies in ESG assessments and ratings, reflecting substantial methodological discrepancies, including the so-called 'rater effect' (e.g. Berg et al., 2022; Christensen et al., 2022; Dimson et al., 2020).

In the context of mounting scepticism towards ESG, particularly evident in the American market, the necessity for a comprehensive and nuanced analysis is paramount. In 2023, a study conducted by The

Conference Board among over 100 large American companies found that nearly half of the respondents had experienced opposition to ESG, and 61% predicted that this trend would continue or intensify over the next two years (The Conference Board, 2023). In 2024, Larry Fink, the Chief Executive Officer of BlackRock—the world's largest asset management company—announced that he would no longer utilise the term 'ESG' in the context of the company's investment strategy (Chatterji & Toffel, 2024). Concurrently, prominent investment banks, including Morgan Stanley, Bank of America, Wells Fargo, Goldman Sachs and Citi, have withdrawn from the Net-Zero Banking Alliance, a UN initiative aimed at achieving zero greenhouse gas emissions by 2050 (Bloomberg, 2025). Meanwhile, Morningstar data indicates that in 2023, American sustainable funds recorded annual capital outflows for the first time—a total of 13 billion dollars was withdrawn from ESG-focused investments (Stankiewicz, 2024). Notwithstanding this trend, larger ESG funds exhibited financial resilience, with the median return for investors amounting to 24.4%, a result that surpassed that achieved by the S&P 500 index in the same year (Stankiewicz, 2024).

Evidence of shifts in the approach to ESG practices is apparent in both the United States and Europe. The European Commission proposed the so-called *Omnibus I* package, a set of simplifications concerning sustainable development reporting, as the first stage of a broader initiative aimed at reducing excessive regulatory complexity and administrative burdens imposed on European enterprises (European Commission, 2025). This initiative was announced in response to mounting opposition from business circles and certain member states, which voiced criticism on the grounds that the existing ESG reporting requirements were overly complex and costly, especially those resulting from the aforementioned directive on sustainability reporting, CSRD (European Parliament & Council, 2022), and the directive on corporate due diligence in the areas of human rights and environmental sustainability, CSDDD (European Parliament & Council, 2024). As scepticism towards ESG grows, leading to the withdrawal from sustainable development initiatives, even by leading institutions, companies find themselves compelled to operate in an increasingly unstable environment, often rife with conflicting expectations. On the one hand, there is a sense of pressure to refrain from engaging in politics; on the other hand, there is a call to actively participate in the pursuit of solutions to the prevalent civilisational challenges (Winston, 2024).

The concept of ESG has been predominantly discussed in the literature from a global or pan-European perspective, while its local context remains relatively underexplored. Research indicates that a localised approach is crucial for interpreting and implementing ESG practices, as geographical conditions and local regulatory frameworks significantly shape how organisations apply ESG principles (see, Adamska et al., 2015; Baldini et al., 2018; Daugaard & Ding, 2022). The cultural context, which is capable of determining the terminology used and the understanding of concepts related to sustainability, remains equally important (Aldowaish et al., 2022). Research indicates that the term 'responsible investing' is predominantly employed in the UK, while in the context of France or the United States, it is frequently disregarded, particularly when it does not incorporate key social dimensions (Sandberg et al., 2009).

This study aims to address a gap in the existing body of literature by examining the experiences of the Polish local market in the context of broader global and European ESG developments. As a long-standing member of the European Union, Poland cannot be considered an 'isolated island'. It joined the EU on 1 May 2004, the same year that the concept of ESG criteria first emerged. Like the ESG dimensions, Poland has now reached a level of maturity that enables it to adapt to European regulations and initiatives, as well as actively contribute to the development of new guidelines.

The primary research focus of this monograph is on the extent and manner in which ESG factors shape organisational practices and financial market development in Poland, with particular attention paid to their relationship with European and global experience. The objective of the analysis is threefold: firstly, to showcase the market specifics and best practices; secondly, to facilitate comparisons of the analysed processes and phenomena; and thirdly, to identify barriers and factors conducive to the effective implementation of ESG aspects in the national context.

As part of the research, detailed questions were formulated with the aim of determining the key factors of ESG aspect integration in the Polish market against the backdrop of the same processes in the European and global markets. The following questions were posed for discussion: firstly, what are the dominant strategies for integrating ESG aspects at the organisational level, and how do these comply with best practices recommended by international, European and local guidelines? The research interest also encompassed the manner in which Polish organisations perceive the role of ESG aspects in management, as well as the factors that facilitate and hinder their implementation. The study also examined the functionality of socially responsible investment (SRI) strategies in Poland, and the extent to which they align with trends observed in global markets, including those in Europe. The research also posed the question of what factors determine the effectiveness of socially responsible investment in Poland compared to other capital markets. The present study seeks to explore the significance of the diversity of ESG financial instruments, such as green bonds or responsible investment funds, for the development of sustainable investments in the Polish and global markets. The purpose of this study is to ascertain the key differences between traditional investing and ESG investing, and their effectiveness in the Polish, European and global market. The analysis also covered the significance of introducing ESG indices on the Warsaw Stock Exchange and their impact on the development of the domestic sustainable investment market. A significant element of the research endeavour was to assess the extent to which the European Union guidelines on non-financial reporting are being implemented by Polish organisations, and the challenges associated with this process. A final attempt was made to evaluate the potential for additional advancement of ESG in Poland within the framework of relevant EU directives and international trends.

The objective of this monograph is to address the research questions by means of an in-depth analysis of the development of the ESG concept and its adoption across global, European and Polish markets. The study further aims to identify the prevailing challenges pertaining to organisational management in the context of environmental, social and corporate governance issues. Furthermore, the monograph functions as a compendium of knowledge, presenting the findings of ESG-related research at the global, European and Polish levels, in addition to leading standards, guidelines, and relevant international, pan-European and local regulations.

The research underlying this monograph was conducted by the author between September 2021 and April 2025 in collaboration with research assistants, who were students of Wolfson College at the University of Cambridge and the Faculty of Management at the University of Warsaw. The assistants, who committed to the project on a voluntary basis and outside of their working hours, assisted in the research process by collecting data, academic studies and papers, expert reports, legal regulations and other relevant documents and source materials.

The present study serves to expand upon and complement the issues presented in the monograph 'Od społecznej odpowiedzialności do ESG w zarządzaniu. Wybrane aspekty' (Łudzińska, 2024), authored by the same researcher and published in Polish by the University of Warsaw Press. In contrast to the preceding study, the present study focuses exclusively on ESG issues, referring to the concept of corporate social responsibility only to the extent necessary to demonstrate its genesis and evolution. Following the publication of the inaugural monograph, considerable changes have transpired within the domain of ESG regulations and practices, particularly at the European Union level. Consequently, this study not only builds upon the foundations laid by preceding research, but also incorporates the most recent regulatory developments, prevailing trends, and current guidelines that are influencing the approach to sustainable management.

The research process underpinning this monograph was based on a set of complementary qualitative methods, allowing for a multifaceted analysis of ESG integration in the Polish context and its connections to international experiences and research findings. A critical review of the scientific literature, prior research results, expert reports and official documents, including EU directives, national regulations and legal acts, played a central role in this process. The narrative review method was utilised, thus facilitating the systematisation and interpretation of a wide spectrum of sources and the capture of the evolution of approaches to ESG in different regulatory and institutional contexts. A pivotal component of the analysis employed the comparative method, utilising this approach to identify both similarities and differences in the development of ESG practices between Poland and a selection of European and global countries. Furthermore, a range of analytical and synthetic methods were employed, facilitating the integration of data from multiple research sources. This approach was complemented by the descriptive method, allowing for an in-depth examination of selected issues, such as the implementation of non-financial reporting or local initiatives related to ESG indices. The methodological triangulation employed in this study yielded a comprehensive and nuanced understanding of the subject matter.

The application of the aforementioned research methodologies enabled the development of a comprehensive and multidimensional approach to the issue under scrutiny. Consequently, this facilitated the identification of pivotal mechanisms and conditions for ESG integration in Poland, whilst also situating these processes within a broader European and global context. Accordingly, this monograph presents up-to-date information, analyses of previous research findings, and the latest guidelines relevant to the

Polish ESG market, primarily within a European context. Concurrently, it provides an original analysis of the evolution of ESG factor integration in Poland, examined in relation to practices adopted in other countries. The study discusses the concept of socially responsible investing, exploring its effectiveness in both Poland and leading global markets. It also examines the introduction of ESG indices on the Warsaw Stock Exchange and global ESG indices. Furthermore, it delves into the status and guidelines for non-financial reporting in the European Union, including Poland, along with the simplifications and deferrals of non-financial reporting obligations planned in the *Omnibus I* package in EU countries.

The analyses presented in this monograph are conducted primarily from an organisational (firm-level) perspective, giving them a micro-level focus centred on the operations of individual entities rather than a macroeconomic approach encompassing the broader economy. This orientation facilitates a more profound comprehension of the processes involved in implementing and adapting ESG aspects within the practices of organisations and markets, with a particular emphasis on the financial market. Nevertheless, the conclusions drawn from the analyses offer a wider range of implications and can provide valuable indications about the level of acceptance and potential for ESG development in a local, sector or national market.

For the purposes of this study, the terms 'enterprise', 'company' and 'organisation' are used interchangeably. Firstly, within the domain of business and management literature, these concepts are frequently employed synonymously. However, it should be noted that these terms may vary in both meaning and scope of reference across different academic disciplines. Secondly, the adoption of such a solution is predicated on the assumption that the monograph focuses on universal aspects of ESG, which apply to different organisational forms, regardless of their legal status or ownership structure. The employment of these terms in an interchangeable manner facilitates a more seamless presentation of content, circumvents superfluous repetitions, and evades excessive terminological precision, which has the potential to distract the reader and compromise the coherence of the message.

The monograph is organised into nine chapters.

- Chapter Two introduces the concept of Environmental, Social and Governance, focusing on its development and integration in both Poland and the global context. It explores the relationship between

ESG and Corporate Social Responsibility (CSR), discusses the core principles and practical applications of ESG, and outlines key milestones in its evolution within management theory and practice. This chapter also addresses the challenges associated with implementing ESG and its acceptance and integration in the Polish market.

- The next chapter analyses the current state and prospects for ESG development both in business operations and in financial markets in Poland, Europe and worldwide. It discusses the scale of ESG assets in Poland and other countries, as well as the degree of their integration in Polish companies, taking into account the global context. This chapter provides an analysis of the current state and possible directions of ESG development on the global and Polish market.
- The fourth chapter focuses on investing in accordance with ESG principles and socially responsible investing (SRI) in the global, European and Polish markets. It discusses the characteristic features of these forms of investing and their specifics in different markets, including the Polish market.
- The fifth chapter discusses ways of financing ESG investments used both in Poland and worldwide. It presents leading ESG financial instruments, their requirements and characteristic features. It also discusses responsible investments in the Polish market, including banking products, real estate, investment funds and debt financing.
- The sixth chapter focuses on ESG indices present on the Polish capital market, analysing 15 years of experience and conclusions drawn from them. It analyses the history of ESG index development on global markets and on the Warsaw Stock Exchange, with particular emphasis on its two indices: RESPECT Index and WIG-ESG, including their composition, methodology and performance assessment.
- The seventh chapter deals with the effectiveness of socially responsible investing and presents research results on this issue both in the markets internationally and in Poland. The effectiveness of SRI investing in leading capital markets and the Polish market is analysed, allowing for an assessment of the effectiveness of these investments in different contexts.
- The penultimate, eighth chapter, is devoted to non-financial reporting, with an emphasis on current international guidelines and challenges associated with their implementation. Non-financial reporting in Poland is also presented, including the current state and guidelines

for non-financial reporting in the Polish market, including proposals for simplifying EU regulations in the field of sustainable development is covered by the *Omnibus I* package.

The monograph concludes with a chapter presenting key findings and recommendations derived from the preceding discussions and analyses. It also introduces an original conceptual model that frames the approach to ESG as a process of continuous improvement. This model not only synthesises the results of previous research but also outlines directions for future inquiry, serving as a foundation for further theoretical and empirical studies. In doing so, the study not only addresses an existing gap in the literature but also encourages continued reflection on the role of ESG in shaping contemporary management theory and practice.

References

Adamska, A., Dąbrowski, T. J., & Grygiel-Tomaszewska, A. (2015). Społecznie odpowiedzialne inwestowanie w Polsce na tle sytuacji w wybranych krajach Unii Europejskiej. *Nauki O Finansach*, *2*(23), 73–95.

Aldowaish, A., Kokuryo, J., Almazyad, O., & Goi, H. C. (2022). Environmental, social, and governance integration into the business model: Literature review and research agenda. *Sustainability*, *14*(5). https://doi.org/10.3390/su14052959 (Article 5).

Baldini, M., Maso, L. D., Liberatore, G., Mazzi, F., & Terzani, S. (2018). Role of country- and firm-level determinants in environmental, social, and governance disclosure. *Journal of Business Ethics*, *150*(1), 79–98. https://doi.org/10.1007/s10551-016-3139-1

Berg, F., Köelbel, J. F., & Rigobon, R. (2022). Aggregate confusion: The divergence of ESG ratings. *Review of Finance*, *26*(6), 1315–1344. https://doi.org/10.1093/rof/rfac033

Bloomberg. (2025, January 2). *Morgan stanley follows Citi, BofA in quitting climate group*. Retrieved January 8, 2025, from https://www.bloomberg.com/news/articles/2025-01-02/morgan-stanley-leaves-net-zero-alliance-for-banks

Boffo, R. R. P. (2020). *ESG investing: Practices, progress and challenges*. OECD. https://www.oecd.org/finance/ESG-Investing-Practices-Progress-Challenges.pdf

Cappucci, M. (2018). The ESG integration paradox. *Journal of Applied Corporate Finance*, *30*(2), 22–28. https://doi.org/10.1111/jacf.12296

Chatterji, A., Ronnie, & Toffel, M. W. (2024, September 20). It's time to unbundle ESG. *Harvard business review*. Retrieved January 9, 2025, from https://hbr.org/2024/09/its-time-to-unbundle-esg

Christensen, D. M., Serafeim, G., & Sikochi, A. (2022). Why is corporate virtue in the eye of the beholder? The case of ESG ratings. *The Accounting Review*, *97* (1), 147–175. https://doi.org/10.1111/jacf.12296

Credit Suisse. (2021). *Credit suisse 2021 global wealth report*. Retrieved February 18, 2025, from https://docs.dpaq.de/17706-global-wealth-report-2021-en.pdf

Daugaard, D., & Ding, A. (2022). Global drivers for esg performance: The body of knowledge. *Sustainability*, *14*(4), 4. https://doi.org/10.3390/su14042322

Dimson, E., Marsh, P., & Staunton, M. (2020). Divergent ESG ratings. *The Journal of Portfolio Management*, *47*(1), 75–87. https://doi.org/10.3905/jpm.2020.1.175

European Commission. (2023). Delegated regulation (EU) 2023/2772 supplementing directive 2013/34/EU as regards sustainability reporting standards. *Official Journal of the European Union*. https://finance.ec.europa.eu/system/files/2023-10/231017-proposal-sustainability-reporting-standards_en.pdf

European Commission. (2025, February 26). *Omnibus I*. https://commission.europa.eu/publications/omnibus-i_en

European Parliament & Council. (2022). Directive (EU) 2022/2464 amending regulation (EU) No 537/2014, directive 2004/109/EC, directive 2006/43/EC and directive 2013/34/EU, as regards corporate sustainability reporting. *Official Journal of the European Union*, *L 322*, 15–80. https://eur-lex.europa.eu/eli/dir/2022/2464/oj/eng

European Parliament & Council. (2024). Directive (EU) 2024/1760 of 13 June 2024 on corporate sustainability due diligence and amending directive (EU) 2019/1937 and regulation (EU) 2023/2859. *Official Journal of the European Union*, *L 1760*, 1–40. Retrieved from https://eur-lex.europa.eu/eli/dir/2024/1760/oj

International Monetary Fund. (2019). Lower for longer. In *Global financial stability report: October 2019*. Retrieved on November 3, 2024. from https://www.imf.org/en/Publications/GFSR/Issues/2019/10/01/global-financial-stability-report-october-2019

IPCC. (2023). Sections. In W. H. Lee & J. Romero (Eds.), *Climate change 2023: Synthesis report. Contribution of working groups I, II and III to the sixth assessment report of the intergovernmental panel on climate change* (35–115). https://doi.org/10.59327/IPCC/AR6-9789291691647

Łudzińska, K. (2024). *Od Społecznej Odpowiedzialności Do ESG W Zarządzaniu. Wybrane Aspekty*. Wydawnictwa Uniwersytetu Warszawskiego Sekcja Wydawnicza Wydziału Zarządzania UW. https://doi.org/10.7172/978-83-235-6498-0.swwz.22

Planetary Health Check. (2025). The planetary boundaries. https://www.planetaryhealthcheck.org/
Sandberg, J., Juravle, C., Hedesström, T. M. & Hamilton, I. (2009). The heterogeneity of socially responsible investment. *Journal of Business Ethics*, *87*(4), 519–533. https://doi.org/10.1007/s10551-008-9956-0
Stankiewicz, A. (2024, January 17). *U.S. sustainable funds register first annual outflows in 2023: Mediocre performance weighed on investor sentiment last year*. Morningstar. Retrieved November 28, 2024, from https://www.morningstar.com/sustainable-investing/us-sustainable-funds-register-first-annual-outflows-2023
The Conference Board. (2023, September 21). *ESG backlash is real and growing. What to know*. Retrieved January 9, 2025, from https://www.conference-board.org/publications/barrons-ESG-backlash-is-real-and-growing
UN. (2004). *Who cares wins. Connecting financial markets to a changing world*. Retrieved January 9, 2025, from https://documents1.worldbank.org/curated/fr/444801491483640669/pdf/113850-BRI-IFC-Breif-whocares-PUBLIC.pdf
Wan, J., Yin, L., & Wu, Y. (2024). Return and volatility connectedness across global ESG stock indexes: Evidence from the time-frequency domain analysis. *International Review of Economics & Finance*, *89*, 397–428. https://doi.org/10.1016/j.iref.2023.10.038
Westveer, J., Freeman, R., McRae, L., Marconi, V., Almond, R. E. A., & Grooten, M. (2022). *A deep dive into the living planet index: A technical report*. WWF.
Winston, A. (2024, December 20). *2024 was a bad year for sustainability*. Harvard business review. Retrieved January 10, 2025, from https://hbr.org/2024/12/2024-was-a-bad-year-for-sustainability
World Bank. (2024, October 15). *Poverty*. Retrieved January 25, 2025, from https://www.worldbank.org/en/topic/poverty/overview
World Inequality Lab. (2023). *Word inequality report 2022*. Retrieved November 14, 2025, from https://wir2022.wid.world/
World Wildlife Fund. (n.d). *The human footprint*. Retrieved February 25, 2025, from https://www.worldwildlife.org/threats/the-human-footprint

CHAPTER 2

Environmental, Social, and Governance: Development of the Concept and its Integration in Poland and Worldwide

2.1 Introduction

This chapter explores the evolution of the Environmental, Social and Governance (ESG) concept within the context of its integration in Poland and globally. Currently the leading approach to business responsibility, ESG evolved from the earlier concept of Corporate Social Responsibility (CSR). It discusses the key stages in the evolution of the ESG concept, its three main dimensions (environmental, social and corporate governance), and its practical application in management. It also addresses the challenges associated with implementing ESG, including ESG assessment and rating issues, and greenwashing. It sets out arguments both for and against integrating ESG into organisational management. While ESG offers many advantages, such as improved risk management and increased investment appeal, some remain sceptical about the potential impact of ESG factors on the financial and operational performance of companies. Finally, the chapter discusses the development and acceptance of CSR and ESG concepts in the Polish market, presenting key events, initiatives and challenges in this area.

K. Łudzińska, *International ESG Perspectives*,
https://doi.org/10.1007/978-3-032-11666-6_2

2.2 Corporate Social Responsibility as a Precursor of the ESG Concept

Although the terms Corporate Social Responsibility (CSR) and Environmental, Social and Governance (ESG) criteria are related and their acronyms are sometimes used interchangeably, they represent distinct characteristics and objectives. CSR refers to the voluntary initiatives, practices and strategies that organisations undertake to ensure a positive impact on society and the environment. ESG factors, on the other hand, represent company actions that take environmental, social and corporate governance factors into account, focusing on strategic and operational aspects in the aforementioned three areas: managing the natural environment, interactions and relations with the social environment, and governance (Robeco, 2020). While CSR initiatives often respond to stakeholder expectations, ESG factors are integral to a company's operational activities and long-term strategy. ESG dimensions provide a comprehensive measure that goes beyond social responsibility to include a company's approach to sustainable development and environmental protection, its relations with the social environment and its ethical behaviour and governance. ESG is also a measurable approach that includes specific indicators used by investors and regulators to evaluate companies' impact on the natural and social environments, as well as corporate governance. Consequently, ESG factors are frequently employed by analysts and investors to evaluate market prospects, anticipate risks and challenges, and pinpoint investment opportunities.

Both concepts: CSR and ESG are largely complementary and can form part of a holistic strategy for sustainable and ethical business practices. According to the widely accepted definition developed by the European Commission, CSR is 'the responsibility of enterprises for their impacts on society [...] to integrate social, environmental, ethical, human rights and consumer concerns into their business operations and core strategy in close collaboration with their stakeholders' (European Commission, 2011, p. 6). The same terms could be applied to the presentation of ESG factors, also referred to interchangeably as 'ESG criteria' or 'ESG aspects' in the literature, supplemented by a corporate governance perspective.

The concept of CSR emerged within contemporary scientific theory across disciplines such as management, economics, sociology and psychology. However, it was philosophy that first emphasised the ethical obligations of human action in response to the need to justify and systematise enterprises' responsibilities towards society. This need was clearly articulated in the literature of the 1960s as a reaction to the limited effectiveness of the market system in addressing social and environmental issues. These issues have contributed to numerous adverse effects and emerging risks (Klimek, 2014; Poniatowska-Jaksch, 2013; Stiglitz, 2013).

Public opinion pressure, both international (represented by anti-globalisation movements) and local, is frequently cited in the literature as a key driver in the development of the concept of corporate social responsibility (Matten & Moon, 2008). At the same time, certain enterprises have undertaken social initiatives not only to meet stakeholder expectations, but also to anticipate them. By engaging voluntarily in socially responsible activities, these companies have helped to prevent various social and environmental risks, taking action in areas where market mechanisms have proven insufficient. This aligns with the view that a company operating under conditions of economic freedom cannot merely exist because it is profitable; rather, its legitimacy stems from being needed by society (Drucker, 2002). Accordingly, economic decisions within an enterprise should prioritise its stakeholders, especially customers, over financial results, efficiency, margins, competitiveness or profit alone.

There are various sources of interest in corporate social responsibility, as well as multiple motivations for its implementation within organisations. The most prominent of these are presented in Table 2.1. Each company undoubtedly has its own specific requirements in this regard. CSR has long since moved beyond being a mere trend and has become an institutionalised element of organisational structures.

When summarising the discussion on social responsibility as the basis for the ESG concept, it is important to emphasise that CSR encompasses integrating environmental and social issues into business management (Liang & Renneboog, 2021). The dimensions, actions and competencies of CSR and ESG are closely linked. Socially responsible companies are expected to generate profit and be financially stable, while also being accountable to shareholders and other stakeholders, such as employees, customers, suppliers and local communities. Furthermore, like ESG, CSR encompasses decision-making processes related to financial management. This convergence raises an important question: what distinguishes ESG from CSR at the organisational level?

Based on an analysis of various empirical studies, the distinction appears to be subtle yet significant, indicating that, although the two frameworks share similar principles, ESG represents a more structured, measurable and

Table 2.1 Key premises of interest in Corporate Social Responsibility in Poland and worldwide

Premises of interest in CSR	*Selected authors of publications (chronologically)*
Disparities in the distribution of global wealth	Prahalad and Hart (2002), Prahalad and Hammond (2002), Bogle (2009), Lakner and Milanovic (2013), Stiglitz (2013), Piketty (2015), Facundo et al. (2018) and Moyer et al. (2022)
Global warming and pollution of the natural environment	Piontek (2002), Rytelewska (2003), Iwacewicz (2004), Chodyński et al. (2008), Kuciński (2009), Pakulska and Poniatowska-Jaksch (2009), Grudzewski et al. (2010), Pietrewicz (2011), Szymański (2015), Jiménez-Parra et al. (2018), Wang et al. (2021) and Hussain et al. (2022)
Increase in ecological awareness of societies	Adamczyk and Nitkiewicz (2007), Żemigała (2007), Pietzner et al. (2011), Gelcich et al. (2014), Korkmaz (2018), McNicholas and Cotton (2019), Glick et al. (2019), Ankamah-Yeboah et al. (2020) and Nastran et al. (2022)
Social, political, demographic and cultural changes in societies	Agle et al. (2008), Szymański (2007), Szymański (2009), Parmar et al. (2010), Scherer and Palazzo (2011), Schmidt and Cracau (2017), Ding et al. (2019), Osuji et al. (2019), Kwon and Ahn (2021)
Technological and social changes resulting from digitisation, digitalisation, computerisation and the availability of new communication channels, including social media	Prahalad and Krishnan (2010), Roszkowska-Śliż (2012), Płoszajski (2012), Adi et al. (2015), Soma et al. (2016), Etter et al. (2019), Lock (2019), Orbik and Zozuľaková (2019), Fotis and Kamariotou (2021), Kong and Liu (2023)
Separation of ownership and management processes and the need for regulation and social supervision of management processes, including the activities of international corporations	Gruszecki (2002), Pakulska and Poniatowska-Jaksch (2009), Orock (2013), Marquis and Raynard (2015), Kolk (2016), Li et al. (2016), Schönherr et al. (2017), Narula (2018), Aguilera et al. (2019), Yuan et al. (2019), Österblom et al. (2022) and Serres et al. (2022)
Increase in consumer awareness and expectations	Prahalad and Ramaswamy (2005), Dobiegała-Korona (2015), Taufique et al. (2016), Cambra-Fierro et al. (2020), Chu

(continued)

Table 2.1 (continued)

Premises of interest in CSR	*Selected authors of publications (chronologically)*
	et al. (2020), Shen and Wang (2022), Aguirre et al. (2023)
Growing recognition of the importance of social responsibility for economic and operational efficiency of businesses	Cochran and Wood (1984), Wartick and Cochran (1985), Wood (1991), Diltz (1995), Feldman et al. (1997), Guerard (1997), Russo and Fouts (1997), King and Lenox (2002), McWilliams and Siegel (2001), Prahalad and Hammond (2002), Prahalad and Hart (2002), Martin (2002), Majewski (2005), Orlitzky et al. (2003), Wheeler et al. (2003), Orlitzky (2005), Porter and Kramer (2006), Margolis et al. (2009), Weber (2008), Orlitzky (2011), Ramchander et al. (2012), Russell and Brockman (2011), Porter and Kramer (2011), Kanter (2011), Jonikas (2012), Juscius and Jonikas (2013), Pavlovich and Corner (2014), Garriga (2014), Wang (2014), Liao et al. (2018), Maqbool and Zameer (2018), Platonova et al. (2018), Wu et al. (2020), Bruna and Lahouel (2022) and Kathayat (2022)

regulatory-driven evolution of CSR practices. ESG dimensions are criteria for assessing an organisation's actions in the social, environmental and governance spheres, while CSR actions form part of an organisation's strategy within its chosen business model and take into account responsible management in economic, social and environmental contexts. These three areas are, in turn, the pillars of the concept of sustainability, in which the three spheres of business activity—economic, social and environmental—interconnect and complement each other (UN, 1987). Therefore, it can be argued that the concept of sustainability integrates and reconciles the assumptions, objectives and principles underlying both the CSR and ESG frameworks (Kaźmierczak, 2022). In practical terms, CSR refers to the actions organisations take to demonstrate environmental and social accountability, thereby striving to act as responsible corporate citizens. ESG criteria, in turn, provide a structured framework for assessing whether an organisation genuinely fulfils this role and for signalling this to markets and stakeholders. Furthermore, a company's performance across the three ESG dimensions is a measurable indicator of the extent to which CSR principles are effectively integrated into its operations and strategies.

2.3 Environmental, Social, and Governance: Foundations and Application

The concept of ESG criteria is considerably more recent than that of CSR. Introduced by the United Nations in 2004, it was first set out in a report entitled Who Cares Wins: Connecting Financial Markets to a Changing World'. The report was produced by 20 leading financial institutions in response to a request from the then Secretary-General of the United Nations, Kofi Annan (UN, 2004). ESG factors were originally developed in response to demand from financial markets for a universal set of criteria with which to evaluate companies' non-financial performance. The aim was to enable investors, analysts, regulators, auditors and other stakeholders to better assess companies' investment attractiveness by taking environmental, social and governance factors into account, as well as financial criteria. Since then, the integration of ESG factors has been recognised as one of the most reliable and frequently used measures of social, environmental and responsible management and investment worldwide. At the same time, ESG criteria have become a leading asset management tool (Edmans, 2023a) rather than merely an element of socially responsible investing, which will be discussed in more detail in subsequent chapters. ESG criteria have also aroused interest in academia, with much attention being given to them in terms of both empirical and theoretical research (e.g. Aldowaish et al., 2022; Baldini et al., 2018; Barrymore & Sampson, 2021; Hughes et al., 2021; Larcker et al., 2022).

In practice, ESG assessments provide data on companies' or financial instruments' sustainable development profiles, assessing their impact on society and the environment, as well as the level of risk associated with sustainable development goals. Consequently, ESG criteria are becoming increasingly influential in the operation of capital markets and in fostering investor confidence in sustainable investment products (European Council, 2024)

Although the aim of ESG is to address key social and environmental challenges, there is no universally accepted definition of ESG factors, nor are there standardised measures for assessing their outcomes. Clément et al. (2023) conducted a systematic literature review to determine how ESG criteria are presented. Of the 4145 articles they examined, they selected 342 particularly influential ones and identified five different definitions relating to the presentation and analysis of ESG results in studies on sustainable development, corporate social responsibility, the disclosure of financial and non-financial information, and company performance in the context of ESG factor analysis.

Nevertheless, the literature identifies two dominant perspectives on integrating ESG factors into economic activity. The first concerns socially responsible investing (SRI) and considers ESG factors from an investment in financial markets perspective. The second evolved from the concept of sustainable development and considers ESG factors from a business operational activities perspective (Aldowaish et al., 2022). While the majority of research so far has focused on integrating ESG factors into investment strategy, the integration of ESG factors into business operations still requires further investigation, particularly with regard to its potential implications for creating business models.

ESG criteria relate to the activities and performance of organisations across three key areas: the environment, society and governance. The environmental criterion (E) assesses how an organisation cares for the natural environment and contributes to mitigating climate change. This includes issues such as greenhouse gas emissions, carbon footprint, waste management, energy consumption, protection of natural resources and animal welfare. The environmental criterion also examines whether the company implements policies and practices that protect the natural environment and address environmental threats and challenges, as well as its contribution to sustainable development.

The social criterion 'S' assesses how well the company manages its relationships with its stakeholders, including employees, suppliers, customers and the local community. This includes fair working conditions and wages, diversity and inclusivity in the workplace, health and safety, customer satisfaction, human rights and engagement with the local community.

Meanwhile, the 'G' criterion, or corporate governance, relates to management processes within the organisation. It covers areas such as leadership and succession, remuneration of employees and managers, audit and internal control processes, shareholder rights and transparency of actions. Good corporate governance is a hallmark of a well-managed company. This is reflected in the organisational structure, balanced board composition and transparent financial and non-financial reporting. It is also demonstrated through high managerial and production standards, including the adoption of codes of conduct and certified processes, as well as operational efficiency.

The number and diversity of ESG criteria are so extensive that it is impossible to list them all, and there is currently no comprehensive list of all possible factors (Matos, 2020). When defining their ESG agendas and selecting relevant criteria for their operations, companies and organisations often rely on various frameworks and guidelines developed by leading institutions, such as the Principles for Responsible Investment (PRI), the Global Sustainability Standards Board, the Global Reporting Initiative (GRI) and the International Integrated Reporting Council (IIRC). Others use their own original agendas and create their own catalogue of actions within the aforementioned three ESG dimensions.

It is worth noting that the 'E' factor, which refers to environmental issues in ESG analysis, has gained particular prominence over the past decade as climate change and environmental degradation have emerged as some of the most pressing challenges facing humanity. During his speech at a conference in New York on 28 July 2023, UN Secretary-General António Guterres stated that the era of global warming has ended and we are now in an 'era of climate boiling' (Sky News, 2023). Furthermore, he emphasised that the pace of changes aimed at limiting this phenomenon is too slow and thus unacceptable. In this context, companies that effectively consider and manage environmental issues contribute to protecting the planet, building a positive image, and gaining the trust of investors and customers. In an era of growing social awareness and pressure for sustainable action, this dimension of ESG criteria is an integral part of responsible, modern management.

In the social dimension, the aim of ESG criteria is to uphold the highest standards of labour practices and cooperation within organisations and across their supply chains. This is important for customers, employees, suppliers, partners and investors, because the results of the social criterion demonstrate how an organisation treats its most important resource: its people. Effective management of social issues can result in a range of benefits. These include greater employee engagement (Chaudhary, 2017; Kim & Kim, 2020), increased productivity (Barrymore & Sampson, 2021), higher job satisfaction (Gu et al., 2020) and an improved company reputation (Murè et al., 2021). In the long term, the 'S' aspect can strengthen a company's competitive position and help it to achieve market success (Kim et al., 2021).

In both literature and business practice, the 'G' factor—the incorporation of corporate governance principles into strategic and operational management—is considered a key element of the ESG concept. Through corporate governance, companies implement responsible management standards and ensure accountability to shareholders and other stakeholders. Enterprises' activities are aligned with local and international legal regulations. Specific procedures are also introduced for managers, including board members, to regulate their cooperation with supervisory bodies such as the supervisory board or board of directors.

In recent decades, considerable research has been devoted to the role of corporate governance in the context of ESG factors. The aim of this research has been to identify synergies between environmental and social management and governance practices (see, for example, Rees & Rodionova, 2015; Rao & Tilt, 2016; Buchetti et al., 2025). Some of this research has focused on integrating ESG aspects into governance structures, examining how organisations adapt or shape their management systems to incorporate sustainable development into decision-making processes (e.g. Mackenzie, 2007; Ricart et al., 2005). Elkington (2006) emphasises that this approach has enriched scientific discourse on topics related to corporate social responsibility, entrepreneurship in local communities, and sustainable development. Research has shown that an increasing number of companies are integrating ESG criteria into their management remuneration systems and establishing committees dedicated to sustainable development (Ricart et al., 2005).

In November 2024, the International Organization for Standardization (ISO) developed and published a new, universally accessible and free set of guidelines titled 'Framework for Implementing Environmental, Social and Governance (ESG) Principles'. These guidelines are aimed at supporting organisations in integrating, measuring and reporting ESG results (ISO, 2024). The guidelines were created in response to an increase in ESG regulations, including the EU's Corporate Sustainability Reporting Directive (CSRD) (European Parliament & Council, 2022), the UK's Modern Slavery Act (2015) and the International Sustainability Standards Board's (ISSB) IFRS S1 and S2 disclosure requirements (International Sustainability Standards Board, 2023a, 2023b). These regulations will be discussed in more detail in subsequent chapters. The ISO ESG guidelines apply to a wide range of organisations, from small businesses to international corporations. They provide a framework to support businesses in implementing and reporting on actions, products, services and commitments towards achieving sustainable development, social justice and good governance.

The ISO document sets out overarching principles and a coherent structure for applying ESG criteria, as well as guidelines for doing so. The flexible framework can be applied to any organisation, regardless of its size, industry or jurisdiction, and reflects changing priorities in the ESG area. Taking regional and economic differences into account, the document has been developed to be accessible to organisations in both developed and developing countries, whether they are required to report on ESG or engage with it on a voluntary basis. The structure of the developed guidelines focuses on non-financial aspects relating to declarations, reporting and the disclosure of information. It recommends considering both material and immaterial values when assessing an organisation's ESG risks and opportunities. These guidelines serve as a compendium of knowledge about ESG principles that can be utilised by businesses, academics, research institutions and non-governmental organisations alike.

In summary, in addition to the aforementioned international guidelines, numerous regional and local environmental protection laws, workers' rights, customers' rights and corporate governance, many countries have adopted rules and standards—including codes of good practice—which outline the behaviour expected of organisations in their interactions with the environment. These guidelines help organisations to create responsible policies and implement procedures that go beyond existing regulations. Although observance is voluntary, many organisations are keen to adopt these guidelines. These primarily include companies listed on the world's largest stock exchanges, as well as those listed on local exchanges such as the Warsaw Stock Exchange. On 1 January 2016, the Warsaw Stock Exchange published the first document describing good practices for listed companies (WSE, 2016). This document presented a set of guidelines based on six fundamental principles, which were then expanded into recommendations and specific rules. These principles covered the company's information policy, communication with investors, management and the supervisory board, internal systems and functions, general meetings and relations with shareholders, conflicts of interest and transactions with related entities, as well as remuneration (Nartowski, 2016, p. 4). After five years, the guidelines were updated, and the new 'Good Practices of Companies Listed on the WSE' came into effect on 1 July 2021. Alongside this, the exchange made the 'Scanner of Good Practices of Listed Companies' available on its website. This tool presents information published by companies about the application of the principles and provides market participants with easy and comprehensive access to this information (WSE, 2021). According to comply or explain principle, the Warsaw Stock Exchange's code of good practice obliges companies to either apply good practices or explain why they do not. Companies that do not adhere to the principles of good practice risk losing their reputation and the trust of investors. Failure to maintain the expected reporting standards may result in regulatory or administrative penalties.

2.4 Milestones in the Development of CSR and ESG Concepts in Practice and Management Theories in the Polish, European and International Markets

Despite numerous studies and analyses being conducted in both the United States and Europe (including Poland) since the 1970s, a single, coherent theory of corporate social responsibility (CSR) has yet to be developed. There is still no universal agreement on which elements should be included in the CSR concept, nor are there any clear guidelines defining its scope. Consequently, CSR remains, at a theoretical level, a collection of many independent management concepts and practices. Nevertheless, the concept has evolved dynamically over the past few decades, which is a positive development, particularly given the incorporation of various significant aspects of economic activity (Dziawgo & Dziawgo, 2017).

In a similar vein, as discussed in Sect. 2.3, the absence of a single, coherent theory describing ESG criteria does not hinder their intensive development, both in academic research and in business practice. The most significant conclusions and pioneering publications demonstrating the evolution of the CSR concept, as well as the ESG criteria, are outlined in Table 2.2.

2.5 Arguments for and Against ESG Integration in Organisational Practice

The integration of ESG factors into management practice has become a central point of discussion for investors, managers, regulators, industry experts and the academic world. Despite the continuous evolution of theory and practice in this domain, the notion of incorporating ESG considerations into organisational management remains a contentious issue, giving rise to divergent viewpoints among proponents and sceptics alike as organisations

Table 2.2 Milestones in the development of CSR and ESG concepts

Author/ Authors	*Groundbreaking publication*	*Key findings*
Bowen (1953)	*Social responsibilities of the businessman*. New York: Harper & Row	Emphasised the ethical and social responsibility of businesses, proposing that they consider the broader impact of their actions on society
Davis and Blomstrom (1975)	*Business and Society: Environment and Responsibility*. New York: McGraw-Hill	CSR is the obligation to make decisions and actions that contribute both to the care of the company's own interest and to the protection and enhancement of social welfare. Davis also proposed the first model of social responsibility
Davis (1975), June	Five propositions for Social Responsibility. *Business Horizons*, No. 18	
Sethi (1975)	Dimensions of Corporate Social Performance: An Analytical Framework. *California Management Review*, Vol. 17 No. 3	CSR can be measured, compared and analysed at three levels: social obligation, responsibility and responsiveness
Carroll (1979)	A Three-Dimensional Conceptual Model of Corporate Social Performance. *Academy of Management Review*, Vol. 4, No. 4	Carroll's Pyramid of Social Responsibility: economic, legal, ethical and philanthropic responsibility
Freeman (1984)	*Strategic management: A Stakeholder Approach*. Boston: Pitman	Stakeholder theory
Wartick and Cochran (1985)	The Evolution of the Corporate Social Performance Model. *Academy of Management Review*, Vol. 10, No. 4	Corporate Social Performance Model (CFP Model)
UN (1987)	*Our Common Future*—Report of the G. H. Brundtland team	First development of the concept of sustainable development
Wood (1991)	Corporate Social Performance Revisited. *Academy of Management Review*, Vol. 16. No. 4	Corporate Social Performance Model II (CSP Model)
Mitchell et al. (1997), October	Towards a Theory of Stakeholder Identification and Salience: Defending the Principle of Who	Stakeholder typology

(continued)

Table 2.2 (continued)

Author/ Authors	*Groundbreaking publication*	*Key findings*
	and What Really Counts. *Academy of Management Review*	
Prahalad and Hammond (2002)	Serving the World's Poor, Profitability. *Harvard Business Review*	CSR as a new, innovative approach providing a competitive market advantage
Prahalad and Hart (2002), December	The Fortune at the Bottom of the Pyramid. *Harvard Business Review*	Reframing poverty alleviation from philanthropic responsibility into a core business opportunity
Porter and Kramer (2002), December	Competitive Advantage of Corporate Philanthropy. *Harvard Business Review*	Strategic approach to corporate philanthropy improving the company's competitive position in the market
UN (2004)	*Who cares wins. Connecting Financial Markets to a Changing World* (Who *cares, wins. Adapting financial markets to a changing world*)	Introduction for the first time to international discourse of ESG criteria: social, environmental and corporate governance related
Porter and Kramer (2006)	Strategy and Society: The Link Between Competitive Advantage and Corporate Social Responsibility. *Harvard Business Review*	CSR can be a source of opportunities, innovations and competitive advantage. If social responsibility is treated as a strategic goal, it could become a source of social progress
Porter and Kramer (2011)	Creating Shared Value. *Harvard Business Review*	The concept of *shared value (Corporate Shared Value, CSV)* involves creating economic value in a way that also creates social value. *Shared value* is a new path to achieving economic and social success
European Parliament and Council (2014)	*Non-Financial Reporting Directive*, NFRD—Directive of the European Parliament and Council 2014/95/EU of 22 October 2014 amending Directive 2013/34/EU as regards disclosure of non-financial information	The first regulation imposing an obligation to report on ESG factors by the largest EU companies
UN (2015)	Sustainable Development Goals (SDGs) and Agenda 2030	*Resolution adopted by the UN General Assembly on 25 September*

(continued)

Table 2.2 (continued)

Author/ Authors	*Groundbreaking publication*	*Key findings*
		2015, adopting 17 sustainable development goals to meet global social and environmental challenges. An initiative undertaken by the European Union, the governments of many countries, and also the management of many companies
European Parliament and Council (2022)	*Corporate Sustainability Reporting Directive (CSRD)*—Directive of the European Parliament and Council of Europe No. 2022/2464/EU of 16 December 2022 on corporate sustainability reporting	Directive amending existing non-financial reporting requirements from 1 January 2024, which replaced the above-mentioned NFRD directive
European Commission (2023a)	European Sustainability Reporting Standards (ESRS)—the first set of 12 European Standards for Sustainability Reporting	The first international non-financial reporting standards, focusing on environmental issues and climate change, dedicated to companies subject to the obligation to report actions in the area of sustainable development
European Commission (2025)	Omnibus I	The first package of simplifications in the area of sustainable development, presented by the European Commission on 26.02.2025, its aim is to reduce administrative burdens for businesses in the European Union. The simplifications concern, among others, the CSRD directive, including a 2-year deferral of the obligation to report sustainable development information for the second and third wave of units, which under the CSRD are required to report for the first time for 2025 or 2026

navigate the tensions between stakeholder expectations, regulatory pressures, and market-driven imperatives.

Proponents of considering ESG factors posit that companies have a societal obligation, as it is this society that grants them a social licence to operate, thereby providing the necessary conditions for conducting business (Boutilier & Thomson, 2011). Consequently, incorporating ESG factors enables companies to operate in a more sustainable and responsible manner, while safeguarding the interests of all stakeholders. Furthermore, the emphasis placed on environmental, social and governance aspects has been demonstrated to enhance the appeal of companies to investors, as evidenced by global trends indicating a growing interest in socially responsible investments (see, Chap. 4 for further details).

ESG assessments have become a significant element of investment decision-making, as they provide investors and regulators with comparable and comprehensive information that helps eliminate information asymmetry (Cappucci, 2018) and minimise reputational and regulatory risk (Humphrey et al., 2012). Furthermore, companies with superior ESG ratings have been shown to achieve elevated excess returns and exhibit diminished volatility (Li et al., 2022). ESG ratings have been demonstrated to enhance environmental awareness among managers, thereby promoting the enhancement of the quality and quantity of green innovations within corporate entities (Tan & Zhu, 2022). The consideration of ESG factors has been demonstrated to engender a number of advantages, including enhanced risk management (van Duuren et al., 2016) and the attainment of superior financial outcomes (Brooks & Oikonomou, 2018; Cahan et al., 2015; Eccles et al., 2014; Fatemi et al., 2015; Filbeck et al., 2009; Friede et al., 2015; Lo & Sheu, 2007; Rodriguez-Fernandez, 2016; Wang & Sarkis, 2017). This approach not only attracts capital but also enables its more efficient use.

Those who are opposed to the incorporation of ESG criteria into organisational management argue that such practices may be associated with higher initial costs resulting from the need to allocate additional resources. The absence of consistent global standards for the consideration and reporting of ESG results represents a significant ongoing challenge, with the potential to engender ambiguity and misunderstanding. Critics have also raised questions regarding the existence of a positive correlation between the implementation of ESG criteria and the financial outcomes of companies. The hypothesis that this relationship may be negative or even non-existent is supported by the findings of Brammer et al. (2006),

Lee et al. (2016), and Duque-Grisales and Aguilera-Caracuel (2021). Moreover, a compelling body of evidence suggests that socially responsible companies benefit from lower discount rates, which in turn leads to lower expected returns on capital for investors. However, these companies do not necessarily generate higher profits or growth (Cornell & Damodaran, 2020). Consequently, the Edelman Trust Barometer (2021) reports that almost three out of four institutional investors lack trust in companies' ability to fulfil their commitments regarding sustainable development, ESG aspects, and diversity, equality and inclusion issues.

Consequently, the rising scepticism towards ESG initiatives in recent years has resulted in numerous actions being critiqued as superficial or merely symbolic, rather than delivering tangible benefits (Winston, 2024). Concurrently, stakeholders are demanding greater transparency from companies regarding the environmental and societal impacts of their activities (de Freitas Netto et al., 2020). In response to these expectations, legislators and market supervisory bodies are increasingly implementing rules and regulations related to ESG. In Europe, initiatives such as the EU Taxonomy (European Commission, 2020) and the CSRD directive (European Parliament & Council, 2022) aim to introduce mandatory non-financial reporting. In the United States, the Federal Trade Commission emphasises the necessity of using clear and precise language when submitting environmental impact statements (Federal Trade Commission, 2012). While these actions are significant, the pursuit of ESG integration often imposes extensive requirements on companies, sometimes leading to substantial economic costs (Porter et al., 2019).

As a result, the discourse transitions from deliberations concerning the imperative for sustainable business practices to a thorough evaluation of their efficacy and execution. Whilst these initiatives affirm the European Union's leading role in sustainable development, concerns have been raised about their execution. Beyond the European continent, there has been a notable escalation in tensions surrounding ESG issues, particularly evident in the United States. It is evident that several prominent investment banks, including Morgan Stanley, Bank of America, Wells Fargo, Goldman Sachs and Citi, have elected to rescind their involvement from the Net-Zero Banking Alliance. This UN initiative is strategically designed to achieve the ambitious target of eliminating greenhouse gas emissions by the year 2050 (Bloomberg, 2025). According to Morningstar research, sustainable funds in the United States recorded annual capital outflows for the first time in 2023, with $13 billion withdrawn from ESG-focused investments (Stankiewicz, 2024).

Notwithstanding this trend, larger ESG funds demonstrated financial resilience, achieving a median investor return of 24.4%, which outperformed the S&P 500 index in the same year.

As scepticism surrounding ESG grows, several significant actors are withdrawing, creating an unstable environment of conflicting pressures. On the one hand, companies are expected to 'stay out of politics'; on the other, they are expected to take action on common social challenges (Winston, 2024). Edmans (2023b) has announced the 'end of ESG' and has argued that ESG should not be privileged. While acknowledging its significance in the long-term value creation of an investment portfolio, it is imperative to recognise its role as an integral component of all investment strategies, rather than perceiving it as a niche concern. The author posits that ESG should not be regarded as exceptional in comparison to other intangible factors, including management quality and innovation. The evaluation of companies should be comprehensive, and should not be based solely on their ESG performance.

According to research by Pérez et al. (2022) for McKinsey, the reservations raised against ESG factors can be divided into four main categories. Firstly, an overemphasis on ESG issues has the potential to divert managerial attention from more pressing concerns related to the core business and its financial performance. Secondly, the implementation of actions that align with ESG criteria is inherently challenging for companies, rendering them unattainable. Achieving a balance between the three dimensions of 'E', 'S' and 'G', to a degree that satisfies all stakeholders, is an overly ambitious undertaking. Furthermore, as Chatterji and Toffel (2024) also observe, the rationale for the equal combination of E, S and G remains ambiguous. This 'unfortunate combination' has become a burden for the ESG movement, especially as it gained popularity.

It is also important to consider the possibility that consultants, bankers and investment managers may promote the consideration of ESG factors to an excessive degree. Pérez et al. (2022) posit that there are undoubtedly companies that benefit from social responsibility, yet there are also companies for which social responsibility incurs costs without yielding commensurate benefits. Investment in ESG that is active in nature does not necessarily result in higher returns than investment that is passive. Moreover, it may be argued that the consideration of ESG criteria is a trend that benefits a select group of individuals, namely consultants, experts and companies that create ESG ratings and indices, without resulting in greater responsibility on the part of companies. In conclusion, Pérez et al. (2022) posit that, despite the capacity to measure ESG outcomes, these demonstrate only a negligible correlation with corporate financial performance. The positive correlation between ESG results and companies' financial performance is attributable to factors other than social, environmental, or corporate governance actions (Whelan et al., 2021). This may also provide a rationale for the inconsistencies observed in research findings concerning the relationship between ESG criteria and companies' financial performance.

Furthermore, the absence of uniform ESG reporting standards, coupled with the evolution of ESG assessments and ratings, is reflected in analysts' reticence to recommend companies that have substantial investments in sustainable development (Porter et al., 2019). Additionally, the presence of inconsistencies in ESG assessments—with an average disagreement level of 56% between agencies—reflects significant methodological discrepancies and biases, including the so-called 'rater effect' (Berg et al., 2022; Christensen et al., 2022; Dimson et al., 2020), which will be discussed in more detail in the next chapter. These discrepancies underscore the necessity for a consensus on the methodologies employed for measuring corporate actions and for identifying those that genuinely contribute to value creation.

A synopsis of the extant research findings pertaining to the critique of ESG criteria reveals the value of referencing the studies of Larcker et al. (2022), who identified seven myths surrounding ESG, categorising them as prevalent yet unsubstantiated by empirical evidence. Primarily, they draw attention to the absence of uniform ESG goals, resulting in inconsistencies in stakeholder expectations. The research indicates that there is no definitive correlation between ESG and company value, and the relationship between ESG and financial results is at least controversial. Moreover, evaluating environmental, social and governance initiatives poses significant challenges. The ESG ratings are intended to assess these initiatives, frequently exhibit inconsistency and unreliability. The notion of a clearly defined ESG agenda within corporate entities has been the subject of scrutiny, highlighting the frequently imperfect implementation of these frameworks in practical contexts. Additionally, although corporate governance is an integral component of ESG, its assessment is not contingent on the other criteria, thereby introducing a layer of complexity to the evaluation process. The authors also observe that mandatory ESG disclosure does not necessarily resolve the assessment problem and, in some cases, may even be detrimental to companies. These findings emphasise the necessity for further research to enhance comprehension and evaluation of the efficacy and tangible advantages of incorporating these criteria.

This is particularly evident in European Union countries, where a primary challenge is the competitiveness of the economy in the era of green transformation. The results of the research presented in the so-called Draghi report on the future competitiveness of Europe demonstrate three key challenges that the European Union must undertake to strengthen its position on the international stage (European Commission, 2024b). Firstly, the creation of an environment conducive to the development of young companies and the support of large enterprises in the implementation of modern technologies, such as artificial intelligence and robotics, are required. This would simplify regulations to facilitate economic activity throughout the Union. Secondly, a joint strategy for decarbonisation and competitiveness is necessary, ensuring access to affordable energy and supporting industry in reducing carbon dioxide emissions. Thirdly, increasing security and reducing excessive dependencies through diversification and strengthening supply chains by establishing new trade and investment partnerships and reviewing public procurement regulations is required, with the aim of increasing the resilience of the EU economy to global challenges. In order to effectively address these challenges, the report underscores the significance of five horizontal factors conducive to competitiveness: namely, the simplification of regulations, the reduction of barriers within the single market, the promotion of competitiveness in terms of finance, the encouragement of skills and high-quality work, and the enhancement of coordination of policies at both the EU and national level.

As a consequence of the observations made in the Draghi report, the European Commission has proposed the first package of regulatory simplifications, designated 'Omnibus I', with the objective of adapting extant financial regulations to new market realities. This proposal refers, inter alia, to the CSRD directive and the obligation of non-financial reporting (European Commission, 2025), a subject which is discussed in more detail in Chap. 8.

The proposed changes will also apply to enterprises operating in Poland. These enterprises have already taken actions in accordance with the CSDR directive, which was incorporated into Polish law through an amendment to the Accounting Act (Parliament of the Republic of Poland, 2024). This amendment was passed on 6 December 2024 and came into effect on 1 January 2025.

2.6 Challenges in Implementing ESG Aspects

2.6.1 *Problematic ESG Assessments and Ratings*

ESG criteria are widely accepted in both academic discourse and business practice as a set of non-financial performance indicators. These indicators are understood to reflect an organisation's commitment to social and environmental responsibility, ethical operation, and adherence to principles of corporate governance. The ESG criteria can be considered a response to the mounting necessity of evaluating organisations based on non-financial metrics. This demand is being driven by market forces that seek to identify companies that demonstrate excellence in the domain of sustainability. As previously stated, ESG assessments were initially developed primarily to satisfy the requirements of financial markets; however, they have also garnered popularity among corporate entities. It was demonstrated that these factors contributed to the enhancement of their reputation (e.g.: Murè et al. (2021). Karwowski and Raulinajtys-Grzybek (2021) found that the companies in question reduced legislative pressure on their operations (Christensen et al., 2022; Porter et al., 2019), financial risk (Chollet & Sandwidi, 2018) and attracted capital (Cheng et al., 2014). Research findings suggest that, from an investor's viewpoint, ESG performance also curtails the risk to which a company is exposed when it finds itself at the centre of an environmental or social scandal (Escrig-Olmedo et al., 2019).

Concurrently, market capitalisation appears to exert an influence on risk reduction, with larger companies generally exhibiting higher ESG scores due to the impact of social pressure (Khan, 2022). As Escrig-Olmedo et al. (2019) critically observe, ESG criteria facilitate the prediction of financial risk associated with the adverse impact of unethical practices (e.g. corruption or child labour) or accidents (e.g. leaks, nuclear failures and destruction of the natural environment) on the financial outcomes of companies. However, they are less apt for analysing the positive outcomes resulting from initiatives undertaken within the ESG framework, i.e. determining the extent to which a company can contribute to social welfare or the preservation of the natural environment. The evaluation of the practical consequences of the implementation of ESG practices, with a particular focus on the impact of organisations on the community and the local environment, continues to represent a significant challenge.

In the context of business practice, the evaluation of companies' ESG performance is conducted by external, independent institutions. The results of these evaluations are presented in the form of ESG ratings. These ratings serve as a tool for investors in selecting companies and are also used to assess the performance of publicly listed firms. Consequently, environmental, social and governance assessment has become a pivotal component of sustainable management strategies, exerting a notable influence on the financial outcomes of corporations (Eccles & Serafeim, 2013).

The construction of ESG scores published by private agencies and commercial firms relies on various types of data, with their primary clients being investment portfolio managers and institutional investors (Escrig-Olmedo et al., 2019). The most prominent international rating agencies that evaluate companies based on ESG factors include, among others: The following sources were consulted for this study: MSCI (MSCI, 2025), Refinitiv, formerly Thomson Reuters ASSET4 ESG (Refinitiv, 2025), (Sustainalytics, 2025), (Robeco, 2025), FTSE Russell, including the FTSE4Good index family (FTSE Russell, 2025), ISS ESG (ISS ESG, ISS ESG, 2025), Moody's, formerly Vigeo Eiris (Moody's, 2025), (S&P Global, 2025), (Bloomberg, 2025) and Morningstar (Morningstar, 2025). The ratings and data they provide fall within the spectrum of scientific research, which, importantly, points to their inconsistency and draws attention to the fact that different agencies assign different weights to different criteria and interpret different data sources in different ways (e.g. Escrig-Olmedo et al., 2019; Kotsantonis & Serafeim, 2019). It is evident that these considerations have the potential to engender considerable variance in the ESG results of a given company, depending on the rating agency responsible for their assessment.

Berg, Kölbel and Rigobon (2022) provide confirmation of a low correlation coefficient between the ESG ratings of six different rating agencies. Furthermore, they demonstrate that the scale of disagreement in the ratings issued by these agencies averages 56%. The primary cause of this phenomenon is identified as discrepancies in measurements and the so-called evaluator effect, in which the overall perspective of the company of the individual preparing the rating influences the selection and methodology of measuring certain ESG categories. Concurrently, there is a mounting demand for greater scrutiny of the methodology employed in generating the underlying data for ESG ratings. Converging conclusions are also reached by Eccles and Stroehle (2018) and Eccles et al. (2020), who in their research confirm that the purpose of developing a rating, as well as its intended recipient, significantly influence the representativeness and scope of the issued ESG result. A problematic level of correlation can also be observed in other studies (e.g. Dimson et al., 2020; Hughes et al., 2021). The existence of discrepancies between companies' ESG results indicates the necessity for greater consensus on the corporate actions that should be measured and the methods by which they should be measured.

The reasons for the observed differences in ratings remain to be elucidated. Christensen et al. (2022) observe that greater disclosure of ESG information leads de facto to greater disagreement in ESG ratings. It is also confirmed that raters disagree more on the ESG results themselves (output indicators) than on the policies for their implementation (input indicators). Furthermore, it appears that disclosure of information leads to an increase in the lack of, in the case of ESG results, i.e., output indicators. The argument is made that, for companies that are listed, a greater lack of consistency in ESG is associated with higher volatility of investment returns, larger absolute changes in share prices and a lower probability of obtaining external financing.

Furthermore, when evaluating a company, it is advisable to consider its geographical location. The availability of qualitative information varies across different countries, and this variation can have a significant impact on the representativeness of ESG results. Baldini et al. (2018) provide evidence that national-level characteristics, including the local political system (legislative framework and level of corruption), labour system (job protection and unemployment rate) and cultural system (social cohesion and equal opportunities), significantly influence companies' practices in disclosing ESG information, which forms the basis of rating assessments. (Daugaard & Ding, 2022)'s study also emphasised the necessity for further research to be conducted into the impact of economic development, the regulatory environment, and responsible investing on ESG dimension results. These research trajectories appear to have considerable ramifications for investment management, corporate strategies, and government policies with regard to ESG outcomes.

Furthermore, research findings emphasise that civil law countries oriented towards stakeholders (i.e. principally European countries) have more detailed regulations on environmental and social issues, leading to more consistent ESG results compared to countries applying common law principles (e.g. in the United States and the United Kingdom), which are shareholder-oriented (Collison et al., 2012; Kock & Min, 2016). Concurrently, (Clément et al., 2023) propose a circumspect approach to the utilisation of ESG outcomes as a metric. ESG criteria were developed for a specific purpose and are significantly limited when applied in other contexts. This may result in a limitation of the scope and representativeness of findings based on

ESG results. For instance, if recommendations for enhancing an organisation's social outcomes, derived from its ESG performance, fail to adequately reflect the positive external effects associated with safeguarding the natural environment, or if their societal impact remains negligible, this could have substantial ramifications. The extant literature indicates that the stock market has a negative reaction to announcements of companies' philanthropic expenditures. This finding suggests that this type of social action is not valued by investors (Masulis & Reza, 2015). Despite the fact that ESG aspects signify a favourable progression in terms of the broader incorporation of the UN Sustainable Development Goals within the domain of financial investments, the primary constraint pertains to the absence of an objective metric to assess companies' performance in this particular domain (Viviers & Eccles, 2012).

Although the regular monitoring of corporate activities is crucial for the assessment of their performance in ESG areas, many studies suggest that such monitoring does not always result in significant changes in corporate behaviour (Hong & Kacperczyk, 2009; Humphrey & Tan, 2014; Salaber, 2013). Furthermore, given the aforementioned discrepancies in the ratings of the same companies, it is challenging to devise indicators that fully reflect the intricacies of the non-financial information they disclose (Camilleri, 2018, 2020). Whilst the specification of indicators has the capacity to counteract the problem of information asymmetry, the establishment of universal criteria for companies wishing to adopt them could result in costs that are disproportionate to the anticipated benefits (Trinks & Scholtens, 2017).

In that context, (Chatterji et al., 2016) advise users of ESG ratings to exercise caution when interpreting them, bearing in mind potential methodological limitations and differences in the evaluation criteria used by different rating institutions. This is of particular importance when considering their actual correlation with companies' actions in the areas of social responsibility, environmental protection and corporate governance. Concurrently, rating agencies are obliged to exercise particular care in developing ratings and conduct regular audits of the rating methodologies used.

It is evident that the intricacies inherent in ESG ratings have not escaped the attention of regulatory authorities. In 2024, the European Council adopted a new regulation to govern activities related to ESG assessments (Council of the European Union, 2024). The objective of the initiative is to enhance the consistency, transparency and comparability of ESG assessments within the European Union, with a view to fostering investor confidence in sustainable financial products. The recently introduced regulations seek to enhance the credibility and comparability of ESG assessments by increasing the transparency of the actions of these assessment providers and also minimising the risk of conflicts of interest. In accordance with the recently introduced regulatory framework, ESG rating providers operating within the European Union will be obligated to obtain the necessary permissions and will be subject to the oversight of the European Securities and Markets Authority (ESMA). Furthermore, they will be required to adhere to stringent transparency requirements, particularly with regard to the methodology employed and the sources of information utilised. Conversely, ESG rating providers from outside the European Union, who wish to offer their services within its territory, are required to have their ratings approved by an authorised EU ESG rating provider, meet requirements based on a specific quantitative criterion, or be entered into the EU ESG provider register as a result of an equivalence decision (European Parliament, & Council, 2024c).

2.6.2 ESG Integration and Market Challenges: Greenwashing and Other Phenomena

The pressure arising from regulatory requirements for non-financial reporting, as well as the growing expectations of investors, clients, partners and other stakeholders regarding ESG disclosure, have the potential to contribute to negative corporate attitudes (Aldowaish et al., 2022). Consequently, this engenders phenomena such as ESG data manipulation, greenwashing (to be discussed in detail below), value washing (Sugai, 2021) and blue washing (Ruiz-Blanco et al., 2022; Zammit, 2003). The primary objective of these phenomena is to attract capital and gain stakeholder acceptance, often at the expense of genuine actions towards sustainable development. The European Securities and Markets Authority (ESMA), in conjunction with other institutions and organisations, has been instrumental in promoting the fight against these phenomena and advocating for transparency in ESG actions and disclosures (ESMA, 2025).

Greenwashing is a complex, multi-faceted phenomenon, which has various causes, takes different forms and can negatively impact both consumer and investor decisions. It is most often associated with green marketing communication, which companies undertake to be perceived as environmentally friendly and socially engaged (e.g. de Freitas Netto et al., 2020; de Jong et al., 2020; Vos, 2009). De facto, companies seek to convince stakeholders that 'the company is doing more for the environment than it actually is' (Dictionary, 2024). It is evident that companies deliberately engage in such practices, and the term 'greenwashing' has been coined to denote the act of orchestrating external allegations against an organisation for the purpose of presenting a deceptive environmental message (Seele & Gatti, 2017). According to Greenpeace, the term 'greenwashing' refers to the practice of misleading consumers about a company's environmental practices or the environmental benefits of a product or service (Greenpeace, 2022). Mitchell and Ramey (2011) specify that for an action to be recognised as greenwashing, it must be intentional. Consequently, the phenomenon of greenwashing is predicated on the assumption of intentional fraudulent activity (Nyilasy et al., 2012). The consequences of this phenomenon extend beyond the immediate stakeholders involved, encompassing the broader societal context. Consequently, the establishment of regulations and rules with the objective of constraining such practices is imperative (Yang et al., 2020). In the context of mounting demands from corporate stakeholders and society at large for greater transparency in disclosing information regarding the environmental impact of companies' activities, organisational communication must evolve to become more dynamic, multifaceted and purposefully directed towards enhancing societal awareness of contemporary environmental and social challenges (de Freitas Netto et al., 2020).

The necessity to consider ESG factors and non-financial reporting has been demonstrated to exert pressure on companies to develop a broad set of social and environmental criteria, regardless of the economic costs (Porter et al., 2019). This pressure has resulted in numerous enhancements; however, it has also served to reinforce the perception among investors that consideration of social and environmental factors may compromise economic efficiency. Consequently, despite the numerous studies and growing acceptance of ESG ratings, it is unclear whether most investors significantly utilise ESG criteria in the investment selection process. A considerable number of these individuals hold the conviction that expenditures made by corporations on social and environmental initiatives constitute a misappropriation of shareholder resources. Research conducted by Serafeim and Ioannou (2019) reveals that investment analysts issue buy recommendations less frequently for companies that heavily invest in sustainable development. Consequently, as asserted by (Porter et al., 2019), numerous investors employ financial analysis as the primary criterion for selecting potential investments, thereby disregarding social and environmental concerns. Subsequently, they utilise the company's extant ESG results as a final screen to mitigate risk.

In view of the aforementioned points, there is a possibility that ESG criteria may be indicative of companies' greenwashing behaviour rather than their genuine pro-environmental actions. Kathan et al. (2025) demonstrated that the correlation between apparent environmental efficiency and ESG ratings is significantly positive, while the correlation between actual environmental efficiency and ESG ratings is significantly negative. Consequently, they argue that ESG ratings are not an appropriate tool for measuring actual environmental impact.

In numerous countries, regulatory authorities are no longer merely passive observers of the phenomenon of greenwashing. Instead, they are proactively implementing measures to safeguard consumers. A significant development at the supranational level was the adoption of the European Union Directive (EU) 2024/825 on 28 February 2024, which came into effect on 27 March 2024 (European Parliament, & Council, 2024a). This act, referred to in public debate as the Empowering Consumers Directive (EmpCo), focuses on combating unfair marketing practices related to false or misleading environmental claims. The directive is intended to amend Directives 2005/29/EC and 2011/83/EU, with the aim of expanding the catalogue of unfair commercial practices to include misleading sustainability statements. It is evident that the utilisation of environmental labels that are not founded upon recognised certification schemes or established by public authorities shall be proscribed. In order to substantiate environmental claims pertaining to products or companies, traders are obligated to furnish clear, verifiable and objective evidence. Furthermore, the use of general and unverifiable declarations such as 'environmentally friendly' or 'green' will be prohibited unless substantiated by recognised evidence. Member States are required to transpose the directive by 27 March 2026, with its provisions applying from 27 September 2026 (European Commission, 2024a, March 27).

In conjunction with the Empowering Consumers Directive, the European Commission had also prepared a further measure to tackle greenwashing—the Green Claims Directive—but its progress has stalled. Since March 2020, the Commission has been engaged in the development of a proposal that aims to mandate scientific substantiation and third-party verification of environmental assertions (European Commission, 2023b, March 22). However, on June 20, 2025, the Commission declared its intention to withdraw the draft proposal in response to mounting political opposition and concerns regarding the disproportionate regulatory burdens it would impose on SMEs, particularly given the failure to exempt micro-enterprises, a provision that had attracted significant criticism (Partner, 2025, August 1). In lieu of a formal withdrawal of the proposal, the Commission opted for a suspension of the legislative process, resulting in the Directive's current state of legal limbo, with no discernible timeline for its revival (Latham & Watkins LLP, 2025). Whilst the Green Claims Directive has been conceived with the intention of complementing the EU Green Deal, the future of the Directive remains uncertain. This is indicative of the difficulty of reconciling robust sustainability standards with economic and political considerations.

To summarise the foregoing discussion, despite the identified limitations, ESG criteria continue to represent the most widely used and pragmatic measure for assessing organisational practices in the field of corporate social responsibility (Cini & Ricci, 2018). They provide a quantitative assessment of the efforts made by organisations to protect their natural and social environment and are widely accepted, which facilitates their use and comparison between companies. Furthermore, ESG is synonymous with corporate responsibility (Larcker et al., 2022). As demonstrated by the findings of the Broadridge study (2021), environmental, social and governance aspects hold particular significance for younger demographics (Broadridge Financial Solutions, Inc., 2021). Conversely, young people advocate for corporations to exclude practices that are deemed socially and environmentally undesirable, and instead promote positive attitudes within the business sector. Notwithstanding the challenges that have been presented, the growing trend of incorporating ESG factors into management and investing strategies indicates that the benefits for businesses, investors and society as a whole outweigh potential losses and risks. A comprehensive analysis of over 2000 empirical research results has indicated that the majority of studies on the inclusion of ESG dimensions have demonstrated a positive impact on the financial results of companies (Friede et al., 2015). A review of empirical research in the literature covering a period of 45 years also demonstrated a positive relationship between ESG and financial performance (Brooks & Oikonomou, 2018).

Consequently, despite the controversies and unresolved issues related to the effectiveness and clear impact of ESG criteria on building economic value, interest in this area is growing in both practice and management theory. Regulations at the national and international level, which require the disclosure of non-financial information, underline the importance of these aspects in assessing the stability and development prospects of markets and companies. In the contemporary era of globalisation and mounting social pressure on business responsibility, it is imperative to acknowledge the significance of ESG aspects. It is evident that companies which demonstrate an understanding of, and capacity to implement, appropriate practices are undoubtedly better prepared to face future challenges and opportunities, thus engendering the trust of their stakeholders. In this context of dynamic change, it is evident that ESG criteria will assume a pivotal role in business strategies and investment decisions in the forthcoming years.

2.7 Development of Acceptance and Integration of CSR and ESG in the Polish Market

The notion of Corporate Social Responsibility began to accrue significance in Poland at the turn of the twenty-first century, largely due to the Responsible Business Forum, a non-governmental organisation founded in 2000 and still active today (Responsible Business Forum, 2025). Furthermore, a number of organisations have expressed support for the promotion of responsible business. These include the Academy for the Development of Philanthropy, the Social Communication Foundation, the Business Ethics Centre (CEBI) and Polish branches of international organisations such as The Conference Board and Business Leaders Forum. In 2001, Poland became the inaugural European nation to accede to the United Nations Global Compact initiative (UN Global Compact Poland, 2024).

The establishment of standards and best practices of corporate social responsibility was also facilitated by the collaborative efforts of multinational corporations, including Deloitte and PwC, as well as domestic entities such as Better and CSR Consulting. The Responsible Business Forum became a partner of CSR Europe in 2002 and has since been actively promoting the idea of CSR in Poland, publishing annual reports entitled Responsible Business in Poland. Good Practices. In 2022, the 21st edition of the report presented a record number of 1705 good practices submitted by 272 companies (Responsible Business Forum, 2022). The Forum, in conjunction with other organisations—including the Sustainable Investment Forum Poland (POLSIF) and the Polish ESG Association—is playing an active role in the development and integration of ESG criteria in organisational activities, as well as non-financial reporting. The mission of POLSIF is to develop and promote the Polish and European market for sustainable investments and finance by creating and disseminating best practices (POLSIF, 2024). The Polish ESG Association is a body that brings together companies, institutions and local government units that are actively implementing ESG ideas. The organisation is responsible for the ESG Good Practices Academy, the Legislation Monitoring Centre and the ESG Trends Barometer (Polish ESG Association, 2023). The subsequent table (Table 2.3) provides a chronological overview of the key milestones in the evolution of the acceptance of the concept of Corporate Social Responsibility (CSR) in Poland. This development ultimately paved the way for the integration of Environmental, Social and Governance (ESG) criteria into organisational practices.

In order to encourage socially and ecologically responsible business practices, the Polish government established the National Reform Programme to support the implementation of the Europe 2020 strategy. The Europe 2020 strategy was the European Union's long-term plan for economic growth and employment for the years 2010–2020 (Republic of Poland Service, 2019). Furthermore, on 21 January 2020, the Minister of Funds and Regional Policy established the Team for Sustainable Development and Corporate Social Responsibility (Ministry of Funds and Regional Policy of the Republic of Poland, 2020). It convenes working groups entrusted with responsibilities including, but not limited to, non-financial reporting, due diligence and the social responsibility of universities.

In 2018, Poland also initiated participation in the Voluntary National Reviews (VNRs) on the implementation of the 2030 Agenda within the United Nations. In 2023, the Polish government presented a report on the progress made in achieving the 17 sustainable development goals in the years 2018–2022 (Ministry of Development and Technology of the Republic of Poland, 2023). The document was produced through a collaborative effort with the UN Global Compact Network Poland, the Responsible Business Forum and the Polish Chamber of Commerce. In achieving sustainable development goals, Poland places particular emphasis on initiatives and actions in the field of sustainable financing in both the public and private sectors, including the financial and insurance industry. It also underscores the priorities of our development cooperation, with a particular emphasis on financing actions for climate protection and the promotion of gender equality. Among Polish investors, there is growing interest in companies that transparently present non-financial information, reflecting both the global trend and the evolution of regulations in developed markets.

Despite the above-mentioned institutional efforts, the integration of ESG criteria in Poland faces a number of challenges, often similar to those

Table 2.3 Development of CSR and ESG concept integration in Poland

Period	*Characteristics*
Up to 2000	• Lack of interest in the issue of Corporate Social Responsibility in public discussion
2000	• Establishment of the Responsible Business Forum—the first non-governmental organisation promoting the idea of CSR in Poland
2000–2002	• Reluctance towards the idea of Corporate Social Responsibility on the part of most companies, economic journalists and academics
2002–2004	• Interest in the concept of Corporate Social Responsibility • First public declarations acknowledging the role of ethics and social responsibility as elements of every company's operation
2004–2005	• Undertaking specific projects related to the implementation of social responsibility, covering selected areas of company operations • The beginnings of companies communicating about actions taken in this area • The emergence of the first corporate social reports and the first Polish-language scientific publications dedicated to CSR
2006–2009	• Linking the concept of Corporate Social Responsibility with other strategies implemented in companies, e.g., communication, personnel, marketing, or corporate governance
2009	• Establishment of the first social responsibility index, RESPECT Index on the Warsaw Stock Exchange
2010–2015	• Formulating corporate social responsibility strategies in companies and undertaking initiatives in line with its objectives • Communicating about social responsibility and dedicating web pages to present such actions • The flourishing of research and scientific publications dedicated to selected aspects of Corporate Social Responsibility
2015–2020	• Citizen monitoring to check whether companies disclose data on key non-financial aspects of their operations • Development of diversity management practices in the workplace, including the publication of the first good practice guide for employing LGBT people in Poland titled *Opening up to Diversity* • Establishment of a working group preparing ethical standards for Polish companies within the UN Global Compact • The flourishing of volunteering, including skills-based volunteering, where employees share their key professional competencies • Development, together with 45 corporate foundations, of operation standards for foundations established by companies and the publication of a handbook for their managers • Enactment of the Social Dialogue Council Act, in force since 11 September 2015 • Organisation of the COP 24 Climate Summit in Katowice (December 2019)

(continued)

Table 2.3 (continued)

Period	*Characteristics*
From 2020	• Introduction of the Diversity Charter in 26 EU countries, including Poland • Further dynamic development of good practices not only among the largest companies but also SMEs • Establishment of the Chapter Zero Poland initiative • Establishment of the Polish Plastic Pact for a circular economy of plastics • The European Commission announced the legislative changes package *Fit for 55*, also widely discussed in Poland • New EU guidelines on mandatory ESG reporting for leading companies—publication of the EU CSRD Directive (2022) and its implementation into Polish legal order (December 2024) • Development and publication of the first EU sustainable development reporting standards (ESRS) in July 2023, also applicable to Polish companies covered by the CSRD directive

Source Based on Responsible Business Forum (2005–2024), European Parliament and the Council (2020–2024)

encountered in other countries, as discussed in Sect. 2.5. The primary concerns pertain to the absence of uniform standards and regulations for ESG reporting, which often results in companies' approaches to these issues being inconsistent and challenging to compare. A paucity of awareness regarding ESG, both among companies and stakeholders (see, Chap. 7), further complicates the understanding of the benefits of these initiatives. For a considerable number of companies, particularly those of a modest to medium size, the challenge of implementing ESG is also characterised by the substantial financial expenditure required for technology, training and reporting. Moreover, the absence of transparency and the minimal pressure from investors have resulted in a limited level of trust in companies with regard to ESG implementation, thereby further hindering the comprehensive integration of these criteria within the Polish business environment. A more thorough examination of these issues is provided in the following chapters.

2.8 Summary and Conclusions

The conclusion of this chapter asserts that the concept of Environmental, Social and Governance (ESG) represents a natural evolution and extension of the notion of Corporate Social Responsibility (CSR). ESG integrates not only aspects of social and ecological responsibility, but also introduces a comprehensive approach to management, taking into account corporate governance issues.

A salient conclusion from the presented analyses is that, despite the numerous benefits resulting from the implementation of ESG, such as comprehensive risk management, increasing investor trust, and improving the organisation's image, there are also significant challenges. These primarily include problems with ESG assessments and ratings, which are often inconsistent and can lead to an incomplete evaluation of companies' actions. The pressure associated with adapting to ESG requirements and expectations, including non-financial reporting, often results in greenwashing. This phenomenon poses a significant threat to the widespread integration and implementation of ESG aspects, undermining the credibility of business actions for sustainable development.

Nevertheless, the chapter asserts that the concept of ESG has withstood criticism and scepticism, as evidenced by the sustained interest it has garnered. This ongoing interest signifies the concept's enduring significance for the development of theory and practice in contemporary organisational management. In the Polish, European and international context, the development of CSR and ESG reflects the growing awareness and commitment of companies to sustainable development, which is becoming an increasingly integrated element of business strategies.

References

Adamczyk, J., & Nitkiewicz, T. (2007). *Programowanie Zrównoważonego Rozwoju Przedsiębiorstw*. Polskie Wydawnictwo Ekonomiczne.

Adi, A., Crowther, D., & Grigore, G. (2015). *Corporate Social Responsibility in the Digital Age* (1st ed.). Emerald Group Publishing Limited.

Agle, B. R., Donaldson, T., Freeman, R. E., Jensen, M. C., Mitchell, R. K., & Wood, D. J. (2008). Dialogue: Toward superior stakeholder theory. *Business Ethics Quarterly*, *18*(2), 153–190.

Aguilera, R. V., Desender, K. A., Bednar, M. K., & Lee, J. H. (2019). Connecting the dots: Bringing external corporate governance into the corporate governance puzzle. *Academy of Management Annals*, *13*(2), 304–339.

Aguirre, C., Ruiz de Maya, S., Palazón Vidal, M., & Rodríguez, A. (2023). Consumer motivations for engaging with corporate social responsibility on social media. *Spanish Journal of Marketing - ESIC*, *27*(2), 202–220. https://doi.org/10.1108/SJME-05-2022-0106

Aldowaish, A., Kokuryo, J., Almazyad, O., & Goi, H. C. (2022). Environmental, social, and governance integration into the business model: Literature review and research agenda. *Sustainability, 14*(5), 2959. https://doi.org/10.3390/su14052959

Ankamah-Yeboah, I., Xuan, B. B., Hynes, S., & Armstrong, C. W. (2020). Public perceptions of deep-sea environment: Evidence from Scotland and Norway. *Frontiers in Marine Science, 7*, Article 137. https://doi.org/10.3389/fmars.2020.00137

Baldini, M., Maso, L. D., Liberatore, G., Mazzi, F., & Terzani, S. (2018). Role of country- and firm-level determinants in environmental, social, and governance disclosure. *Journal of Business Ethics, 150*, 79–98. https://doi.org/10.1007/s10551-016-3139-1

Barrymore, N., & Sampson, R. C. (2021). ESG performance and labor productivity: Exploring whether and when ESG affects firm performance. *Academy of Management Proceedings, 2021*(1), 13997. https://doi.org/10.5465/AMBPP.2021.13997abstract

Berg, F., Köelbel, J. F., & Rigobon, R. (2022). Aggregate confusion: The divergence of ESG ratings. *Review of Finance, 26*(6), 1315–1344. https://doi.org/10.1093/rof/rfac033

Bloomberg. (2025). *ESG data and analytics.* Retrieved September 20, 2025, from https://www.bloomberg.com/professional/product/esg-data/

Bloomberg. (2025, January 2). Morgan Stanley follows Citi, BofA in quitting climate group. Retrieved January 8, 2025, from https://www.bloomberg.com/news/articles/2025-01-02/morgan-stanley-leaves-net-zero-alliance-for-banks

Bogle, J. C. (2009). *Dość. Prawdziwe Miary Bogactwa, Biznesu I Życia.* Polskie Towarzystwo Ekonomiczne.

Boutilier, R., & Thomson, I. (2011). *Modelling and measuring the social licence to operate: Fruits of a dialogue between theory and practice.* Retrieved December 5, 2021, from http://socialicense.com/publications/Modelling%20and%20Measuring%20the%20SLO.pdf

Bowen, H. R. (1953). *Social Responsibilities of the Businessman.* Harper & Row.

Brammer, S., Brooks, C., & Pavelin, S. (2006). Corporate social performance and stock returns: UK evidence from disaggregate measures. *Financial Management, 35*(3), 97–116. https://doi.org/10.1111/j.1755-053X.2006.tb00149.x

Broadridge Financial Solutions, Inc. (2021). *From the retail trading frenzy to growing ESG trends, what will be in proxy season 2021?* Retrieved July 20, 2023, from https://www.prnewswire.com/news-releases/from-the-retail-trading-frenzy-to-growing-esgtrends-what-will-be-in-proxy-season-2021-301281582.html

Brooks, C., & Oikonomou, I. (2018). The effects of environmental, social and governance disclosures and performance on firm value: A review of the literature in accounting and finance. *The British Accounting Review*, *50*(1), 1–15. https://doi.org/10.1016/j.bar.2017.11.005

Bruna, M. G., & Lahouel, B. (2022). CSR & financial performance: Facing methodological and modeling issues commentary paper to the eponymous FRL article collection. *Finance Research Letters*, *44*, 102036. https://doi.org/10.1016/J.FRL.2021.102036

Buchetti, B., Arduino, F. R., & Perdichizzi, S. (2025). A literature review on corporate governance and ESG research: Emerging trends and future directions. *International Review of Financial Analysis*, *97*, 103759. https://doi.org/10.1016/j.irfa.2024.103759

Cahan, S. F., Chen, C., Chen, L., & Nguyen, N. H. (2015). Corporate social responsibility and media coverage. *Journal of Banking and Finance*, *59*, 409–422. https://doi.org/10.1016/j.jbankfin.2015.07.004

Cambra-Fierro, J. J., Flores-Hernández, J. A., Pérez, L., & Valera-Blanes, G. (2020). CSR and branding in emerging economies: The effect of incomes and education. *Corporate Social Responsibility and Environmental Management*, *27*(6), 2765–2776. https://doi.org/10.1002/csr.2000

Camilleri, M. A. (2018). Theoretical insights on integrated reporting: The inclusion of non-financial capitals in corporate disclosures. *Corporate Communications: An International Journal*, *23*(4), 567–581. https://doi.org/10.1108/CCIJ-01-20180016

Camilleri, M. A. (2020). The market for socially responsible investing: A review of the developments. *Social Responsibility Journal*, *17*(3), 412–428. https://doi.org/10.1108/SRJ-06-2019-0194

Cappucci, M. (2018). The ESG integration paradox. *Journal of Applied Corporate Finance*, *30*(2), 22–28. https://doi.org/10.1111/jacf.12296

Carroll, A. B. (1979). A Three-Dimensional Conceptual Model of Corporate Social Performance. *Academy of Management Review*, *4*(4), 497–505.

Chatterji, A. K., Durand, R., Levine, D. I., & Touboul, S. (2016). Do ratings of firms converge? Implications for managers, investors and strategy researchers. *Strategic Management Journal*, *37*(8), 1597–1614. https://doi.org/10.1002/smj.2407

Chatterji, A. K., & Toffel, M. W. (2024, September 20). It's time to unbundle ESG. *Harvard Business Review*. https://hbr.org/2024/09/its-time-to-unbundle-esg

Chaudhary, R. (2017). Corporate social responsibility and employee engagement: Can CSR help in redressing the engagement gap? *Social Responsibility Journal*, *13*(2), 323–338. https://doi.org/10.1108/SRJ-07-2016-0115

Cheng, B., Iannou, I., & Serafeim, G. (2014). Corporate social responsibility and access to finance. *Strategic Management Journal*, *35*(1), 1–23.

Chodyński, A., Jabłoński, A., & Jabłoński, M. (2008). ECSR – Koncepcja strategiczna oparta o ekologiczną i społeczną odpowiedzialność biznesu. In W. W. M. Grudzewski & I. K. Hejduk, *W Poszukiwaniu Nowych Paradygmatów Zarządzania* (pp. 63–72). Oficyna Wydawnicza SGH w Warszawie.

Chollet, P., & Sandwidi, B. W. (2018). *CSR Engagement and Financial Risk: A Virtuous Circle?* International evidence.

Christensen, D. M., Serafeim, G., & Sikochi, A. (2022). Why is corporate virtue in the eye of the beholder? The case of ESG ratings. *The Accounting Review*, *97*(1), 147–175. https://doi.org/10.2308/TAR-2019-0506

Chu, S.-C., Chen, H.-T., & Gan, C. (2020). Consumers' engagement with corporate social responsibility (CSR) communication in social media: Evidence from China and the United States. *Journal of Business Research*, *110*, 260–271. https://doi.org/10.1016/j.jbusres.2020.01.036

Cini, A. C., & Ricci, C. (2018). CSR as a driver where ESG performance will ultimately matter. *Symphonya. Emerging Issues in Management*, *1*(1). https://doi.org/10.4468/2018.1.05cini.ricci

Clément, A., Robinot, É., & Trespeuch, L. (2023). The use of ESG scores in academic literature: A systematic literature review. *Journal of Enterprising Communities: People and Places in the Global Economy*, ahead-of-print. https://doi.org/10.1108/JEC-10-2022-0147

Cochran, P. L., & Wood, R. A. (1984). Corporate social responsibility and financial performance. *Academy of Management Journal*, *27*, 42–56.

Collison, D., Cross, S., Ferguson, J., Power, D., & Stevenson, L. (2012). Legal determinants of external finance revisited: The inverse relationship between investor protection and societal well-being. *Journal of Business Ethics*, *108*(3), 393–410. https://doi.org/10.1007/s10551-011-1098-0

Cornell, B., & Damodaran, A. (2020). Valuing ESG: Doing good or sounding good? *New York University – Stern School of Business*. https://doi.org/10.2139/ssrn.3557432

Council of the European Union. (2024, November 19). *Environmental, social and governance (ESG) ratings: Council greenlights new regulation*. Retrieved January 8, 2025, from https://www.consilium.europa.eu/en/press/press-releases/2024/11/19/environmental-social-and-governance-esg-ratings-council-greenlights-new-regulation/

Daugaard, D., & Ding, A. (2022). Global drivers for ESG performance: The body of knowledge. *Sustainability*, *14*(4), 2322. https://doi.org/10.3390/su14042322

Davis, K. (1975). Five propositions for Social Responsibility. *Business Horizons*, *18*, 19–24.

Davis, K., & Blomstrom, R. (1975). *Business and Society: Environment and Responsibility* (3rd ed.). McGraw-Hill.

de Freitas Netto, S. V., Sobral, M. F. F., Ribeiro, A. R. B., & Soares, G. R. D. L. (2020). Concepts and forms of greenwashing: A systematic review. *Environmental Sciences Europe*, *32*(1), 19. https://doi.org/10.1186/s12302-020-0300-3

de Jong, M. D. T., Huluba, G., & Beldad, A. D. (2020). Different shades of greenwashing: Consumers' reactions to environmental lies, half-lies, and organizations taking credit for following legal obligations. *Journal of Business and Technical Communication*, *34*(1), 38–76. https://doi.org/10.1177/1050651919874105

Dictionary, C. (2024). *Greenwashing*. Retrieved July 30, 2024, from https://dictionary.cambridge.org/dictionary/english/greenwashing?q=Greenwashing

Diltz, J. D. (1995). The private cost of socially responsible investing. *Applied Financial Economics*, *5*, 69–77.

Dimson, E., Marsh, P., & Staunton, M. (2020). Divergent ESG ratings. *The Journal of Portfolio Management*, *47*(1), 75–87. https://doi.org/10.3905/jpm.2020.1.175

Ding, D. K., Ferreira, C., & Wongchoti, U. (2019). The geography of CSR. *International Review of Economics & Finance*, *59*, 265–288. https://doi.org/10.1016/j.iref.2018.09.003

Dobiegała-Korona, B. (2015). Uwarunkowania i wyzwania budowy wartości klienta. W B. Dobiegała-Korona (Red.). In *Budowa Wartości Klienta* (pp. 19–38). Wydawnictwo Difin.

Drucker, P. F. (2002). *Myśli Przewodnie Druckera*. MT Biznes.

Duque-Grisales, E., & Aguilera-Caracuel, J. (2021). Environmental, social and governance (ESG) scores and financial performance of Multilatinas: Moderating effects of geographic international diversification and financial slack. *Journal of Business Ethics*, *168*(2), 315–334. https://doi.org/10.1007/s10551-019-04177-w

Dziawgo, D., & Dziawgo, L. (2017). *Private Banking – Wealth Management: Ecological Aspects*. Uniwersytet Ekonomiczny we Wrocławiu. https://doi.org/10.15611/pn.2017.478.14

Eccles, R. G., Ioannou, I., & Serafeim, G. (2014). The impact of corporate sustainability on organizational processes and performance. *Management Science*, *60*(11), 2835–2857. https://doi.org/10.1287/mnsc.2014.1984

Eccles, R. G., Lee, L.-E., & Stroehle, J. C. (2020). The social origins of ESG: An analysis of Innovest and KLD. *Organization & Environment*, *33*(4), 575–596. https://doi.org/10.1177/1086026619888994

Eccles, R. G., & Serafeim, G. (2013). A tale of two stories: Sustainability and the quarterly earnings call. *Journal of Applied Corporate Finance*, *25*(3), 8–19. https://doi.org/10.1111/jacf.12023

Eccles, R. G., & Stroehle, J. C. (2018). Exploring social origins in the construction of ESG measures (SSRN Scholarly Paper No. 3212685). *Social Science Research Network.* https://doi.org/10.2139/ssrn.3212685

Edelman Trust Barometer. (2021). *Special report: Institutional investors.* Retrieved July 20, 2023, from https://www.edelman.com/trust/2021-trust-barometer/investor-trust

Edmans, A. (2023a). Applying economics—not gut feel—to ESG. *Financial Analysts Journal, 79*(4), 16–29.

Edmans, A. (2023b). The end of ESG. *Financial Management, 52*(1), 3–17. https://doi.org/10.1111/fima.12413

Elkington, J. (2006). Governance for Sustainability. *Corporate Governance: An International Review, 14*(6), 522–529. https://doi.org/10.1111/j.1467-8683.2006.00527.x

Escrig-Olmedo, E., Fernández-Izquierdo, M. Á., Ferrero-Ferrero, I., Rivera-Lirio, J. M., & Muñoz-Torres, M. J. (2019). Rating the raters: Evaluating how ESG rating agencies integrate sustainability principles. *Sustainability, 11*(3), 915. https://doi.org/10.3390/su11030915

ESMA. (2025). *Sustainable finance.* Retrieved February 29, 2025, from https://www.esma.europa.eu/esmas-activities/sustainable-finance

Etter, M., Fieseler, C., & Whelan, G. (2019). Sharing economy, sharing responsibility? Corporate social responsibility in the digital age. *Journal of Business Ethics, 159*(4), 935–942. https://doi.org/10.1007/s10551-019-04212-w

European Commission. (2011). *A renewed EU strategy 2011–14 for corporate social responsibility* (COM(2011) 681 final). https://eur-lex.europa.eu/legal-content/EN/TXT/?uri=celex:52011DC0681

European Commission. (2020). *Taxonomy: Final report of the Technical Expert Group on Sustainable Finance. March 2020.* https://finance.ec.europa.eu/system/files/2020-03/200309-sustainable-finance-teg-final-report-taxonomy_en.pdf

European Commission. (2023a). Delegated Regulation (EU) 2023/2772 supplementing Directive 2013/34/EU as regards sustainability reporting standards. *Official Journal of the European Union.* https://finance.ec.europa.eu/system/files/2023-10/231017-proposal-sustainability-reporting-standards_en.pdf

European Commission. (2023b, March 22). *Proposal for a Directive on Green Claims.* https://environment.ec.europa.eu/publications/proposal-directive-green-claims_en

European Commission. (2024a, March 27). *New EU rules to empower consumers for the green transition enter into force* [News announcement]. Directorate-General for Energy. https://energy.ec.europa.eu/news/new-eu-rules-empower-consumers-green-transition-enter-force-2024-03-27_en

European Commission. (2024b). *Report on the future of European competitiveness* [Draghi Report]. https://commission.europa.eu/topics/eu-competitiveness/draghi-report_en

European Commission. (2025). *Omnibus: New rules to enhance transparency and consumer protection in the digital economy*. European Commission Press Corner. Retrieved March 3, 2025, from https://ec.europa.eu/commission/presscorner/detail/en/ip_25_614

European Council. (2024). *Environmental, social and governance (ESG) ratings: Council greenlights new regulation*. Press Release. Retrieved November 19, 2025, from https://www.consilium.europa.eu/en/press/press-releases/2024/11/19/environmental-social-and-governance-esg-ratings-council-greenlights-new-regulation/

European Parliament & Council. (2022). Directive (EU) 2022/2464 of the European Parliament and of the Council of 14 December 2022 amending Regulation (EU) No 537/2014, Directive 2004/109/EC, Directive 2006/43/EC and Directive 2013/34/EU, as regards corporate sustainability reporting. *Official Journal of the European Union, L 322*, 15–61. https://eur-lex.europa.eu/legal-content/EN/TXT/?uri=CELEX%3A32022L2464

European Parliament, & Council. (2024a). *Directive (EU) 2024/825 of 28 February 2024 on empowering consumers for the green transition through better protection against unfair practices and better information*. Official Journal of the European Union, L 2024/825, 6 March 2024, 1–22. https://eur-lex.europa.eu/eli/dir/2024/825/oj

European Parliament, & Council. (2024b). Directive (EU) 2024/1760 of 13 June 2024 on corporate sustainability due diligence and amending Directive (EU) 2019/1937 and Regulation (EU) 2023/2859 (Text with EEA relevance). *Official Journal of the European Union, L 2024/1760*, 5 July 2024. https://eur-lex.europa.eu/eli/dir/2024/1760/oj

European Parliament & Council. (2024c). Regulation (EU) 2024/3005 of 27 November 2024 on the transparency and integrity of environmental, social, and governance (ESG) rating activities and amending Regulations (EU) 2019/2088 and (EU) 2023/2859. *Official Journal of the European Union, L 3005*, 1–20. 12 December 2024. https://eur-lex.europa.eu/eli/reg/2024/3005/oj/eng

Facundo, A., Chancel, L., Piketty, T., Saez, E., & Zucman, G. (2018). The elephant curve of global inequality and growth. *AEA Papers and Proceedings, 108*, 103–108. https://doi.org/10.1257/pandp.20181073

Fatemi, A., Fooladi, I., & Tehranian, H. (2015). Valuation effects of corporate social responsibility. *Journal of Banking and Finance, 59*, 182–192. https://doi.org/10.1016/j.jbankfin.2015.04.028

Federal Trade Commission. (2012). *Guides for the use of environmental marketing claims*. https://www.ftc.gov/sites/default/files/documents/federal_register_notices/guides-use-environmental-marketing-claims-green-guides/greenguidesfrn.pdf

Feldman, S. J., Soyka, P. A., & Ameer, P. G. (1997). Does improving a firm's environmental management system and environmental performance result in a higher stock price? *Journal of Investing*, *6*(4), 87–97.

Filbeck, G., Gorman, R., & Zhao, X. (2009). The "Best Corporate Citizens": Are They Good for Their Shareholders? *Financial Review*, *44*(2), 239–262. https://doi.org/10.1111/j.1540-6288.2009.00217.x

Fotis, K., & Kamariotou, M. (2021). Artificial intelligence and business strategy towards digital transformation: A research agenda. *Sustainability*, *13*(4). https://doi.org/10.3390/su13042025 (2025).

Freeman, E. R. (1984). *Strategic Management: A Stakeholder Approach.*

Friede, G., Busch, T., & Bassen, A. (2015). ESG and financial performance: Aggregated evidence from more than 2000 empirical studies. *Journal of Sustainable Finance & Investment*, *5*(4), 210–233. https://doi.org/10.1080/20430795.2015.1118917

Garriga, E. (2014). Beyond stakeholder utility function: Stakeholder capability in the value creation process. *Journal of Business Ethics*, *120*, 489–507.

Gelcich, S., Buckley, P., Pinnegar, J. K., & Duarte, C. M. (2014). Public awareness, concerns, and priorities about anthropogenic impacts on marine environments. *Proceedings of the National Academy of Sciences of the United States of America*, *111*(42), 15042–15047. https://doi.org/10.1073/pnas.1417344111

Glick, D. M., Goldfarb, J. L., Heiger-Bernays, W., & Kriner, D. L. (2019). Public knowledge, contaminant concerns, and support for recycled water in the United States. *Resources, Conservation and Recycling*, *150*, 11.

Greenpeace, U. K. (2022). What is greenwashing? Greenpeace UK. Retrieved June 11, 2025, from https://www.greenpeace.org.uk/news/what-is-greenwashing/

Grudzewski, W. M., Hejduk, I. K., Sankowska, A., & Wańtuchowicz, A. (2010). *Sustainability W Biznesie, Czyli Przedsiębiorstwo Przyszłości.* Poltext.

Gruszecki, T. (2002). *Współczesne Teorie Przedsiębiorstwa.* Wydawnictwo Naukowe PWN.

Gu, Y., Yang, Y., & Wang, J. (2020). Research on employee sense of gain: The development of scale and influence mechanism. *Frontiers in Psychology*, *11*, 568609. https://www.frontiersin.org/articles/10.3389/fpsyg.2020.568609.Pozyskanoz.

Guerard Jr, J. B. (1997). Is there a cost to being socially responsible in investing? *Journal of Investing*, *6*, 87–97.

Hong, H., & Kacperczyk, M. (2009). The price of sin: The effects of social norms on markets. *Journal of Financial Economics*, *93*(1), 15–36. https://doi.org/10.1016/j.jfineco.2008.09.001

Hughes, A., Urban, M. A., & Wójcik, D. (2021). Alternative ESG ratings: How technological innovation is reshaping sustainable investment. *Sustainability*, *13*(6), 3551. https://doi.org/10.3390/su13063551

Humphrey, J. E., Lee, D. D., & Shen, Y. (2012). Does it cost to be sustainable? *Journal of Corporate Finance*, *18*(3), 626–639. https://doi.org/10.1016/j.jcorpfin.2012.03.002

Humphrey, J. E., & Tan, D. T. (2014). Does it really hurt to be responsible? *Journal of Business Ethics*, *122*(3), 375–386. https://doi.org/10.1007/s10551-013-1741-z

Hussain, Y., Abbass, K., Usman, M., Rehan, M., & Asif, M. (2022). Exploring the mediating role of environmental strategy, green innovations, and transformational leadership: The impact of corporate social responsibility on environmental performance. *Environmental Science and Pollution Research*, *29*(51), 7686–76880. https://link.springer.com/article/10.1007/s11356-022-20922-7

International Sustainability Standards Board. (2023a). *IFRS S1 General Requirements for Disclosure of Sustainability-related Financial Information*. IFRS Foundation. Retrieved March 4, 2025, from https://www.ifrs.org/issued-standards/ifrs-sustainability-standards-navigator/ifrs-s1-general-requirements/

International Sustainability Standards Board. (2023b). *IFRS S2 Climate-related Disclosures*. IFRS Foundation. Retrieved March 4, 2025, from https://www.ifrs.org/issued-standards/ifrs-sustainability-standards-navigator/ifrs-s2-climate-related-disclosures/

Ioannou, I., & Serafeim, G. (2019). Corporate Sustainability: A Strategy? (January 1, 2019). *Harvard Business School Accounting & Management Unit Working Paper* No. 19065, https://doi.org/10.2139/ssrn.3312191

ISO. (2024). *IWA 48:2024 - Framework for implementing environmental, social and governance (ESG) principles*. ISO. Retrieved February 12, 2025, from https://www.iso.org/standard/89240.html

ISS ESG. (2025). *ESG corporate ratings*. Retrieved September 20, 2025, from https://www.issgovernance.com/esg/ratings/

Iwacewicz, A. (2004). Certyfikaty i oznakowania ekologiczne jako metoda poprawy wiarygodności przedsiębiorstwa. In W. A. Kopczuk (red.), *Wiarygodność Ekonomiczna Przedsiębiorstwa – Ocena I Kształtowanie* (pp. 182–188). Wydawnictwo Wyższej Szkoły Finansów i Zarządzania w Białymstoku.

Jiménez-Parra, B., Alonso-Martínez, D., & Godos-Díez, J.-L. (2018). The influence of corporate social responsibility on air pollution: Analysis of environmental regulation and eco-innovation effects. *Corporate Social Responsibility and Environmental Management*, *25*(6), 1029–1416. https://doi.org/10.1002/csr.1645

Jonikas, D. (2012). Value Creation Through CSR at Stakeholders Level. *Economics and Management*, *17*(20), 693–698.

Juscius, V., & Jonikas, D. (2013). Integration of CSR into value creation chain: Conceptual framework. *Inzinerine Ekonomika-Engineering Economics*, *24*(1), 63–70.

Kanter, R. M. (2011). How Great Companies Think Differently. *Harvard Business Review*. Nov. 66–78.

Karwowski, M., & Raulinajtys-Grzybek, M. (2021). The application of corporate social responsibility (CSR) actions for mitigation of environmental, social, corporate governance (ESG) and reputational risk in integrated reports. *Corporate Social Responsibility and Environmental Management*, *28*(4). https://doi.org/10.1002/csr.2137 (Article 4).

Kathan, M. C., Utz, S., Dorfleitner, G., Eckberg, J., & Chmel, L. (2025). What you see is not what you get: ESG scores and greenwashing risk. *Finance Research Letters*, *74*, 106710. https://doi.org/10.1016/j.frl.2024.106710

Kathayat, A. (2022). A case against CSR initiatives. *Open Journal of Business and Management*, *10*(2), 2. https://doi.org/10.4236/ojbm.2022.102039

Kaźmierczak, M. (2022). A literature review on the difference between CSR and ESG. *Zeszyty Naukowe Politechniki Śląskiej. Organizacja I Zarządzanie*, *162*, 162. https://doi.org/10.29119/1641-3466.2022.162.16

Khan, M. A. (2022). A bibliometric analysis of ESG performance in the banking industry: From the current status to future directions. *Research in International Business and Finance*, *61*(10). https://doi.org/10.1016/j.ribaf.2022.101668

Kim, J., Kim, M., Im, S., & Choi, D. (2021). Competitiveness of e-commerce firms through ESG logistics. *Sustainability*, *13*(20). https://doi.org/10.3390/su132011548 (Article 20).

Kim, M., & Kim, J. (2020). Corporate social responsibility, employee engagement, well-being and the task performance of frontline employees. *Management Decision*, *59*(8), 2040–2056. https://doi.org/10.1108/MD-03-2020-0268

King, A., & Lenox, M. (2002). Exploring the Locus of Profitable Pollution Reduction. *Management Science*, *48*(2), 289–299. https://doi.org/10.1287/mnsc.48.2.289.258

Klimek, J. (2014). *Etyka Biznesu. Teoretyczne Założenia, Praktyka Zastosowań*. Wydawnictwo Difin.

Kock, C. J., & Min, B. S. (2016). Legal origins, corporate governance, and environmental outcomes. *Journal of Business Ethics*, *138*(3), 507–524. https://doi.org/10.1007/s10551-015-2617-1

Kolk, A. (2016). The social responsibility of international business: From ethics and the environment to CSR and sustainable development. *Journal of World Business*, *51*(1), 23–34. https://doi.org/10.1016/j.jwb.2015.08.010

Kong, D., & Liu, B. (2023). Digital technology and corporate social responsibility: Evidence from China. *Emerging Markets Finance and Trade*, *59*(9), 2967–2993. https://doi.org/10.1080/1540496X.2023.2199122

Korkmaz, M. (2018). Public awareness and perceptions of climate change: Differences in concern about climate change in the West Mediterranean region of Turkey. *Applied Ecology and Environmental Research*, *16*(4), 4039–4050.

Kotsantonis, S., & Serafeim, G. (2019). Four things no one will tell you about ESG data. *Journal of Applied Corporate Finance*, *31*(2), 50–58. https://doi.org/10.1111/jacf.12346

Kuciński, K. (2009). Wprowadzenie. In W. K. Kuciński (Ed.), *Strategie Przedsiębiorstw Wobec Wymogów Zrównoważonego Rozwoju*. Oficyna Wydawnicza Szkoły Głównej Handlowej w Warszawie.

Kwon, J., & Ahn, J. (2021). Socio-demographic characteristics and green consumption behavior in developing countries: The case of Malaysia. *Social Responsibility Journal*, *17*(8), 1213–1231. https://doi.org/10.1108/SRJ-02-2020-0071

Lakner, C., & Milanovic, B. (2013). Global income distribution: From the fall of the Berlin Wall to the Great Recession. *Policy Research Working Paper* No. 6719. World Bank. Pozyskano z: http://hdl.handle.net/10986/16935

Larcker, D. F., Tayan, B., & Watts, E. M. (2022). Seven myths of ESG. *European Financial Management*, *28*(4), 869–882. https://doi.org/10.1111/eufm.12378

Latham & Watkins LLP. (2025, June). European Commission announces intention to withdraw EU Green Claims Directive proposal, although the status remains unclear. https://www.lw.com/en/insights/european-commission-announces-intention-to-withdraw-eu-green-claims-directive-proposa

Lee, K.-H., Cin, B. C., & Lee, E. Y. (2016). Environmental responsibility and firm performance: The application of an environmental, social, and governance model. *Business Strategy and the Environment*, *25*(1), 40–53. https://doi.org/10.1002/bse.1855

Li, F., Li, T., & Minor, D. (2016). CEO power, corporate social responsibility, and firm value: A test of agency theory. *International Journal of Managerial Finance*, *12*(5), 611–628. https://doi.org/10.1108/IJMF-05-2015-0116

Li, X., Xu, F., & Jing, K. (2022). Robust enhanced indexation with ESG: An empirical study in the Chinese stock market. *Economic Modelling*, *107*, 105711. https://doi.org/10.1016/j.econmod.2021.105711

Liang, H., & Renneboog, L. (2021). Corporate social responsibility and sustainable finance: A review of the literature. *Corporate Social Responsibility and Sustainable Finance*. https://doi.org/10.1093/acrefore/9780190625979.013.592

Liao, P.-C., Shih, Y.-N., Wu, C.-L., Zhang, X.-L., & Wang, Y. (2018). Does corporate social performance pay back quickly? A longitudinal content analysis on international contractors. *Journal of Cleaner Production*, *170*, 1328–1337. https://doi.org/10.1016/j.jclepro.2017.09.230

Lo, S.-F., & Sheu, H.-J. (2007). Is corporate sustainability a value-increasing strategy for business? *Corporate Governance: An International Review*, *15*(2), 345–358. https://doi.org/10.1111/j.1467-8683.2007.00565.x

Lock, I. (2019). Explicating communicative organization-stakeholder relationships in the digital age: A systematic review and research agenda. *Public Relations Review*, *45*(4), 101829. https://doi.org/10.1016/j.pubrev.2019.101829

Mackenzie, C. (2007). Boards, incentives and corporate social responsibility: The case for a change of emphasis. *Corporate Governance: An International Review*, *15*(5), 935–943. https://doi.org/10.1111/j.1467-8683.2007.00623.x

Majewski, S. (2005). Społeczna odpowiedzialność spółek publicznych czy celowy wybór towarzystw funduszy inwestycyjnych. *Zeszyty Naukowe Uniwersytetu Szczecińskiego*, *415*(16), 199–209.

Maqbool, S., & Zameer, M. N. (2018). Corporate social responsibility and financial performance: An empirical analysis of Indian banks. *Future Business Journal*, *4*(1), 84–93. https://doi.org/10.1016/J.FBJ.2017.12.002

Margolis, J. D., Elfenbein, H. A., & Walsh, J. P. (2009). Does it pay to be good ... and does it matter? A meta-analysis of the relationship between corporate social and financial performance. *SSRN Scholarly Paper* 1866371. https://doi.org/10.2139/ssrn.1866371

Marquis, C., & Raynard, M. (2015). Institutional strategies in emerging markets. *Academy of Management Annals*, *9*(1), 291–335.

Martin, R. L. (2002). The virtue matrix: Calculating the return on corporate responsibility. *Harvard Business Review*, *80*(3), 3–9.

Masulis, R. W., & Reza, S. W. (2015). Agency problems of corporate philanthropy. *Review of Financial Studies*, *28*(2), 592–636. https://doi.org/10.1093/RFS/HHU082

Matos, P. (2020). ESG and responsible institutional investing around the world: A critical review. *CFA Institute Research Foundation Literature. Reviews*. https://doi.org/10.2139/ssrn.3668998

Matten, D., & Moon, J. (2008). "Implicit" and "explicit" CSR: A conceptual framework for a comparative understanding of corporate social responsibility. *Academy of Management Review*, *33*(2), 404–424.

McNicholas, G., & Cotton, M. (2019). Stakeholder perceptions of marine plastic waste management in the United Kingdom. *Ecological Economics*, *163*, 77–87. https://doi.org/10.1016/J.ECOLECON.2019.04.022

McWilliams, A., & Siegel, D. (2001). Corporate social responsibility: A theory of the firm perspective. *The Academy of Management Review*, *26*(1), 117–127.

Ministry of Development and Technology of the Republic of Poland. (2023). *Implementation of the Sustainable Development Goals in Poland: 2023 report under the monitoring programme of the 2030 Agenda*. Retrieved July 14, 2024, from https://www.gov.pl/web/rozwoj-technologia/monitoring-realizacji-agendy-2030

Ministry of Funds and Regional Policy of the Republic of Poland. (2020, January 21). *Order of the Minister of Funds and Regional Policy on the establishment of the Team for Sustainable Development and Corporate Social Responsibility*. Ministerial Official Gazette. Retrieved from https://sip.lex.pl/akty-prawne/dzienniki-resortowe/powolanie-zespolu-do-spraw-zrownowazonego-rozwoju-i-spolecznej-35725408

Mitchell, L., & Ramey, W. (2011). Look how green I am! An individual-level explanation for greenwashing. *Journal of Applied Business and Economics*, *12*(6), 40–45. https://papers.ssrn.com/abstract=2409956

Mitchell, R. K., Agle, B. R., & Wood, D. J. (1997). Toward a Theory of Stakeholder Identification and Salience: Defending the Principle of Who and What Really Counts. *Academy of Management Review*, *22*(4), 853–886.

Modern Slavery Act. (2015). c. 30. https://www.legislation.gov.uk/ukpga/2015/30/enacted

Moody's. (2025). *ESG and climate risk capabilities.* Retrieved September 20, 2025, from https://www.moodys.com/web/en/us/capabilities/esg.html

Morningstar. (2025). *Morningstar ESG solutions.* Retrieved September 20, 2025, from https://www.morningstar.com/business/brands/esg

Moyer, J. D., Verhagen, W., Mapes, B., Bohl, D. K., Xiong, Y., Yang, V., et al. (2022). How many people is the COVID-19 pandemic pushing into poverty? A long-term forecast to 2050 with alternative scenarios. *PLOS ONE*, *17*(7), e0270846. https://doi.org/10.1371/journal.pone.0270846

MSCI. (2025). Sustainable investing powered by insight. Retrieved September 20, 2025, from https://www.msci.com/data-and-analytics/sustainability-solutions

Murè, P., Spallone, M., Mango, F., Marzioni, S., & Bittucci, L. (2021). ESG and reputation: The case of sanctioned Italian banks. *Corporate Social Responsibility and Environmental Management*, *28*(1), 265–277. https://doi.org/10.1002/csr.2047

Nartowski, A. S. (2016). *Dobre Praktyki Spółek Notowanych Na GPW 2016. Podręcznik GPW W Warszawie*. Giełda Papierów Wartościowych w Warszawie.

Narula, R. (2018). Multinational firms and the extractive sectors in the twenty-first century: Can they drive development? *Journal of World Business*, *53*(1), 85–91. https://doi.org/10.1016/j.jwb.2017.09.004

Nastran, M., Pintar, M., Železnikar, Š., & Cvejić, R. (2022). Stakeholders' perceptions on the role of urban green infrastructure in providing ecosystem services for human well-being. *Land*, *11*(2), 299. https://doi.org/10.3390/land11020299

Nyilasy, G., Gangadharbatla, H., & Paladino, A. (2012). Greenwashing: A consumer perspective. *Economics & Sociology*, *5*(2), 116–123, 153–154.

Orbik, Z., & Zozuľaková, V. (2019). Corporate social and digital responsibility. *Management Systems in Production Engineering*, *27*(2), 79–83. https://doi.org/10.1515/mspe-2019-0013

Orlitzky, M. (2005). Payoffs to social and environmental performance. *The Journal of Investing*, *14*(3), 48–52.

Orlitzky, M. (2011). Institutional Logics in the Study of Organizations: The Social Construcion of the Relationship between Corporate Social and Financial Performance. *Business Ethics Quarterly*, *21*(3), 409–444.

Orlitzky, M., Schmidt, F. L., & Rynes, S. L. (2003). Corporate social and financial performance: A meta-analysis. *Organization Studies*, *24*(3), 403–441.

Orock, R. T. E. (2013). Less-told stories about corporate globalization: Transnational corporations and CSR as the politics of (ir)responsibility in Africa. *Dialectical Anthropology*, *37*(1), 27–50. https://doi.org/10.1007/s10624013-9293-2

Österblom, H., Bebbington, R., Blasiak, M., Sobkowiak, M., & Folke, C. (2022). Transnational corporations, biosphere stewardship, and sustainable futures. *Annual Review of Environment and Resources*, *47*(1), 609–635. https://doi.org/10.1146/annurev-environ-120120-052845

Osuji, O., Ngwu, F., & Jamali, D. (2019a). CSR and sustainable development cross-country studies. In O. Osuji, F. Ngwu, & D. Jamali (Eds.), *Corporate Social Responsibility in Developing and Emerging Markets: Institutions, Actors and Sustainable Development* (131–278). Cambridge University Press.

Pakulska, T., & Poniatowska-Jaksch, M. (2009a). *Korporacje Transnarodowe a Globalne Pozyskiwanie Zasobów*. Oficyna Wydawnicza Szkoły Głównej Handlowej.

Parliament of the Republic of Poland. (2024). Act of 6 December 2024 amending the Accounting Act, the Act on Statutory Auditors, Audit Firms, and Public Oversight, and certain other acts. *Journal of Laws*, 2024, item 1863. https://isap.sejm.gov.pl/isap.nsf/DocDetails.xsp?id=WDU20240001863

Parmar, B. L., Freeman, R. E., Harrison, J. S., Wicks, A. C., Purnell, L., & De Colle, S. (2010). Stakeholder theory: The state of the art. *The Academy of Management Annals*, *4*(1), 403–445.

Partner, C. (2025, August 1). Green Claims Directive on hold: Much ado about nothing? Retrieved September 14, 2025, from https://www.climatepartner.com/en/knowledge/blog/green-claims-directive-on-hold#:~:text=ClimatePartner-,Green%20Claims%20Directive%20on%20hold:%20Much%20ado%20about%20nothing?,directive%20intended%20to%20step%20in

Pavlovich, K., & Corner, P. D. (2014). Conscious enterprise emergence: Shared value creation through expanded conscious awareness. *Journal of Business Ethics*, *121*(3), 341–351.

Pérez, L., Hunt, V., Samandari, H., Nuttall, R., & Biniek, K. (2022). Does ESG really matter—and why? *McKinsey Quarterly*. Retrieved from https://www.mckinsey.com/~/media/mckinsey/business%20functions/sustainability/our%20insights/does%20esg%20really%20matter%20and%20why/does-esg-really-matter-and-why-vf.pdf

Pietrewicz, J. W. (2011). *Ochrona Środowiska W Warunkach Procesów Globalizacji*. Oficyna Wydawnicza Szkoły Głównej Handlowej.

Pietzner, K., & Schumann, K. (2011). Public awareness and perceptions of carbon dioxide capture and storage (CCS): Insights from surveys administered to representative samples in six European countries. *Energy Procedia*, *4*, 6300–6306. https://doi.org/10.1016/j.egypro.2011.02.645

Piketty, T. (2015). *Ekonomia Nierówności*. Wydawnictwo Krytyki Politycznej.

Piontek, B. (2002). *Koncepcja Rozwoju Zrównoważonego I Trwałego Polski*. Wydawnictwo Naukowe PWN.

Platonova, E., Asutay, M., Dixon, R., & Mohammand, S. (2018). The impact of corporate social responsibility disclosure on financial performance: Evidence from the GCC Islamic banking sector. *Journal of Business Ethics*, *151*(2), 451–471. https://doi.org/10.1007/s10551-016-3229-0

Płoszajski, P. (2012). Ruchomy cel: O konieczności redefinicji teorii i praktyki społecznej odpowiedzialności przedsiębiorstw w warunkach nowej gospodarki. In W. P. Płoszajski (Ed.), *Społeczna Odpowiedzialność Biznesu W Nowej Gospodarce* (11–27). Oficyna Wydawnicza Szkoły Głównej Handlowej, Wydawnictwo Open Links.

POLSIF. (2024). *Sustainable Investment Forum Poland*. Retrieved December 20, 2024, from https://www.polsif.org/

Poniatowska-Jaksch, M. (2013). Przesłanki nowego myślenia strategicznego. In W. M. Duczkowska-Piasecka, M. Poniatowska-Jaksch, & K. Duczkowska-Małysz (Eds.), *Model Biznesu. Nowe Myślenie Strategiczne* (21–62). Wydawnictwo Difin.

Porter, M. E., & Kramer, M. R. (2002). The competitive advantage of corporate philanthropy. *Harvard Business Review*, *80*(12), 56–68.

Porter, M. E., & Kramer, M. R. (2006). Strategy and society: The link between competitive advantage and corporate social responsibility. *Harvard Business Review*, *84*(12), 78–92.

Porter, M. E., & Kramer, M. R. (2011). Creating shared value: How to reinvent capitalism—and unleash a wave of innovation and growth. *Harvard Business Review*, *89*(1/2), 62–67.

Porter, M. E., Kramer, M. R., & Serafeim, G. (2019). Where ESG fails. *Institutional Investor*. Retrieved from https://www.institutionalinvestor.com/article/2bswdin8nvg922puxdzwg/opinion/where-esg-fails

Prahalad, C. K., & Hammond, A. (2002). Serving the world's poor, profitably. *Harvard Business Review*, *80*(9), 48–57.

Prahalad, C. K., & Hart, S. (2002). The fortune at the bottom of the pyramid. *Harvard Business Review*, *80*(12), 55–67.

Prahalad, C. K., & Krishnan, M. S. (2010). *Nowa Era Informacji*. Wydawnictwo Profesjonalne PWN.

Prahalad, C. K., & Ramaswamy, V. (2005). *Przyszłość Konkurencji*. Polskie Wydawnictwo Ekonomiczne.

Ramchander, S., Schwebach, R. G., & Staking, K. (2012). The informational relevance of corporate social responsibility: Evidence from DS400 Index reconstructions. *Strategic Management Journal*, *33*(3), 303–314. https://doi.org/10.1002/smj.952

Rao, K., & Tilt, C. (2016). Board composition and corporate social responsibility: The role of diversity, gender, strategy and decision making. *Journal of Business Ethics*, *138*(2), 327–347. https://doi.org/10.1007/s10551-015-2613-5

Rees, W., & Rodionova, T. (2015). The influence of family ownership on corporate social responsibility: An international analysis of publicly listed companies. *Corporate Governance: An International Review*, *23*(3), 184–202. https://doi.org/10.1111/corg.12086

Refinitiv. (2025). *ESG scores*. Retrieved September 20, 2025, from https://www.refinitiv.com/en/sustainable-finance/esg-scores

Republic of Poland Service. (2019). *Capital Market Development Strategy*. Retrieved July 18, 2024, from https://www.gov.pl/web/finanse/strategia-rozwoju-rynku-kapitalowego

Responsible Business Forum. (2005–2024). Responsible business in Poland. Good practices [Annual report series]. Warsaw: Responsible Business Forum. https://raportyzr.pl/

Responsible Business Forum. (2025). *Forum Odpowiedzialnego Biznesu*. Retrieved July 18, 2025. https://odpowiedzialnybiznes.pl/

Ricart, J. E., Rodríguez, M. Á., & Sánchez, P. (2005). Sustainability in the boardroom: An empirical examination of Dow Jones Sustainability World Index leaders. *Corporate Governance: The International Journal of Business in Society*, *5*(3), 24–41. https://doi.org/10.1108/14720700510604670

Robeco. (2020). *Sustainability Report*. Robeco. Retrieved 21, 2024, from https://www.robeco.com/en-int/insights/2018/08/the-big-book-of-sustainable-investing?z=%5B%2asearchterm%2a%5D&cmp=se_3_12160&gclid=Cj0KCQjwqs6lBhCxARIsAG8YcDhBmdB56wF12BbaZ-gWmha9H1cZZj4vzB5dx9cRJVAFvayiywJJousaAp8eEALw_wcB

Robeco. (2025). *Indices and sustainability themes*. Retrieved September 20, 2025, from https://www.robeco.com/en-int/themes/indices.

Rodriguez-Fernandez, M. (2016). Social responsibility and financial performance: The role of good corporate governance. *BRQ Business Research Quarterly*, *19*(2), 137–151. https://doi.org/10.1016/j.brq.2015.08.001

Roszkowska-Śliż, M. (2012). CSR 2.0, czyli społeczna odpowiedzialność biznesu w czasach Web 2.0. In P. Płoszajski (Ed.), *Społeczna Odpowiedzialność Biznesu W Nowej Gospodarce* (77–95). Oficyna Wydawnicza Szkoły Głównej Handlowej & Wydawnictwo Open Links.

Ruiz-Blanco, S., Romero, S., & Fernandez-Feijoo, B. (2022). Green, blue or black, but washing–What company characteristics determine greenwashing? *Environment, Development and Sustainability, 24*(3), 4024–4045. https://doi.org/10.1007/s10668-021-01602-x

Russell, F. T. S. E. (2025). *FTSE4Good Index Series*. Retrieved September 20, 2025, from https://www.ftserussell.com/products/indices/ftse4good

Russell, J. W., & Brockman, C. M. (2011). Do shareholders benefit from sound corporate citizenship? *Review of Business Research, 11*(5), 21–32.

Russo, M. V., & Fouts, P. A. (1997). A resource-based perspective on corporate environmental performance and profitability. *Academy of Management Journal, 40*(3), 534–559.

Rytelewska, G. (2003). Proekologiczne postawy społeczne w warunkach globalizacji a konkurencja na rynkach finansowych. In L. Pawłowicz & R. Wierzba (Eds.), *Rynki Finansowe Wobec Procesów Globalizacji* (235–244). Gdańska Akademia Bankowa przy Instytucie Badań nad Gospodarką Rynkową; CeDeWu.

S&P Global. (2025). *Trucost environmental data and risk analysis*. Retrieved September 20, 2025, from https://www.spglobal.com/esg/trucost

Salaber, J. (2013). Religion and returns in Europe. *European Journal of Political Economy, 32*, 149–160. https://doi.org/10.1016/j.ejpoleco.2013.07.002

Scherer, A. G., & Palazzo, G. (2011). The new political role of business in a globalized world: A review of a new perspective on CSR and its implications for the firm, governance, and democracy. *Journal of Management Studies, 48*(4), 899–931. https://doi.org/10.1111/j.1467-6486.2010.00950.x

Schmidt, M. A., & Cracau, D. (2017). A cross-country comparison of the corporate social responsibility orientation in Germany and Qatar: An empirical study among business students. *Business & Professional Ethics Journal, 37*(1), 1–30. https://doi.org/10.5840/bpej201712866

Schönherr, N., Findler, F., & Martinuzzi, A. (2017). Exploring the interface of CSR and the Sustainable Development Goals. *Transnational Corporations, 24*(3), 33–47.

Seele, P., & Gatti, L. (2017). Greenwashing revisited: In search of a typology and accusation-based definition incorporating legitimacy strategies. *Business Strategy and the Environment, 26*(2), 239–252. https://doi.org/10.1002/bse.1912

Serres, C., Hudon, M., & Maon, F. (2022). Social corporations under the spotlight: A governance perspective. *Journal of Business Venturing, 37*(3), 106192. https://doi.org/10.1016/j.jbusvent.2022.106192

Sethi, P. (1975). Dimensions of Corporate Social Performance: An Analytical Framework. *California Management Review, 17*(3), 58–64.

Shen, M., & Wang, J. (2022). The impact of pro-environmental awareness components on green consumption behavior: The moderation effect of consumer perceived cost, policy incentives, and face culture. *Frontiers in Psychology, 13*, 1–13. https://doi.org/10.3389/fpsyg.2022.580823

Sky News. (2023, July 28). *Speech by António Guterres, Secretary-General of the United Nations* [Video]. YouTube. https://www.youtube.com/watch?v=nWbdXl4XSiI (Accessed: May 30, 2025).

Soma, K., Termeer, C. J. A. M., & Opdam, P. (2016). Informational governance – A systematic literature review of governance for sustainability in the Information Age. *Environmental Science & Policy, 56*, 89–99. https://doi.org/10.1016/j.envsci.2015.11.006

Stankiewicz, A. (2024, January 17). *U.S. sustainable funds register first annual outflows in 2023: Mediocre performance weighed on investor sentiment last year.* Morningstar. Retrieved November 28, 2024, from https://www.morningstar.com/sustainable-investing/us-sustainable-funds-register-first-annual-outflows-2023

Stiglitz, J. E. (2013). *The Price of Inequality: How Today's Divided Society Endangers Our Future.* Penguin Books.

Sugai, P. (2021). The Definition, Identification and Eradication of Value Washing. *Journal of Creating Value, 7*(2), 165–169. https://doi.org/10.1177/23949643211032073

Sustainalytics. (2025). *ESG ratings.* Retrieved September 20, 2025, from https://www.sustainalytics.com/esg-ratings

Szymański, W. (2007). *Czy Globalizacja Musi Być Irracjonalna?* Oficyna Wydawnicza Szkoły Głównej Handlowej.

Szymański, W. (2009). *Kryzys Globalny. Pierwsze Przybliżenie.* Wydawnictwo Difin.

Szymański, W. (2015). *Świat I Polska Wobec Wyzwań.* Wydawnictwo Difin.

Tan, Y., & Zhu, Z. (2022). The effect of ESG rating events on corporate green innovation in China: The mediating role of financial constraints and managers' environmental awareness. *Technology in Society, 68*, 101906. https://doi.org/10.1016/j.techsoc.2022.101906

Taufique, K. M. R., Siwar, C., Chamhuri, N., & Sarah, F. H. (2016). Integrating general environmental knowledge and eco-label knowledge in understanding ecologically conscious consumer behavior. *Procedia Economics and Finance, 37*, 39–45. https://doi.org/10.1016/S2212-5671(16)30090-9

Trinks, P. J., & Scholtens, B. (2017). The opportunity cost of negative screening in socially responsible investing. *Journal of Business Ethics, 140*(2), 193–208. https://doi.org/10.1007/s10551-015-2684-3

UN. (1987). *Our Common Future.* World Commission on Environment and Development. Retrieved April 17, 2024, from https://sustainabledevelopment.un.org/content/documents/5987our-common-future.pdf

UN. (2004). *Who cares wins. Connecting Financial Markets to a Changing World.* Retrieved May 20, 2024, from https://efaidnbmnnnibpcajpcglclefindmkaj/https://www.unepfi.org/fileadmin/events/2004/stocks/who_cares_wins_-global_compact_2004.pdf
UN. (2015). *Resolution adopted by the General Assembly on 25 September 2015 (A/RES/70/1)*. Retrieved from https://docs.un.org/en/A/RES/70/1
UN Global Compact Poland. (2024). *Homepage*. Retrieved August 20, 2024, from http://ungc.org.pl/
van Duuren, E., Plantinga, A., & Scholtens, B. (2016). ESG integration and the investment management process: Fundamental investing reinvented. *Journal of Business Ethics, 138*(3), 525–533. https://doi.org/10.1007/s10551-015-2610-8
Viviers, S., & Eccles, N. S. (2012). 35 years of socially responsible investing (SRI) research: General trends over time. *South African Journal of Business Management, 43*(4), 4. https://doi.org/10.4102/sajbm.v43i4.478
Vos, J. (2009). Actions speak louder than words: Greenwashing in corporate America. *Notre Dame Journal of Law, Ethics & Public Policy, 23*, 673.
Wang, S. (2014). On the Relationship between CSR and Profit. *Journal of Business Ethics, 7*(1), 51–57.
Wang, Y., Lu, T., & Qiao, Y. (2021). The effect of air pollution on corporate social responsibility performance in high energy-consumption industry: Evidence from Chinese listed companies. *Journal of Cleaner Production, 280*, 124345. https://doi.org/10.1016/j.jclepro.2020.124345
Wang, Z., & Sarkis, J. (2017). Corporate social responsibility governance, outcomes, and financial performance. *Journal of Cleaner Production, 162*, 1607–1616. https://doi.org/10.1016/j.jclepro.2017.06.142
Wartick, S. L., & Cochran, P. L. (1985). The evolution of the corporate social performance model. *Academy of Management Review, 10*(4), 758–769.
Weber, M. (2008). The business case for corporate social responsibility: A company-level measurement approach for CSR. *European Management Journal, 26*(4), 247–261.
Wheeler, D., Colbert, B., & Freeman, R. E. (2003). Focusing on value: Reconciling corporate social responsibility, stakeholder theory and sustainability in a network world. *Journal of General Management, 28*(3), 1–28.
Whelan, T., Atz, U., Van Holt, T., & Clark, C. (2021). *ESG and financial performance: Uncovering the relationship by aggregating evidence from 1000 plus studies published between 2015–2020.* NYU Stern Center for Sustainable Business. Retrieved September 19, 2024, from https://www.stern.nyu.edu/sites/default/files/assets/documents/NYU-RAM_ESG-Paper_2021%20Rev0.pdf
Winston, A. (2024). *2024 was a bad year for sustainability. Harvard Business Review*. Retrieved December 27, 2024, from https://hbr.org/2024/12/2024-was-a-bad-year-for-sustainability

Wood, D. J. (1991). Corporate social performance revisited. *Academy of Management Review*, *16*(4), 691–718.

WSE. (2016). *Dobre praktyki spółek notowanych na GPW*. Retrieved August 14, 2022, from https://www.gpw.pl/pub/GPW/files/PDF/GPW_1015_17_DOBRE_PRAKTYKI_v2.pdf

WSE. (2021). *Dobre praktyki spółek notowanych na GPW 2021*. Retrieved August 14, 2022, from https://www.gpw.pl/pub/GPW/files/PDF/GPW_1015_17_DOBRE_PRAKTYKI_v2.pdf

Wu, L., Shao, Z., Yang, C., Ding, T., & Zhang, W. (2020). The impact of CSR and financial distress on financial performance – Evidence from Chinese listed companies of the manufacturing industry. *Sustainability*, *12*(17), 6799. https://doi.org/10.3390/su12176799

Yang, Z., Nguyen, T. T. H., Nguyen, H. N., Nguyen, T. T. N., & Cao, T. T. (2020). Greenwashing behaviours: Causes, taxonomy and consequences based on a systematic literature review. *Journal of Business Economics and Management*, *21*(5), 1486–1504. https://doi.org/10.3846/jbem.2020.13225

Yuan, Y., Tian, G., Lu, L. Y., & Yu, Y. (2019). CEO ability and corporate social responsibility. *Journal of Business Ethics*, *157*(2), 391–411.

Zammit, A. (2003). *Development at Risk: Rethinking UN-business Partnerships*. United Nations Research Institute for Social Development & South Centre.

Żemigała, M. (2007). *Społeczna Odpowiedzialność Przedsiębiorstwa*. Oficyna Wydawnicza Wolters Kluwer Business.

CHAPTER 3

ESG in Businesses and Financial Markets in Poland, Europe and the World

3.1 Introduction

The present chapter is devoted to analysing the role and significance of the ESG concept in the marketplace, both from the perspective of businesses and financial markets, at the national (Polish), European and global levels. The initial section provides a comprehensive overview of the key international and pan-European initiatives in the field of ESG, which have a direct impact on the activities of organisations in the context of transformation towards sustainable development. The current state of implementation and main challenges associated with integrating ESG factors in the activities of Polish companies are then discussed, with particular emphasis on the results of locally conducted research.

The subsequent part of the chapter focuses on financial markets, presenting the current state of development of ESG assets in Poland and globally. The degree of integration of ESG aspects in investment strategies and their growing influence on decisions made by institutional and individual investors are analysed. Particular attention is given to the dynamic growth in the value of assets managed according to ESG criteria, indicating regional differences and local conditions, including European and Polish specifics.

The chapter identifies the main challenges associated with implementing the ESG concept in both the real economy and the financial sector. In

K. Łudzińska, *International ESG Perspectives*,
https://doi.org/10.1007/978-3-032-11666-6_3

conclusion, the importance of further education and promotion of environmental, social and governance aspects as necessary conditions to meet the growing market expectations and achieve sustainable development goals are emphasised.

3.2 Key International and Pan-European ESG Initiatives and Regulations

Globally, a growing number of initiatives and regulatory frameworks aim to standardise the integration of ESG aspects into both business operations and financial markets, with particular emphasis on sustainability reporting. The most important of these include the SFDR regulation, EU Taxonomy, the EU NFRD directive and its successor—the CSRD directive, European Sustainable Reporting Standards (ESRS), the EU CSDDD directive, as well as international frameworks, such as the recommendations of the Carbon Disclosure Project (CDP), Task Force on Climate-Related Financial Disclosures (TCFD) and non-financial reporting standards IFRS S1 and S2 developed by the International Sustainability Standards Board (ISSB). These issues are discussed in detail in Chap. 8.

This chapter complements this picture with other significant international and pan-European initiatives, which, although not always having the status of binding regulations, are already having, or will have in the near future, a significant impact on market practices in the ESG area. The most important of these include: UN Sustainable Development Goals (SDGs), Science Based Targets initiative (SBTi), Greenhouse Gas Protocol (GHG Protocol), the European Union regulation on Eco-Design for Sustainable Products (ESPR) including Digital Product Passports (DPPs) and the Regulation on Packaging and Packaging Waste (PPWR), as well as two particularly important EU regulations in the context of the Polish economy—Carbon Border Adjustment Mechanism (CBAM) and the Regulation on Preventing Deforestation (EUDR). Although these initiatives differ in scope and legal form, they share a common goal: to support economic transformation towards sustainable development—both on a European and global scale.

The concept of sustainability is the foundation for a range of international initiatives in the ESG area, and it is from this standpoint that this review should commence. The concept of sustainable development, also referred to as sustainability, was pioneered by the United Nations, which in 1987 published a report by the World Commission on Environment and Development, chaired by former Norwegian Prime Minister Gro Harlem Brundtland, titled 'Our Common Future' (World Commission on Environment and Development, 1987). This document instigated a comprehensive discourse on the future of the planet, culminating in the inaugural United Nations Conference on Environment and Development, otherwise referred to as the 'Earth Summit', which was held in 1992 in Rio de Janeiro (United Nations, 1992).

The report formulated the first universally recognised definition of sustainable development: 'meeting the needs of the present generation without compromising the ability of future generations to meet their own needs' (World Commission on Environment and Development, 1987). It was emphasised that an integrated approach encompassing three interrelated dimensions—social (People), environmental (Planet) and economic (Profit)—is required to establish the framework for sustainable economic growth, protection of natural resources and social development.

The concept of sustainability has been further articulated through the 17 Sustainable Development Goals (SDGs), which were established by the United Nations (UN) in 2015 as part of the 2030 Agenda. The 2030 Agenda constitutes a global action plan for peace, prosperity and environmental protection, which was adopted unanimously by all member states of the United Nations (United Nations, 2015). The aforementioned goals comprise 169 specific tasks and 232 indicators, the purpose of which is to monitor progress in their implementation.

The European Union has adopted sustainable and durable development as one of its key strategic objectives, as clearly stated in the most important programmatic documents concerning the economic and social policy of the Community. One such strategy is entitled *Towards a Sustainable Europe by 2030* and was published by the European Commission in 2019 (European Commission, 2019b). This document encompasses a broad spectrum of actions and initiatives that establish the framework for the European strategy for economic growth oriented towards sustainable development. Concurrently, it upholds a degree of adaptability, thereby enabling member states to adopt an individualised approach to the implementation of the Sustainable Development Goals (SDGs), in accordance with their respective socio-economic and energy conditions.

The varied pace of transformation, especially in terms of transitioning to renewable energy sources, has been highlighted by member states, for whom the full transition to a low-emission economy will require a greater investment of time than for countries already largely using green technologies. Poland, for instance, is facing the challenge of a prolonged transition to renewable energy sources, necessitating a more extended timeframe than that required by countries that have already attained a high level of advancement in sustainable energy systems. In response to these challenges, the European Union has developed the European Green Deal, a comprehensive action plan announced in December 2019, which aims to achieve climate neutrality by 2050 (European Commission, 2019a). The Green Deal constitutes a series of policies and legislative initiatives with the objective of transforming the European Union into a modern, resource-efficient and competitive economy. This document integrates climate, environmental and social issues, thereby establishing itself as a cornerstone of European ESG policy.

Among the international initiatives for the implementation of the UN's sustainable development goals, the Science Based Targets initiative (SBTi) is distinguished as a global initiative that supports businesses and financial institutions in establishing greenhouse gas emission reduction targets in accordance with current scientific knowledge and the objectives of the Paris Agreement (Science Based Targets initiative, 2025b). The objective of SBTi is to empower companies to ascertain the magnitude and pace at which they should curtail their emissions to avert the deleterious consequences of climate change and attain emission neutrality by 2050 at the latest. The initiative was constituted in 2015 as a joint venture among several organisations, namely the Carbon Disclosure Project (CDP), the United Nations Global Compact, the World Resources Institute (WRI) and the World Wide Fund for Nature (WWF). In 2023, SBTi was registered as a charity in the United Kingdom (Science Based Targets initiative, 2025a).

SBTi develops standards, tools and guidelines that enable companies to establish greenhouse gas emission reduction targets in accordance with the necessity to restrict global warming to well below 2 °C, preferably to 1.5 ° C compared to the pre-industrial era. In October 2021, the Science Based Targets initiative (SBTi) published the world's first 'Net-Zero' standard, which defines the framework and tools for companies to set emission neutrality goals based on scientific foundations (Science Based Targets initiative, 2021). The organisation also develops sector-specific guidelines, tailored to the specifics of various industries, such as the steel, cement, chemical, aviation and financial sectors (Science Based Targets initiative, 2024).

Notwithstanding its increasing popularity, the SBTi faces challenges, including the debate surrounding the role of offsets in achieving climate goals, and the need to increase transparency and operational efficiency throughout supply chains. In 2025, the organisation proposed new rules that allow companies to purchase emission removals for difficult-to-reduce residual emissions, while maintaining a rigorous approach to the use of offsets (Khan, 2025). Despite the challenges faced, SBTi continues to be a leading organisation in establishing emission reduction standards for businesses. It provides them with credible, science-based frameworks to support the transition towards sustainable development.

In the context of greenhouse gas emissions, the aforementioned Carbon Disclosure Project (now operating solely under the name CDP) is another leading initiative. It is an international non-profit organisation running a global disclosure system for environmental information for companies, cities, countries and regions (CDP, 2025). Its main goal is to encourage economic entities to disclose data on their impact on the climate, water resource consumption and deforestation, enabling investors and stakeholders to make more informed decisions in the field of sustainable development and environmental risk management (more on this in Chap. 8 on non-financial reporting).

The need to standardise the rules for reporting greenhouse gas emissions is also addressed by the GHG Protocol (Greenhouse Gas Protocol)—a global standard for accounting and reporting emissions, developed in 1998 by the aforementioned World Resources Institute (WRI) in cooperation with the World Business Council for Sustainable Development (WBCSD) (Greenhouse Gas Protocol, 2025a, b). The aim of the protocol is to provide consistent and transparent frameworks for organisations to identify, measure and manage greenhouse gas emissions. The GHG Protocol standard is the foundation of many international climate initiatives, such as the aforementioned Science Based Targets initiative (SBTi). It also forms the basis for corporate reporting under EU directives, such as CSRD or the EU taxonomy. Thanks to its universality and transparency, the GHG Protocol plays a key role in efforts to decarbonise the economy and achieve climate goals.

In the context of greenhouse gas emissions and climate change, the Carbon Border Adjustment Mechanism (CBAM) is an important instrument, particularly from the perspective of the Polish market. It was established by European Parliament and Council Regulation (EU) 2023/956 of 10 May 2023 and is a tool of the European Union's climate policy (European Parliament & Council, 2023a). The mechanism aims to prevent so-called 'carbon leakage', i.e. the transfer of production to countries with less stringent environmental regulations. CBAM introduces an obligation to purchase certificates reflecting the greenhouse gas emissions associated with the import of certain goods to EU countries, including cement, steel, aluminium, fertilisers, hydrogen and electricity (European Commission, 2023).

This mechanism is intended to balance the climate costs borne by EU producers covered by the EU ETS (European Emission Trading System), while promoting decarbonisation at a global level. From 1 October 2023 to the end of 2025, there is a transitional period during which importers must report emission data. However, the obligation to purchase certificates is set to come into effect from 1st January 2026 (European Commission, 2023). CBAM is a key element of the European Green Deal and is the first mechanism of its kind in the world, combining trade and climate policy to level the playing field and promote sustainable production (European Commission, 2023). At the same time, it has become part of the so-called Omnibus 1 simplification package, more on this in Chap. 8.

Another pillar of the European Green Deal is the Ecodesign for Sustainable Products Regulation (ESPR) (European Parliament and Council, 2024). This significantly expands the scope of ecodesign requirements to cover almost all physical goods introduced to the EU market. Certain categories, such as food, feed and medicinal products, are excluded as they are covered by other detailed regulations (European Commission, 2024). The aim of the regulation is to enhance the durability, repairability, reusability and recyclability of products, as well as their energy efficiency, throughout their entire life cycle (White & Case, 2024).

Furthermore, one of the key tools of the ESPR is the introduction of digital product passports (Digital Product Passports, DPPs), which will contain detailed information about the composition, origin, environmental impact and the possibilities of processing or disposal after the end of use (European Commission, 2024). In addition, the regulation introduces a ban on the destruction of unsold consumer goods, aimed at strengthening the transition to a circular economy (Ecochain, 2024).

Although the ESPR regulation came into effect on 18 July 2024, its provisions will be implemented gradually over the next few years (Noerr, 2024). The digital product passport is expected to be fully implemented by 19 July 2026 (White & Case, 2024). Similarly, the ban on the destruction of unsold consumer products will apply to large enterprises from 19 July 2026 and to medium-sized enterprises from 19 July 2030 (White & Case, 2024). In April 2025, the European Commission published the first ESPR action plan, identifying priority product groups and implementation measures for the next five years (European Commission, 2025a). The ESPR regulation therefore, represents a significant change for businesses in the European Union. Manufacturers, importers and distributors will need to adapt their production and logistics practices to the new standards, which will certainly require significant changes and investments.

In a similar vein, the Packaging and Packaging Waste Regulation (PPWR), adopted by the European Union in February 2025, represents a significant step towards sustainable packaging management (European Commission, 2025c). Replacing Directive 94/62/EC from 1994 (European Parliament and Council, 1994), the PPWR introduces uniform rules applicable in all Member States without the need for implementation into national law (European Parliament and Council, 2025). The regulation's primary objectives are to reduce packaging waste, increase the proportion of recycled materials and promote a circular economy. It sets basic targets to reduce the amount of packaging waste by 5% by 2030, 10% by 2035 and 15% by 2040 compared to the 2018 level (Packaging Dive, 2024). By 2030, all packaging introduced to the EU market must be fully recyclable in an economically viable way. Additionally, the PPWR introduces restrictions on single-use plastic packaging, including that used for fresh fruit and vegetables weighing less than 1.5 kg, as well as individual spice portions in the catering sector. Furthermore, businesses offering takeaway meals will be required to allow customers to use their own containers free of charge. The PPWR also foresees a ban on the use of per- and polyfluoroalkyl substances (PFAS) in food contact packaging from August 2026 (Packaging Dive, 2024). These new regulations not only aim to protect the environment, but also to ensure consistency in the internal market by unifying packaging standards across the European Union.

To further mitigate climate change, the Accountability Framework Initiative (AFi) was established. This is an agreement between non-governmental organisations that have developed common principles and guidelines aimed at eliminating deforestation, ecosystem degradation and human rights violations in the supply chains of agricultural and forestry products (AFi, 2025a). The AFi framework provides companies with tools and guidelines to help them formulate, implement and monitor commitments related to responsible sourcing, in line with the United Nations Sustainable Development Goals (AFi, 2019). These guidelines emphasise the protection of natural forests, avoiding the conversion of other ecosystems and respecting the rights of indigenous peoples and local communities. The AFi framework is used by hundreds of companies, financial institutions and organisations worldwide as a common platform for implementing and assessing progress in ethical supply chains (AFi, 2025b). The AFi guidelines provide organisations with guidance on how to report progress effectively, based on existing systems such as CDP and consistent with AFi principles. This enables companies to better manage environmental and social risk and demonstrate transparency and compliance with stakeholder expectations.

These efforts are also supported by new EU-level regulations. Adopted in 2023, the EU Deforestation Regulation (EUDR) is an important step towards reducing the European Union's impact on global deforestation and forest degradation (European Parliament and Council, 2023b). Under the regulations, companies must demonstrate that products introduced to the EU market, including soy, cocoa, coffee, palm oil, timber, rubber and beef, were not produced after 31 December 2020 in a way that contributed to deforestation or forest degradation (European Commission, 2025d). Companies will be required to conduct a due diligence process involving gathering information about the origin of products, assessing risk and taking preventive measures. In practice, this means tracing supply chains back to the farm where the raw materials were sourced. The regulation aims to protect tropical forests and biodiversity, and to combat climate change by reducing greenhouse gas emissions associated with the loss of forest areas.

The EUDR regulations were due to come into effect at the end of 2024. However, the European Commission is currently working with partner countries and companies to simplify the regulations and ensure an effective transition to deforestation-free supply chains. On 15 April 2025, the European Commission presented a number of simplifications to the EUDR regulations with the aim of reducing administrative burdens and facilitating their implementation (European Commission, 2025b).

These are intended to support companies, EU member state authorities and partner countries in demonstrating that their products do not contribute to deforestation. The ongoing work is subject to public consultation, with the aim of including further clarifications and simplifications regarding the scope of the EUDR. It is worth noting that the EUDR and the Corporate Sustainability Due Diligence Directive (CSDDD), which is discussed in Chap. 8, complement each other as part of the EU's strategy for sustainable development and strengthening corporate responsibility.

In addition to forestry-related issues, the sustainable management of water resources is becoming an increasingly important element of the ESG agenda and of corporate environmental responsibility. Launched in 2007 by the UN Secretary-General and the UN Global Compact in collaboration with the Pacific Institute, the CEO Water Mandate is a global initiative (UN-Water, 2025). It aims to encourage business leaders to implement responsible water resource management as part of sustainable development initiatives (CEO Water Mandate, 2025a). The initiative supports companies in developing, implementing and reporting on sustainable water management policies and offers a platform for sharing best practices and establishing partnerships to address urgent issues related to water scarcity, water quality and access to water and sanitation facilities. The initiative provides tools and resources such as the Water Stewardship Toolbox to help companies fulfil their water management commitments (CEO Water Mandate, 2024). By joining the CEO Water Mandate, companies can better manage water-related risks and actively participate in global efforts to achieve the Sustainable Development Goals, particularly Goal 6 relating to clean water and sanitation (CEO Water Mandate, 2025b).

In summary, sustainable development is a fundamental reference point for organisational activities within the ESG concept. At the corporate level, it can be defined as the effective adaptation to dynamic environmental changes, alongside the provision of valuable services in a manner that is consistent with the principles of sustainable development and considers environmental, social and economic factors (Schalock et al., 2016). In the context of corporate operations, this encompasses areas such as product recycling, the implementation of sustainable strategies and business processes, and the development of business models based on principles of efficiency and responsibility (Aldowaish et al., 2022). Literature also identifies key management pillars associated with sustainable development, including corporate strategy, human resource management, knowledge and innovation management, the use of indicators and assessment tools, the disclosure of non-financial data and integrated management systems (Nunhes et al., 2020).

As Abhayawansa and Mooneeapen (2022) note, organisations can take various paths towards sustainable development, but these require a systemic approach to be effective. The authors identify a set of systems that are beginning to influence the business environment. Implementing these systems requires a fundamental change in the way business objectives are approached. These systems include those that limit excessive consumption through resource usage limits or quotas; those focused on maximising social and environmental benefits instead of economic growth alone; and closed-loop systems that promote reuse, repair and resource processing as an alternative to recycling. Additionally, the authors emphasise the importance of models centred on functionality and user experience rather than product ownership; an example of this could be the sharing economy. The proposed solutions also include systems that promote professional development, creativity and employee skills, as well as systems based on collaboration and knowledge sharing rather than aggressive competition. Implementing these concepts requires a fundamental rethinking of a company's purpose and how it creates value.

3.3 Integrating ESG Aspects into the Activities of Polish Companies

Implementing the 17 Sustainable Development Goals (SDGs), which were adopted by the United Nations as part of the 2030 Agenda, requires coordinated action at many levels, including from international organisations, governments, public institutions, the private sector, and civil society and its stakeholders. Based on the principle of 'leave no one behind', this agenda promotes development that considers the needs of everyone, regardless of their socio-economic status, place of residence, or cultural, religious, or national affiliation.

Poland has declared the implementation of the 2030 Agenda to be a key part of its development strategy, integrating the SDGs with public policies. According to data from 2024, Poland ranks tenth in the world for progress in implementing the SDGs, behind countries such as Finland, Sweden, Denmark, Germany, Austria, France, Norway, Croatia and the United Kingdom (Sustainable Development Report, 2025).

Responsibility for monitoring and reporting on Poland's progress in implementing the 2030 Agenda lies with the Central Statistical Office, which runs a dedicated portal containing relevant data, indicators and analyses (Statistics Poland, 2024). This includes international indicators adopted by the UN, as well as national indicators reflecting Polish specifics, such as 'Poland on the path to sustainable development', which is published electronically. The latest available study covers data for 2024 (Statistics Poland, 2024).

Integrating ESG aspects into the activities of Polish companies remains a significant challenge, particularly in the context of energy transformation. The Polish energy sector's reliance on hard coal significantly limits the potential for a swift transition to more sustainable energy sources (Forum Energii, 2025). Another challenge is that Poland has not yet implemented any nuclear power plant projects, which complicates efforts to reduce emissions and decarbonise the economy. As a member of the European Union, Poland is subject to the same regulations as more developed European economies that are already further advanced in the energy transition process. As part of the European Green Deal, the European Commission has set ambitious goals, such as reducing greenhouse gas emissions by 55% by 2030 (the 'Fit for 55' programme) and achieving net-zero greenhouse gas emissions by 2050 (European Commission, 2021). This plan also includes key assumptions such as increasing the share of renewable energy sources to 40% of the European Union's energy mix and improving energy efficiency by 36–39%. As a member state, Poland faces the challenge of adapting its economy to these requirements, necessitating intensified efforts towards energy transformation and the integration of ESG into business strategies.

In October 2024, the international research institute Ayming conducted a study on the integration of ESG practices and strategies among 723 CEOs, CFOs, and ESG and sustainable development managers in eight countries, including Poland (Ayming, 2025). The study covered the Belgian, French, German, Italian, Portuguese, Spanish, British and Polish markets. It examined how companies incorporate ESG into their business strategies, the impact on their operations, the obstacles encountered in this process, and the extent to which organisations are prepared to report in accordance with the requirements of the Corporate Sustainability Reporting Directive (CSRD). Respondents represented four sectors: industrial production, the food industry, financial services, and IT and technology. They were also divided into two categories based on company size: large companies employing over 500 workers and medium-sized companies employing between 250 and 500 people. In Poland, the study covered 150 companies equally distributed across the aforementioned sectors. The study showed that 69% of Polish companies have a clearly defined ESG strategy, close to the European average of 72%. 61% of Polish companies currently meet the requirements of the CSRD directive, while a further 31% plan to do so within the next 12 months. 74% of Polish companies recognise the positive impact of ESG strategies on their business results, while 31% cite insufficient funding as the primary obstacle to implementing these strategies. This is the highest proportion among the countries surveyed (Ayming, 2025).

The Ayming study (2025) clearly indicates that companies are becoming more aware of and knowledgeable about ESG. They are also recognising more and more that ESG aspects affect their operations, both directly and indirectly. ESG is no longer merely a reporting obligation; it is evolving into a comprehensive organisational transformation process based on education and engagement at all levels of the company. The study results also show that, in terms of ESG, companies have primarily focused on the environmental aspect ('E'). Responsibility for protecting the natural environment is a priority for 35% of companies. This is not surprising, given that regulations in this area are becoming increasingly restrictive and that additional pressure is being exerted by growing social expectations and consumer demand.

Furthermore, according to the Ayming study (2025), 13% of Poland's largest companies allocate more than 10% of their revenues to investments in sustainable development, while 83% allocate more than 5%. Almost half (48%) of the organisations surveyed have set up dedicated ESG teams, supported by external partnerships (41%) and collaboration with subcontractors (25%). Polish companies focus on implementing key initiatives such as education and employee engagement, process automation and ESG risk management, including climate risk. The surveyed Polish companies see the greatest potential in artificial intelligence (AI) and machine learning (ML). According to 37% of respondents, these technologies enable process optimisation and improvement of ESG strategies.

The results of a study conducted by a team from the National Bank of Poland and published in January 2023 also shed light on the status of incorporating ESG criteria into companies' operations in Poland. The 100th edition of the Quick Monitoring report not only presents a summary of annual macroeconomic data and indicators, but also the results of a survey of Polish companies on energy and environmental issues (NBP, 2023). Conducted in December 2022, the study covered 1696 companies from across the country and various sectors of the economy, excluding agriculture, forestry and fishing. Large enterprises (those employing over 250 people) were the main focus, while micro-enterprises (those employing up to nine people) were underrepresented in the study. The issue of financing the green energy transformation also recurs in the study results. As many as 57% of Polish companies cited a lack of funds as the main obstacle.

Unfortunately, the analysis of the study results reveals some worrying trends. Most Polish companies do not prioritise strategic planning for energy use, including renewable energy. Only around a quarter of them have a defined energy management strategy, and just 12% use renewable energy or heat sources (NBP, 2023). Figure 3.1 shows that the vast majority of companies (73%) operate without an energy carrier management policy, while 20% have implemented a current policy and only 7% have adopted a long-term policy. This indicates limited strategic commitment to energy management across firms in Poland (Fig. 3.1).

Only one third of the surveyed enterprises undertook actions aimed at reducing CO_2 emissions and striving for climate neutrality. Of these enterprises, 11% considered these actions to be a key part of their strategy (NBP, 2023). The main motivations for these actions were environmental responsibility (63%), reducing costs (61%), ensuring energy supply continuity (56%), and legal obligations (51%). Nevertheless, almost half of the companies cited the unprofitability of such actions (49%) and financing difficulties (47%) as

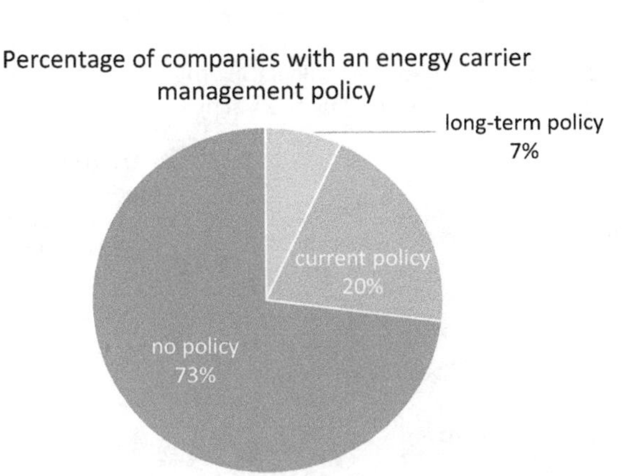

Fig. 3.1 Policy on the management of energy carriers in enterprises in Poland. *Source* Based on data from the National Bank of Poland (NBP, 2023)

obstacles. Furthermore, 34% of companies did not perceive their actions as having a significant impact on the climate, while 24% were not interested in this topic. Notably, 35% of enterprises were unaware of their CO_2 emissions. Only 14% analysed their carbon footprint, while a further 16% planned to do so in the near future (Fig. 3.2).

Despite the challenges associated with the transformation of the energy market, 73% of companies did not have an established energy carrier policy (NBP, 2023). Only 30% use renewable energy sources, the majority of which (17%) do so on a limited scale (Fig. 3.3). However, the report states that 34% of companies intend to establish their own renewable energy sources by the end of 2023. Enterprises also plan to invest in higher-efficiency machinery (36%), improve energy efficiency in production (33%) and modernise transport to be more ecological (31%).

Similar research results were obtained by EY, which conducted a telephone survey of a representative sample of 200 key Polish enterprises operating on at least a national scale and employing at least 200 people in February 2022 (EY, 2022). The study focused on the perception and implementation of sustainable development principles. The results revealed that 90% of the surveyed companies indicated that their mission included ESG aspects. Meanwhile, 67% of companies said they actively implement these aspects in their daily operations and 48% have integrated sustainable development principles into various business activities. The

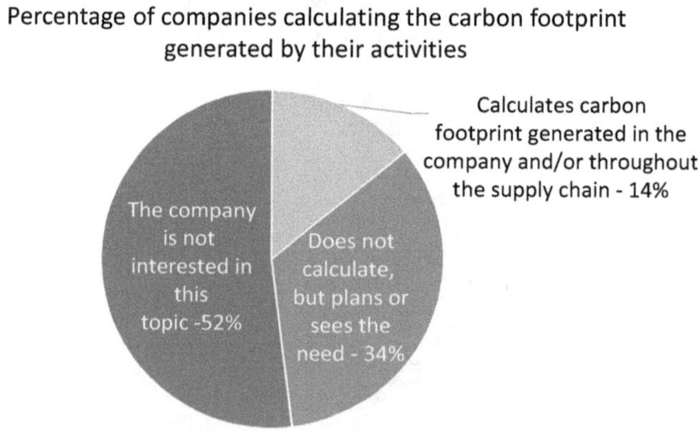

Fig. 3.2 Percentage of enterprises in Poland calculating their carbon footprint. *Source* Based on data from the National Bank of Poland (NBP, 2023)

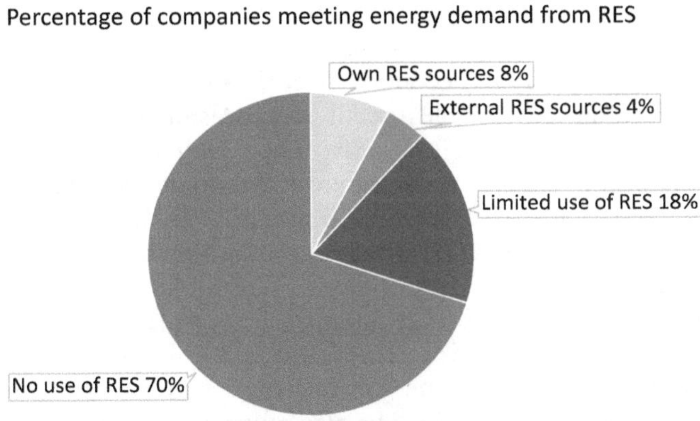

Fig. 3.3 Percentage of enterprises in Poland using renewable energy sources (RES). *Source* Based on data from the National Bank of Poland (NBP, 2023)

main motivators for these actions were consumer expectations (71%) and trade partners (59%). Despite these positive results, however, only 17% of companies publish non-financial reports. According to the study's authors, incorporating ESG issues into a company's strategy enables it to adapt its offerings to meet the demands of a growing group of environmentally conscious consumers. Taking stakeholder expectations and new regulations into account can contribute to long-term growth in company value. The financial sector plays a significant role in this process, as its needs and expectations of enterprises are increasing. For the largest global players, reducing the carbon footprint is a key ESG consideration, but this is not commonly implemented in Poland. This may be due to a lack of understanding of the impact of climate risks on businesses. While enterprises in Poland prioritise environmental protection for their development, compliance with standards is no longer sufficient. Many leaders recognise that sustainable development issues are becoming increasingly important in their sectors and are entering supply chains. More than half of Polish companies already emphasise that sustainable development criteria are key when choosing energy and technology suppliers (EY, 2022).

In response to global challenges, the Bank Gospodarstwa Krajowego (BGK) created the 3 W initiative (3 W: water, hydrogen, coal) (BGK, 2025). This pioneering, large-scale international project brings together representatives from science, business and public administration to work on innovations in water management, hydrogen and advanced coal technologies. The 3 W initiative is a long-term project that aims to guide the transformation of the Polish economy over the next few decades. It will do this by promoting sustainable use of water resources, accelerating the energy transition based on green hydrogen technologies and creating and implementing carbon nanostructure technologies with versatile applications in many industrial sectors (BGK Team, 2023).

In light of the current geopolitical situation, the European Commission has launched the REPowerEU initiative, which will directly impact the energy transition in Poland. The initiative aims to make Europe independent of fossil fuel imports from Russia by 2030, focusing on renewable energy sources, increased energy efficiency and green technologies (European Commission, 2022). The plan involves allocating an additional €30 billion for investment over the next five years, which is expected to stimulate a further €115 billion of investment by 2027.

The European Investment Bank Group (EIB) is committed to climate action, planning to invest 1 trillion euros by 2030. In 2022, it invested a record-breaking 17 billion euros in clean energy projects within the EU. Poland is participating in these initiatives, too: in 2022, 4.9 billion euros out of the 10 billion euros allocated to ecological initiatives were earmarked for Poland (Rabsztyn, 2023). The Polish Development Fund (PFR) is accelerating the energy transition in Poland through the PFR Green Hub programme (PFR Green Hub, 2023). A key element of this is supporting innovative ecological technology projects. However, rather than financing such projects directly, PFR funds are directed to specialist investors, such as venture capital and growth equity funds. This approach leverages the investors' experience and expertise in selecting and developing the most promising ventures.

In 2022, PFR Ventures, responsible for investing EU and national funds in venture capital (VC) and private equity (PE) funds, signed agreements with several key funds, including Contrarian Ventures, Eurazeo, BeyondNetZero and Polish Montis Capital. PFR Ventures' total contribution to these funds amounts to approximately 250 million PLN. Notably, all of these funds prioritise 'green strategies', investing in projects that address climate challenges (Walczak, 2023). At the same time, each fund has a direct impact on the Polish market by investing in local companies. Thanks to its broad spectrum of activities, PFR Green Hub provides financial support for companies at every stage of their development, thereby strengthening the Polish ecosystem of green innovations. Working with these funds' experienced investment teams also facilitates the transfer of knowledge and best practices to the local market, thereby benefiting Poland.

The second edition of the nationwide ESG Report (Polish ESG Association, 2024) indicates that an increasing number of companies are developing ESG strategies, with large enterprises requiring their contractors to implement them. Banks and financial institutions are also setting ESG as a condition for granting financing, making it a key element of competitiveness and market survival. However, companies are concerned about the potential high costs of transformation, estimated at 15% of revenues. They also note the growing demand for ESG advisors and a shortage of qualified experts, which is one of the biggest challenges. Many organisations therefore choose to train their own specialists instead of hiring external consultants. The report also shows that 46% of companies have already developed an ESG strategy and that almost half of these expect contractors to require its implementation. ESG is no longer just seen as a burden; 50% of companies now view it as an opportunity for development and gaining new customers. Nevertheless, the surveyed companies still face difficulties with non-financial reporting, particularly with regard to carbon footprints and sustainable development. While ESG covers many operational aspects, the social area poses the greatest challenge for surveyed Polish companies, particularly with regard to working conditions and supply chain relations. Changes are progressing dynamically, and companies are increasingly recognising that adapting to new realities may be necessary for their future functioning and development.

The results of the Warsaw School of Economics' research on ESG in the activity of investment funds in Poland, presented in the previous chapter, also included companies listed on the Warsaw Stock Exchange. As part of the project, a proprietary tool was used to measure the level of maturity in managing ESG factors and determine this maturity level among Polish stock exchange companies (Warsaw School of Economics, 2024). The results of the research showed that companies listed on the Warsaw Stock Exchange are increasingly taking strategic action in the management of ESG aspects in order to adapt to growing regulatory requirements and stakeholder expectations. The highest level of maturity was achieved by entities included in the WIG20 index, mainly due to the implementation schedule of the CSRD directive. Larger companies demonstrate greater proficiency in managing ESG risk, with nearly 70% of surveyed companies possessing formalised processes and dedicated personnel for this purpose. However, there is still a need for ESG to be better integrated into the overall risk management strategy, including the financial and capital perspectives. Additionally, ESG integration in business process management is most advanced in internal operations, where companies set, achieve and measure the effects of their goals. An increasing number of entities are also attempting to integrate ESG into their supply chains, beginning with key partners, although there is significant potential for further development in this area.

Research by the Warsaw School of Economics also indicates that most companies have achieved a high level of organisational structuring of ESG activities, incorporating them into job descriptions and management structures. However, there is still a lack of tools to enable ESG units to effectively influence other departments within the company, and there is a need for further development of systematic internal communication on this subject. It is worth emphasising that engagement in ESG initiatives is positively evaluated by both employees and boards alike, thereby promoting the development of an organisational culture that supports sustainable practices. Although companies implement training programmes, access to knowledge about ESG should be promoted more widely, especially among employees not directly involved in these activities. The study also indicates that larger companies with greater capital resources achieve a higher level of ESG maturity despite being subject to more restrictive regulations. Nevertheless, they can serve as a reference point for smaller entities, who can model their actions and gradually develop their own ESG strategies.

A study by the consultancy firm ManpowerGroup in October 2024 among employees of Polish companies has also provided insights into the current level of integration of ESG aspects, with a particular focus on small and medium-sized enterprises (ManpowerGroup, 2024). The survey involved 750 Polish company representatives from various sectors and of different sizes, including small enterprises employing fewer than 50 workers (27% of respondents) and medium-sized enterprises employing between 50 and 249 workers (36% of respondents). In response to the question regarding the identification of the ESG domain deemed most significant from the employees' viewpoint, respondents predominantly indicated the social domain (37%), closely followed by the environmental (26%) and governance (28%) domains. The implementation of ESG strategies is evident in just under a quarter of the represented companies (22%), while nearly a fifth do not plan to develop such a strategy at all (19%). Concurrently, 33% of respondents selected the option 'I don't know, hard to say', suggesting a lack of familiarity with this particular domain. It is encouraging to note that

26% of respondents admitted that their organisations do not yet have a formal ESG strategy, but plan to implement one in the near future. As illustrated in Fig. 3.4, the majority of companies that have or will implement an ESG strategy are still in the preliminary planning stage.

In addition, respondents were invited to specify the advantages that their employers have identified in relation to the integration of ESG principles. As the analysis demonstrates, companies primarily benefit from enhanced organisational image, augmented transparency of actions and superior risk management (Fig. 3.5).

In summary, the Polish market in the context of ESG aspects is still in the initial phase of development compared to other economically advanced European Union countries. Despite the commitment demonstrated by authorities and various organisations, there is still a necessity for greater understanding of the importance of social, environmental and corporate governance issues. It is becoming increasingly evident that the promotion of the ESG concept among entrepreneurs and investors, in addition to the provision of active support for sustainable development initiatives, is a pivotal factor in the process of raising awareness of ESG

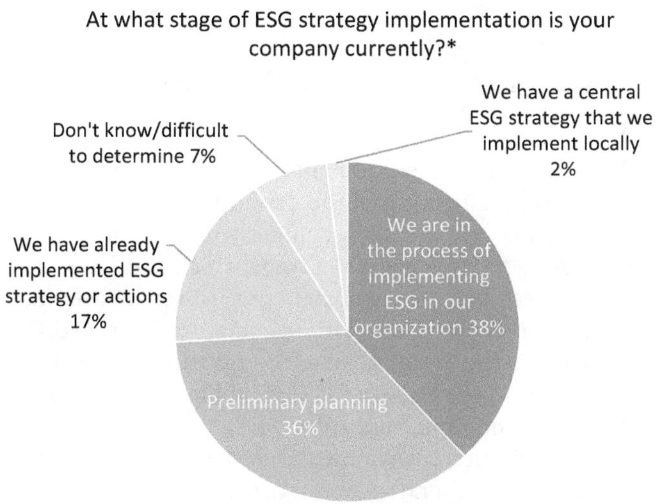

Fig. 3.4 Stages of ESG implementation in companies in Poland. *Note* *Single choice question. *Source* Based on data from ManpowerGroup (2024)

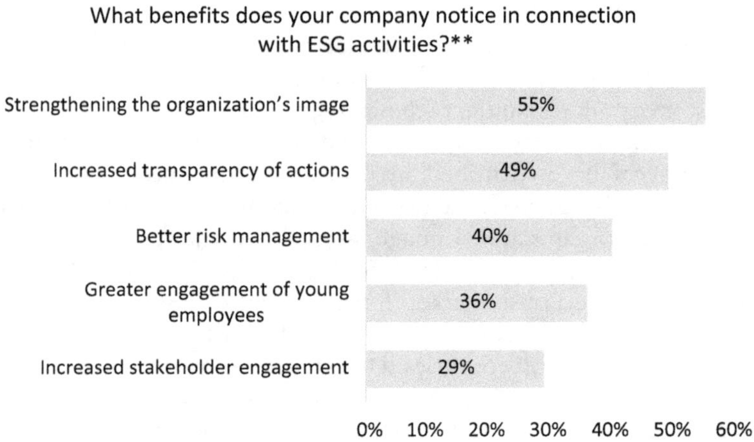

Fig. 3.5 Benefits of implementing ESG in organisations from the perspective of their employees. **Multiple choice question. *Source* Based on data from ManpowerGroup (2024)

issues and ensuring their more effective integration into business culture and investment practices.

3.4 Scale and Scope of ESG Dimensions in Financial Markets

The notion of sustainable development of companies is also reflected in financial markets, primarily through the development of socially responsible investments, so-called 'green' and ecological investments, as well as the growing importance of ESG indices (a topic which is discussed in detail in Chap. 6). The Robeco Group, a company specialising in asset management and promoting responsible investment practices, has indicated that sustainable development in the financial market constitutes a business strategy aimed at creating long-term value for shareholders (Robeco, 2023). This strategy is based on the skilful use of opportunities and risk management resulting from economic, environmental and social challenges. The approach outlined here is founded upon two fundamental principles. The initial assumption is that management practices aligned with the concept of sustainable development serve as the foundation for establishing enduring value in conditions of mounting pressure on finite natural resources. The second aspect pertains to the necessity of identifying and responding to sustainable development challenges, including climate change, social expectations, demographic pressures and energy transformation. These challenges serve as both a source of risk and potential benefits. Consequently, competitive companies must concentrate their efforts on quality, innovation and efficiency growth, in order to effectively transform these challenges into strategic advantages and generate long-term value for stakeholders.

In a broader context, the role of sustainable development in financial markets extends beyond the actions of individual companies. In the era of globalisation, the financial sector, and more specifically the capital market, has emerged as a pivotal component of the contemporary economy, functioning as a significant catalyst for dynamic economic growth. The sentiments and choices of investors have a direct impact on the real economy, influencing the developmental trajectories of individual sectors, the composition of investments, and the rate of implementation of innovative and sustainable solutions. In this intricate and multi-tiered network of connections, the significance of investments grounded in ESG criteria, which have become an integral component of contemporary investment strategies and capital allocation policies, is becoming increasingly evident.

According to research conducted by EY (2022), it is projected that by 2025, the value of assets under the management of financial institutions that are focused on ESG investments will amount to 53 trillion USD. This represents a substantial increase from the 2016 figure of 22.8 trillion USD, and the 2021 figure of 37.8 trillion USD (EY, 2022). According to the latest report of the international organisation Global Sustainable Investment Alliance, published on 30 January 2025, global sustainable investment assets under management (AuM) reached 30.3 trillion USD in 2022, reflecting a 20% increase compared to 2020 across all markets except for the US (Global Sustainable Investment Alliance, 2023). In the event of the American market being included in the analysis, it is estimated that total global assets would have decreased by 14% between 2022 and 2020. This is partly due to a change in the methodology of collecting data on sustainable investments by the Global Sustainable Investment Alliance. Concurrently, in 2022, sustainable assets constituted 37.9% of all managed assets (AUM) on a global scale, signifying a 20% increase in comparison with 2020. As demonstrated in Table 3.1, there was an increase in sustainable investment assets in Japan, Australia and Asia, as well as in Europe, between 2022 and 2020.

Table 3.1 Global sustainable investment assets (in 2016, 2018, 2020, 2022, in billion USD)

Region	*2016*	*2018*	*2020*	*2022*
Europe	12,040	14,075	12,017	14,054
USA	8723	11,995	17,081	8400
Canada	1086	1699	2423	2358
Australia and Asia	516	734	906	1220
Japan	474	2180	2874	4289
Total	**22,839**	**30,683**	**35,301**	**30,321**

Source Based on Global Sustainable Investment Alliance (2023, p. 9)

The value of sustainable investments in Europe increased from 12 trillion USD in 2020 to 14 trillion USD in 2022 (Global Sustainable Investment Alliance, 2023). However, their growth did not keep pace with the overall market increase. This is a long-term trend in Europe, where the share of assets classified as sustainable is decreasing by approximately 5% per annum. This phenomenon may be partly attributable to mounting regulatory imperatives for transparency and a more circumspect approach to risk reporting. This phenomenon is part of a broader process of maturing definitions and methodologies of sustainable investing, along with the evolution of the entire industry.

The most recent data compilation on sustainable investments by the European Social Investment Forum (Eurosif) was published on 30 January 2025. According to this compilation, the European market for socially responsible investments was valued at over €20,000 billion in 2017 (Eurosif, 2019, pp. 16–17). In Europe, the United Kingdom has consistently dominated the field of socially and environmentally responsible investments, with investments amounting to approximately 7138 billion euros. France and the Netherlands have also demonstrated notable commitment to this area, with investments reaching 3875 billion euros and 2800 billion euros, respectively. In Poland, the market for sustainable and responsible investments is also gradually developing, with these investments being estimated at nearly 22 billion euros in 2017 (see Table 3.2).

In Poland, the development of the capital market in the context of integrating ESG aspects proved crucial with the adoption of the Capital Market Development Strategy by the Polish government on October 1,

Table 3.2 Socially responsible investments in selected European countries in 2017 (in million euros)

European countries	*Total*
Austria	118,512
Belgium	421,420
Denmark	301,640
France	3,875,451
Germany	1,716,130
Italy	1,924,508
Netherlands	2,800,676
Poland	**21,953**
Spain	300,014
Sweden	2,231,838
Switzerland	2,642,931
United Kingdom	7,138,315
Total in million EUR	**23,493,388**

Source Based on Eurosif (Eurosif, 2019, p. 83)

2019 (Council of Ministers, 2019). A significant aspect of this strategy is the increased role of the capital market in financing businesses, particularly small and medium-sized enterprises (SMEs), and improving their access to capital. The strategy emphasises the importance of economic and financial education to raise awareness and competence in investing. The objective of the initiative is twofold: firstly, to streamline regulatory frameworks and processes for market participants; and secondly, to enhance the market's competitiveness and appeal to investors. The promotion of the Polish capital market is also planned, with the Warsaw Stock Exchange designated as the primary financial centre in the Central and Eastern Europe region. The document also anticipates the growth of the corporate bond segment, with the objective of diversifying the financing sources available to companies. The strategy was developed to strengthen the role of the capital market in the Polish economy, stimulate investment, and support long-term, sustainable economic growth.

In conclusion, it is evident that the consideration of ESG is now pervasive in financial markets worldwide. Despite a discernible decline in the level of interest in such investments within the American market, there is evidence of their development in other markets. In addition to the leading markets presented above, including Poland, investments that consider sustainable development criteria, and social and environmental responsibility, can also be found in Africa, mainly in South Africa, Nigeria and Kenya, as well as in South American countries (Global Sustainable Investment Alliance, 2020). Despite the fact that their development remains comparatively limited in relation to the predominant markets of North America, Asia and Europe, the numerous regulations introduced in these markets pertaining to the attainment of sustainable development goals established by the UN, in conjunction with initiatives undertaken by governments and companies, indicate that socially responsible investments will continue to be cultivated with greater intensity in these regions. According to Bloomberg Intelligence (2021), forecasts indicate that socially responsible investments based on ESG results will exceed 53 trillion USD in 2025, constituting more than one-third of assets under management worldwide. Consequently, companies will be under increasing pressure to demonstrate that they are achieving superior results in the areas of environmental, social and corporate governance (Clément et al., 2023).

3.5 The Polish Financial Market and the Integration of ESG

The consideration of environmental, social and corporate governance aspects is also gaining importance in the Polish financial market, where their understanding and adaptation take on unique characteristics. An analysis of these factors facilitates an understanding of the impact of ESG issues on corporate strategy formation and investor expectations within the Polish market, as well as the evaluation of various initiatives that promote and facilitate their advancement.

Despite the growing importance of ESG factors in Poland, many companies still regard them as a challenge rather than an opportunity. A number of obstacles have been identified that hinder full integration of ESG factors. These include a paucity of knowledge, a limited number of specialists, the costs associated with specialists, and a lack of appropriate reporting tools. These challenges are further compounded by external factors, including the ongoing war in Ukraine, the ongoing transformation of the energy sector, and inflation in the economy.

In July 2022, the team at the Warsaw Stock Exchange (WSE) conducted a study investigating the impact of ESG factors on investment decisions made by investors on the WSE trading floor (WSE, 2022). The study's findings suggest that ESG issues are becoming increasingly important and are receiving more attention from equity market investors. However, almost 40% of respondents recognise that the relationship between ESG practices and the financial performance of companies is unclear. A similar proportion of respondents cannot indicate the direction of this correlation, which may suggest a lack of interest in this aspect of business operations. The vast majority (81%) of professional investors believe that companies implementing ESG strategies are characterised by a lower level of risk. Nevertheless, the percentage of investors who have noticed this relationship has decreased slightly compared to the previous study conducted in 2019. The Good Practices of Listed Companies, developed by the WSE team, proved significant for investors—81% of respondents regard them as a valuable source of knowledge, particularly with regard to analyses and investment recommendations. They also indicate that certain issues reported as a result of these regulations are key to their analyses. Furthermore, the WIG-ESG index (see, Sect. 6.3.2 for more information) has gained recognition among respondents. Three years after its launch, 90% of respondents were familiar with it, highlighting the importance of the Polish WIG-ESG index as a tool for promoting and developing ESG criteria. Notably, a record 84% of respondents declare that they consider ESG data when making investment decisions, representing a substantial increase compared to previous years. Awareness of sustainable funds on the domestic market has also increased, rising from 44 to 75%. Finally, the results of the 2022 GPW study show that more than two-thirds of respondents see sustainable funds as an attractive investment option within pension schemes, reflecting the global trend of paying attention to ESG aspects in investment strategies.

Despite the efforts of leading companies and various organisations, research conducted by the Polish ESG Association in cooperation with the Market and Social Research Institute (IBRiS) and the research company Quality Watch among medium and large Polish companies in 2022 and again in 2023 shows that knowledge of ESG issues remains unsatisfactory in Polish companies (Polish ESG Association, 2023; 2024). The research revealed that 53% of the companies surveyed were not familiar with the concept of 'ESG'. Only 14% of respondents were well acquainted with the topic, while 32% had heard of non-financial reporting at least once. The industrial and construction sectors proved to be the least aware of the issue: 62% of companies in the industrial sector and 57% in the construction sector were unfamiliar with ESG issues. Interestingly, of the 46% of companies with at least basic knowledge of ESG, only 28% produce social reports. The construction industry stands out in this respect, with reports being prepared in 33% of cases, perhaps due to investor expectations. In the industrial sector, only 13% of companies prepare these reports. Furthermore, companies' main activities in the context of ESG tend to be limited to specific areas such as energy saving, thermal modernisation and preventing workplace bullying.

A survey of investment fund companies (TFI) in Poland, conducted by the Warsaw School of Economics (2024), produced similar results. The actions of TFIs in the ESG area are primarily driven by the need to comply with legal regulations. While most TFIs implement strategies that are consistent with sustainable development, they do not view ESG as a source of competitive advantage. ESG criteria are seen more as a means of limiting portfolio risk than as a tool for increasing investment returns. At the same time, the proper application of these criteria in the decision-making process still raises many questions, making it difficult to assess future rates of return. The importance of ESG factors is assessed differently by investment funds, and their significance in management depends on the fund category. In the real estate sector, a significant component of many investment portfolios, ESG remains underdeveloped—many assets lack EPC certificates and plans to reduce energy consumption and CO_2 emissions. There is a lack of energy consumption monitoring and zero-emission transition strategies, making it difficult to implement sustainable practices. Investment fund managers in the Polish market view ESG as an additional burden associated with costs and increased workload, with no short-term benefits. In the long term, however, ESG-compliant investing may be beneficial for environmental and economic reasons. Currently, the challenges are insufficient returns, low data quality and rapidly changing regulations, which make ESG seem more like a cost than a competitive advantage (Warsaw School of Economics, 2024).

In conclusion, the Polish market, in the context of the integration of ESG factors, remains in its early stages of development compared to other, more developed markets in the European Union. Despite the commitment demonstrated by authorities and various organisations, awareness of the importance of social, environmental and corporate governance issues still requires intensification. The promotion of the ESG concept among entrepreneurs and investors, as well as the active support for sustainable development initiatives, are becoming crucial factors.

3.6 Summary and Conclusions

This chapter presents an overview of the current state and future directions of the development of the ESG concept, as perceived by companies and financial markets in Poland, Europe and the world. Issues pertaining to environmental protection, social responsibility and corporate governance are becoming an integral part of operational and investment strategies, directly influencing business decisions and capital allocation. Globally, the development of the ESG approach is characterised by a varied dynamic. On the one hand, there is a decrease in interest in ESG-compliant investments, especially in the American market. On the other hand, there is an intense growth in the value of assets managed according to these criteria in other regions. In the European context, including Poland, there has been a gradual increase in the acceptance and implementation of ESG standards, although the pace of these processes varies depending on the economic sector and regional conditions.

In Poland, despite an increasing awareness of the significance of ESG, many companies still regard this concept as a challenge rather than an opportunity. The absence of adequate knowledge and the necessary tools for comprehensive integration of ESG into business strategies poses a considerable challenge. Moreover, research findings suggest a paucity of familiarity with ESG issues among Polish companies, thereby emphasising the necessity to augment educational and promotional initiatives in this domain.

The findings of the present study indicate that the ESG concept is becoming an indispensable element of both the product market and the financial market. In order to maintain competitiveness and credibility, companies must adapt their strategies to the growing expectations of investors and regulatory requirements. Despite the evident progress, Poland continues to lag behind more developed economies with regard to the scale of ESG-compliant assets managed and the level of integration of this concept with business practices. The development of educational activities and the provision of support for companies, especially in the area of non-financial information reporting and the implementation of sustainable management models, are crucial for accelerating these processes. Regulations and initiatives, both national and EU-wide, which not only promote responsible investing but also support the transition towards a low-emission and socially responsible economy, play a particularly important role in this context. It is asserted that the full potential of ESG can only be realised through comprehensive, coordinated actions that combine education, institutional support and regulatory frameworks. This assertion is made with regard to both the Polish market and the global market.

References

Abhayawansa, S., & Mooneeapen, O. (2022). Directions for future research to steer environmental, social and governance (ESG) investing to support sustainability: A systematic literature review. In *Handbook of accounting and sustainability* (pp. 318–341). Edward Elgar Publishing. https://www.elgaronline.com/edcollchap/book/9781800373518/book-part-9781800373518-27.xml

AFi. (2019). *The accountability framework: Operational guidance on deforestation and ecosystem conversion*. Retrieved April 16, 2025, from https://accountability-framework.org/fileadmin/uploads/afi/Documents/Deforestation-and-Conversion-Accountability-Framework.pdf

AFi. (2025a). *About the AFi*. Retrieved April 16, 2025, from https://accountability-framework.org/about/about-the-afi/

AFi. (2025b). *How companies can use the framework*. Retrieved April 16, 2025, from https://accountability-framework.org/news-events/news/catalysing-progress-towards-responsible-supply-chains/

Aldowaish, A., Kokuryo, J., Almazyad, O., & Goi, H. C. (2022). Environmental, social, and governance integration into the business model: Literature review and research agenda. *Sustainability*, *14*(5), 2959. https://doi.org/10.3390/su14052959

Ayming. (2025). *Międzynarodowy bartometr ESG 2025. Wdrożenie ESG i zgodność z dyrektywą CSRD: gdzie aktualnie jest Twoja firma?* Retrieved February 3, 2025, from https://www.ayming.pl/analizy-i-aktualnosci/raporty/miedzynarodowy-barometr-esg-2025/

BGK. (2025). *3W initiative—Water, hydrogen, carbon*. Retrieved April 22, 2025, from https://www.bgk.pl/3w/

BGK Team. (2023). Finansowanie w formule sustainability linked katalizatorem zrównoważonej transformacji w realnej gospodarce. In L. Kotecki (Ored.), *Zielone Finanse W Polsce 2023* (pp. 110–111). Instytut Odpowiedzialnych Finansów. Retrieved February 14, 2025, from https://ungc.org.pl/wp-content/uploads/2023/06/Zielone-Finanse-w-Polsce-2023.pdf

Bloomberg Intelligence. (2021). *ESG assets may hit $53 trillion by 2025, a third of global AUM Bloomberg professional services*. Retrieved May 16, 2024, from: http://www.bloomberg.com/professional/blog/esgassets-may-hit-53-trillion-by-2025-a-third-of-global-aum/

CDP. (2025). *About us*. Retrieved April 15, 2025, from https://www.cdp.net/en/about

CEO Water Mandate. (2024). *WASH benefits accounting framework: A standardized approach for estimating and valuing the multiple benefits of corporate investments in drinking water, sanitation and hygiene access—Introduction and summary report*. Retrieved April 16, 2025, from https://ceowatermandate.org/publications/WASH-Framework-Summary.pdf

CEO Water Mandate. (2025a). *What is the mandate?* Retrieved April 16, 2025, from https://ceowatermandate.org/about/what-is-the-mandate/

CEO Water Mandate. (2025b) *Water stewardship toolbox*. Retrieved April 16, 2025, from https://www.ceowatermandate.org/toolbox/

Clément, A., Robinot, É., & Trespeuch, L. (2023). The use of ESG scores in academic literature: A systematic literature review. *Journal of Enterprising Communities: People and Places in the Global Economy*, https://doi.org/10.1108/JEC-10-2022-0147

Council of Ministers. (2019). Resolution No. 114 of 1 October 2019 on the adoption of the Capital Market Development Strategy (Monitor Polski, item 1027). Official Journal of the Republic of Poland. http://www.monitorpolski.gov.pl/M2019000102701.pdf

Ecochain. (2024). *The EU's Ecodesign for Sustainable Products Regulation (ESPR): What you need to know*. https://ecochain.com/blog/espr-2024-overview/

European Commission. (2019a). *The European green deal*. European Commission COM(2019) 640 final. https://eur-lex.europa.eu/legal-content/EN/TXT/?uri=CELEX%3A52019DC0640

European Commission. (2019b). *Towards a sustainable Europe by 2030*. https://commission.europa.eu/publications/towards-sustainable-europe-2030_en

European Commission. (2021). *European green deal*. Retrieved April 21, 2025, from https://ec.europa.eu/info/strategy/priorities-2019-2024/european-green-deal_en

European Commission. (2022). *REPowerEU at a glance*. Retrieved August 17, 2024, from https://commission.europa.eu/strategy-and-policy/priorities-2019-2024/european-green-deal/repowereu-affordable-secure-and-sustainable-energy-europe_pl

European Commission. (2023). *Carbon Border Adjustment Mechanism (CBAM)*. Retrieved April 15, 2025, from https://taxation-customs.ec.europa.eu/carbon-border-adjustment-mechanism_en

European Commission. (2024). *Ecodesign for sustainable products regulation (ESPR)*. https://commission.europa.eu/energy-climate-change-environment/standards-tools-and-labels/products-labelling-rules-and-requirements/ecodesign-sustainable-products-regulation_en

European Commission. (2025c). *Packaging waste*. Retrieved April 16, 2025, from https://environment.ec.europa.eu/topics/waste-and-recycling/packaging-waste_en

European Commission. (2025d). *Regulation on deforestation-free products environment*. Retrieved April 16, 2025, from https://environment.ec.europa.eu/topics/forests/deforestation/regulation-deforestation-free-products_en

European Commission. (2025a, April 16). *Commission rolls out plan to boost circular and efficient products in the EU [Press release]*. https://ec.europa.eu/commission/presscorner/detail/en/ip_25_1071

European Commission. (2025b, April 15). *Commission takes action to simplify the implementation of the EU deforestation regulation* [Press release]. https://ec.europa.eu/commission/presscorner/detail/en/ip_25_1063

European Parliament and Council (1994). Directive 94/62/EC of 20 December 1994 on packaging and packaging waste. *Official Journal of the European Union*, L 365, 10–23. http://data.europa.eu/eli/dir/1994/62/oj

European Parliament and Council. (2023a). Regulation (EU) 2023/956 of the European Parliament and of the Council of 10 May 2023 establishing a carbon border adjustment mechanism. *Official Journal of the European Union*, (L 130), 52–104. https://eur-lex.europa.eu/legal-content/EN/TXT/?uri=CELEX%3A32023R0956

European Parliament and Council. (2023b). Regulation (EU) 2023/1115 of 31 May 2023 on the making available on the Union market and the export from the Union of certain commodities and products associated with deforestation and forest degradation and repealing regulation (EU) No 995/2010. *Official Journal of the European Union*, L 150, 206–247. https://eur-lex.europa.eu/eli/reg/2023/1115/oj/eng

European Parliament and Council. (2024). Regulation (EU) 2024/1781 of the European Parliament and of the Council of 13 June 2024 establishing a framework for the setting of ecodesign requirements for sustainable products, amending directive (EU) 2020/1828 and regulation (EU) 2023/1542 and repealing directive 2009/125/EC. *Official Journal of the European Union*,L 1781, 1–89. https://eur-lex.europa.eu/legal-content/EN/TXT/?uri=CELEX%3A32024R1781

European Parliament and Council. (2025). Regulation (EU) 2025/40 of 19 December 2024 on packaging and packaging waste, amending regulation (EU) 2019/1020 and directive (EU) 2019/904, and repealing directive 94/62/EC (Text with EEA relevance). *Official Journal of the European Union, L 2025*(40). Retrieved January 22, 2025, from http://data.europa.eu/eli/reg/2025/40/oj

Eurosif. (2019). *Report. European Sri study 2018*. Bruksela. Retrieved March 12, 2023, from http://www.eurosif.org

EY. (2022). *Czy polski biznes jest zrównoważony? Strategie zrównoważonego rozwoju polskich przedsiębiorstw*. Retrieved June 30, 2023, from https://www.ey.com/pl_pl/climate-change-sustainability-services/badanie-ey-czy-polski-biznes-jest-zrownowazony

Forum Energii. (2025). *2024 wrapped*. Retrieved March 14, 2025, from https://www.forum-energii.eu/2024_wrapped

Global Sustainable Investment Alliance. (2020). *Global sustainable investment review 2020*. Retrieved June 30, 2024, from https://www.gsi-alliance.org/wp-content/uploads/2021/08/GSIR-20201.pdf

Global Sustainable Investment Alliance. (2023). *Global sustainable investment review 2022* (p. 9). Retrieved September 14, 2024, from https://www.gsi-alliance.org/wp-content/uploads/2023/12/GSIA-Report-2022.pdf

Greenhouse Gas Protocol. (2025a). *About WRI & WBCSD*. Retrieved April 15, 2025, https://ghgprotocol.org/about-wri-wbcsd

Greenhouse Gas Protocol. (2025b). *Standards & guidance*. World Resources Institute and World Business Council for Sustainable Development. Retrieved April 15, 2025, from https://ghgprotocol.org/standards-guidance

Khan, Y. (2025, March 18). *Corporate climate targets group mulls changes to net-zero standard. The Wall Street Journal.* https://www.wsj.com/articles/sbti-proposes-opening-the-door-to-carbon-removals-8af40233

ManpowerGroup. (2024). *ESG w polskich organizacjach 2024*. Retrieved February 2, 2025, from https://www.manpowergroup.pl/2024/11/27/raport-esg-w-polskich-organizacjach-2024/?utm_source=organic_company_page&utm_medium=social_media&utm_campaign=raport_ESG&utm_term=11_24

National Bank of Poland (NBP). (2023, January 2023). Quick monitoring, 100th edn. Retrieved August 16, 2024, from https://nbp.pl/publikacje/cykliczne-materialy-analityczne-nbp/szybki-monitoring/

Noerr. (2024). *Ecodesign for Sustainable Products Regulation now in force*. https://www.noerr.com/en/insights/ecodesign-for-sustainable-products-regulation-now-in-force

Nunhes, T. V., Bernardo, M., & Oliveira, O. J. D. (2020). Rethinking the way of doing business: A reframe of management structures for developing corporate sustainability. *Sustainability*, *12*(3), 1177. https://doi.org/10.3390/su12031177

Packaging Dive. (2024, December 16). *EU packaging regulation clears final legislative hurdle*. Retrieved April 16, 2025, from https://www.packagingdive.com/news/eu-council-adopts-packaging-waste-regulation/735602/

PFR Green Hub. (2023). Retrieved August 17, 2025, from https://pfrventures.pl/program-dla-vc/podsumowanie-green-hub

Polish ESG Association. (2023). *Raport. Koszty i wyzwania ESG*. Retrieved June 20, 2024, from https://polskiestowarzyszenieesg.pl/raport-koszty-i-wyzwania-esg/

Polish ESG Association. ESG. (2024). *Raport ESG: Szanse i ryzyka*. Retrieved February 12, 2025, from https://polskiestowarzyszenieesg.pl/raport-szanse-i-ryzyka-esg/

Rabsztyn, G. (2023). REPowerEU kluczem do uniezależnienia od paliw kopalnych. In (L. Kotecki) (Ed.), *Zielone Finanse W Polsce* (112–113). Instytut Odpowiedzialnych Finansów

Robeco. (2023, August 22). *The new big book of sustainable investing* [Insight]. Retrieved September 29, 2024, from https://www.robeco.com/en-int/insights/2023/08/the-new-big-book-of-sustainable-investing

Schalock, R. L., Verdugo, M., & Lee, T. (2016). A systematic approach to an organization's sustainability. *Evaluation and Program Planning*, *56*, 56–63. https://doi.org/10.1016/j.evalprogplan.2016.03.005

Science Based Targets initiative. (2021). *Net-zero standard*. https://sciencebasedtargets.org/net-zero

Science Based Targets initiative. (2024, March). *Getting started guide for science-based target setting* (Version 1.1). https://sciencebasedtargets.org/resources/files/Getting-Started-Guide.pdf

Science Based Targets initiative. (2025a). *About us*. Retrieved April 15, 2025, from https://sciencebasedtargets.org/about-us

Science Based Targets initiative. (2025b). *Science based targets initiative: Ambitious corporate climate action*. Retrieved April 15, 2025, from https://sciencebasedtargets.org/

Statistics Poland. (2024). *Sustainable Development Goals (SDGs)—Poland*. Retrieved April 20, 2025, from https://sdg.gov.pl/

Sustainable Development Report. (2025). *SDG Index rankings*. Retrieved April 20, 2025, from https://dashboards.sdgindex.org/rankings

United Nations. (1992). *United Nations conference on environment and development, Rio de Janeiro, Brazil, 3–14 June 1992*. Retrieved May 25, 2024, from https://www.un.org/en/conferences/environment/rio1992

United Nations. (2015). *Transforming our world: The 2030 Agenda for Sustainable Development (A/RES/70/1)*. https://sdgs.un.org/2030agenda

UN-Water. (2025). *UN global compact's CEO water mandate—UN global compact*. Retrieved April 16, 2025, from https://www.unwater.org/about-un-water/members-and-partners/un-global-compacts-ceo-water-mandate-un-global-compact

Walczak, M. (2023). Zielony wehikuł dla innowacji zmieniających świat. In W. L. Kotecki, (red.), *Zielone Finanse W Polsce* (116–117). Instytut Odpowiedzialnych Finansów

Warsaw School of Economics. (2024). *Dojrzałość zarządzania ESG a kryzys klimatyczny 2024: Raport z badań*. Retrieved January 14, 2025, from https://gazeta.sgh.waw.pl/sites/gazeta.sgh.waw.pl/files/zalaczniki-2024/382-GAZETA-SGH-raport-EGS.pdf

White & Case. (2024). *Eight key aspects to know about the EU ecodesign for sustainable products regulation*. Retrieved April 21, 2025, from https://www.whitecase.com/insight-alert/eight-key-aspects-know-about-eu-ecodesign-sustainable-products-regulation

World Commission on Environment and Development. (1987). *Our common future*. United Nations. https://sustainabledevelopment.un.org/content/documents/5987our-common-future.pdf

WSE. (2022). *Komunikat prasowy z dn. 22.07.2022. Inwestorzy stawiają na ESG*. Retrieved July 23, 2022, from https://www.gpw.pl/aktualnosc?cmn_id=112787&title=Inwestorzy+stawiaj%C4%85+na+ESG

CHAPTER 4

ESG and SRI Investing: Characteristics and Investment Practice in Poland, Europe and Beyond

4.1 Introduction

The present chapter is dedicated to the analysis of the development and significance of socially responsible investing (SRI) and ESG-compliant investing in global, European and Polish markets. ESG investing is a trend that can be understood as an integration of environmental, social and corporate governance factors into the investment decision-making process. This integration is understood within the broader concept of SRI. The objective of such strategies is not solely to achieve competitive and long-term financial returns, but also to generate positive social and environmental impact.

Moreover, the discussion encompasses the terminological and conceptual diversity associated with SRI investing and the key investment strategies employed in capital markets, including ESG criteria integration, exclusions, thematic investing, as well as approaches based on shareholder engagement and positive impact. Concurrently, it provides a concise exposition on innovative ESG investing instruments, namely green cryptocurrencies, while also addressing the critical discourse surrounding the incorporation of ESG criteria in investment decision-making, predominantly from the American market.

K. Łudzińska, *International ESG Perspectives*,
https://doi.org/10.1007/978-3-032-11666-6_4

4.2 Characteristics of Socially Responsible and ESG Investing

Socially responsible investing (SRI) denotes the practical implementation of environmental, social and governance criteria integration in financial markets. The term *Socially Responsible Investing* encompasses a variety of expressions, including Socially Responsible, Environmental, Sustainable, and Sustainable & Responsible Investing. The acronym SRI is commonly used to describe all approaches to socially and environmentally responsible investing, emphasising the importance of considering social and environmental factors in investment decisions. Furthermore, SRI places significant emphasis on ethical considerations, and at times, on the personal convictions of investors and asset managers who utilise their investment strategies, which may encompass positive (e.g., best-in-class selection) or negative (e.g., exclusions) approaches, to guide their investment selection. The International Finance Corporation (IFC) places particular emphasis on the positive impact aspect of SRI investing, underlining the point that investing should not only generate profits but also deliver measurable benefits for society and the environment (International Finance Corporation, 2023).

Conversely, ESG investing incorporates environmental, social and governance criteria with a view to achieving long-term, competitive financial returns. This analytical and comprehensive approach is utilised by individual and institutional investors, as well as asset managers, who employ ESG performance and ratings to evaluate companies. The primary focus of this analysis is the evaluation of potential investments based on ESG indicators, facilitating their quantitative comparison. However, with the increasing acceptance of the ESG concept as a broader approach to responsible management and investing, it is often equated with SRI investing. Nevertheless, the two differ in their underlying motivations: ESG investing focuses on financial materiality and risk management, while SRI investing is often driven by ethical, social, or environmental values.

In the literature, the concept of socially responsible investing is referred to by various terms, including ethical, green, sustainable and mission-driven investing (Czerwonka, 2013). Aldowaish et al. (2022) hypothesise that the diversity of terminology in the context of SRI may have a cultural basis. The term 'responsible investing' is frequently employed in the United Kingdom, yet it is eschewed in France and the United States if the strategies under discussion neglect to incorporate substantial social dimensions (Sandberg et al., 2009). Research findings also suggest that there is no universal standard defining the structure of the socially responsible investment market, indicating the significant importance of local institutional conditions, and thus terminological ones (Adamska et al., 2015). Nevertheless, the contemporary trend of combining sustainable development with ESG criteria in the field of finance is referred to by the common term SRI (Nagel et al., 2017; Widyawati, 2020).

In practice, socially responsible investing refers to the process of systematically integrating ESG factors, which take into account environmental, social and corporate governance criteria in investment decision-making (Widyawati, 2020; Global Sustainable Investment Alliance, 2020; Abhayawansa & Mooneeapen, 2022). Irrespective of the nomenclature adopted, the fundamental concept of socially responsible investing is to integrate the financial objectives of investors, such as the anticipated rate of return, with the generation of positive social and environmental impacts. The mounting cognisance among investors, regulators and other stakeholders regarding the potential ramifications of imprudent investment decisions, including the possibility of long-term adverse consequences, serves to accentuate the significance of this concept. The development process of this approach is presented in Table 4.1.

A discernible trend towards impact investing is also evident in the market. While impact investing and socially responsible investing both aim to have a positive impact on the environment and community, as highlighted by the Global Impact Investing Network (GIIN, 2019), there are some significant differences between them. Impact investing is an investment strategy that prioritises the generation of measurable social and environmental benefits, often placing a higher value on these benefits than on financial returns. Investors are adopting strategies that are proactive in nature, electing to pursue actions that have a beneficial social or environmental impact, as opposed to merely avoiding the adverse effects. A fundamental aspect of impact investing is the monitoring and evaluation of the achieved impact, encompassing support for initiatives such as sustainable agriculture, biodiversity conservation, renewable energy, microfinance and access to fundamental services, including housing, healthcare and education (GIIN, 2023).

Regenerative investing is a recent development in the field of socially responsible investing. Its characteristics extend beyond the conventional pursuit of resource conservation or sustainable development. Rather, the focus of regenerative investing is on proactive measures intended to compensate, renew and revitalise social and ecological systems (Regenerators, 2023).

Table 4.1 Milestones in the development of ESG investing

Year	*Event*
2004	The emergence of the ESG concept in the UN report 'Who cares wins. Connecting Financial Markets to a Changing World' (UN, 2004)
2005	UNEP FI (United Nations Environment Programme Finance Initiative, a global partnership between the United Nations Environment Programme, UNEP and the financial sector) and the law firm Freshfields, Bruckhaus and Deringer jointly present the definition of ESG investments
2006	UN PRI (UN Principles for Responsible Investing) presented six principles of ESG investing
2008	Goldman Sachs promotes a sustainable equity portfolio: UBS, Blackrock, HSBC, Allianz, which expanded the practice of ESG investing
2009	UNCTAD (United Nations Conference on Trade and Development), UN PRI, UN EPFI jointly launched the UN SEE initiative, Sustainable Stock Exchanges, or Sustainable Stock Exchanges (United Nations Sustainable Stock Exchanges Initiative, 2024a)
2012	International Finance Corporation (IFC), a member institution of the World Bank Group published Environmental and Social Standards (ESS), which are widely used guidelines for analysing infrastructure programmes (IFC, 2012, World Bank, 2025b)
2015	UN SSE promotes a voluntary stock exchange instrument that helps issuers report on ESG issues (United Nations Sustainable Stock Exchanges Initiative, 2024b)
2016	The World Bank publishes ESG guidelines for financial institutions to assess infrastructure projects
2019	The World Bank creates a national-level ESG data platform: ESG Sovereign Data Portal (World Bank, 2025a)
	The European Commission introduces the SFDR regulation (Sustainable Finance Disclosure Regulation) on disclosing information about sustainable financing
2020	UNEP and PSI, Principles for Sustainable Insurance, jointly published the first ESG guidelines for the global insurance sector
	The European Commission approved the EU Taxonomy to promote the development of ESG investments in the European market (European Commission, 2020b)
2021	The European Commission proposes a new European standard for green bonds
2023	The European Commission introduces the European Sustainability Reporting Standards (ESRS)

Source Based on European Commission (2021, 2023a, 2023b); European Parliament and Council of the European Union (2019); Eurosif (2018, 2019); International Finance Corporation (2012); Li (2022); United Nations Sustainable Stock Exchanges Initiative (2024a, 2024b); World Bank (2025a, 2025b)

Adopting a holistic approach, regenerative investments treat the economy, community and ecosystem as interconnected elements of a whole. Consequently, their actions are multifaceted, as opposed to a focus on single, isolated solutions. In addition to conventional profitability indicators, they utilise metrics to evaluate social health, ecological regeneration and resilience. The effectiveness of these investments is measured not only through the prism of negative actions they have avoided, but primarily through the positive impact they have had on the environment and society. These principles find application in a wide range of sectors, including agriculture, where practices such as agroforestry and soil regeneration are promoted, and the real estate market, where the design of ecological buildings and the promotion of social well-being are becoming increasingly important. To illustrate this point, it is important to note that financing initiatives directed towards the agricultural sector can result in the restoration of biodiversity and the soil's capacity to retain water. Concurrently, in the domain of social investment, the primary focus is not solely on job creation, but rather on implementing comprehensive strategies to enhance the quality of life for local communities (Capital Institute, 2023).

4.3 The Practice of ESG Investing in Global and European Markets

Initially, investments based on ESG criteria were mainly the domain of institutional investors. However, in recent years, a dynamic increase in interest in this form of investing from individual investors, especially in Europe, has become evident—in 2019 their share reached 31% (Matczak et al., 2019). The integration of ESG factors into investment strategy is commonly manifested through the adoption of one of three primary approaches: investment screening, which involves the analysis of potential investments with consideration for the individual investor's preferences; the integration of ESG aspects into the analysis and decision-making process of investing; and thematic investing, which focuses on specific environmental or social challenges that a given investment product addresses (Principles for Responsible Investment, 2023b) (Table 4.2).

Concurrently, the investment process in the ESG area has become relatively standardised, and can be divided into four main stages, as presented in Table 4.3.

The integration of ESG criteria within investment strategies is indicative of the distinct preferences of investors, encompassing both individual and institutional entities. Investors may opt to implement an exclusion strategy, thereby eliminating companies, funds or sectors that do not align with sustainable development standards. This could, for instance, include sectors associated with coal or weapons production. Such an approach may include fundamental analysis, taking into account both financial and non-financial indicators related to ESG. Alternatively, other investors may favour thematic investments, focusing on solutions addressing ESG challenges, such as green technologies or social innovations. Furthermore, an engagement strategy has been developed in which investors collaborate with company boards, encouraging them to adopt more sustainable practices. A range of financial products is available, including ESG funds and green bonds, which incorporate these criteria. The selection of strategy is contingent upon the investor's preferences: some opt to proactively engage in ESG initiatives, while others prefer a more passive approach, allocating funds to sustainable financial products.

In addition to considering ESG factors when making investment decisions, institutional investors are currently paying increasing attention to

Table 4.2 Integration of ESG factors in existing investment practices

Investment Screening	*ESG Integration*	*Thematic Investing*
Involves applying filters to a set of securities, issuers, sectors or other financial instruments to decide whether to consider investing in them. It is based on criteria such as investor preferences or specific investment indicators, defined in the investment process or reflecting the mandate of the client or fund. Screening can be positive, norm-based or negative (i.e., exclusions)	Involves considering ESG issues in analyses and investment decisions to better manage risk and improve returns	Involves seeking opportunities created by long-term ESG trends, such as the transition to renewable energy or a circular economy. This may mean choosing a thematic product, such as a fund or index, or constructing a portfolio around such a trend

Source Based on Principles for Responsible Investment (2023a)

Table 4.3 Framework stages of the ESG investment process in the capital market

Stage	*Process*	*Description*
Stage 1	Disclosure of ESG aspects by companies	Listed companies disclose ESG information, based on selected standards. Their main sources are regulations of international organisations (e.g., Global Reporting Initiative (GRI, 2023)), stock exchange requirements (e.g., guidelines of the New York Stock Exchange contained in NYSE Best Practices for Sustainability Reporting (NYSE, 2023), and government policies (e.g., the so-called ESG Taxonomy introduced by the European Commission in 2020: Taxonomy: Final Report of the Technical Expert Group on Sustainable Finance (European Commission, 2020a)
Stage 2	Preliminary analysis of ESG results	Rating agencies conduct a preliminary analysis of company results, based on ESG criteria. After this initial assessment, the data is further processed in the context of the investment portfolio, ESG indices or SRI investment funds. It is worth noting that this process encounters certain difficulties, mainly due to the lack of standardisation in the disclosure of non-financial information and insufficient transparency of the assessment process, leading to a low correlation of ESG assessment results between leading rating agencies, as discussed in Sect. 6.1
Stage 3	Inclusion/exclusion of companies in ESG indices	Companies specialising in creating investment portfolios, ESG indices, or SRI funds, such as Sustainalytics (Sustainalytics, 2025), Thomson Reuters (Thomson Reuters, 2025), construct these indices based on rating results
Stage 4	Investment decisions	Using various possible ESG investment strategies, investors integrate ESG criteria and ESG rating results into the investment decision-making process, expecting them to consider, in addition to ESG factors, other important criteria such as risk and return on investment

Source Based on Leite and Cortez (2014); van Duuren et al. (2016); Trinks et al. (2018); Camilleri (2020); Li (2022); Sustainalytics (2025); Thomson Reuters (2025)

shareholder engagement. The Principles for Responsible Investment (PRI) define this as the use of influence by institutional investors to maximise long-term value, including the value of economic, social and environmental assets on which returns and the interests of clients and beneficiaries depend (Principles for Responsible Investment, 2024). In practice, investors are able to fulfil their commitments to active asset management through the utilisation of various methods and tools, which can be divided into investee relations and broader stewardship. A significant proportion of these instruments and activities is utilised in conjunction by investors. The specific tools employed and actions undertaken may vary depending on the asset class or investment entities, but frequently encompass, among other aspects, engagement in cooperation with investors (both current and potential); voting at shareholder meetings; submission of, co-submission of, or presentation of shareholder resolutions or proposals; nomination of directors to boards; service on boards or board committees; direct supervision of portfolio companies or assets; cooperation with standard-setting entities and engagement in industry groups, etc. (Principles for Responsible Investment, 2024).

As demonstrated in Table 4.4, the majority of the most frequently employed decision criteria in socially responsible investment strategies in the European market have been developed by the non-governmental organisation Eurosif. The highest aggregated annual return rate in Europe is achieved by the strategy of integrating ESG criteria, followed by investments in industry leaders, i.e. companies that stand out from the competition. Subsequent categories comprise shareholder engagement and investments that are intended to have a positive impact on the natural environment and society. A marked decline in return rates was evident in instances of investments based on compliance with norms and standards and strategies excluding certain industries, companies or countries.

In the literature, negative selection is classified as the first generation of SRI strategies, i.e. the one that appeared on the market first. The second generation incorporates positive selection, the third generation comprises engagement strategy, and the fourth generation consists of the ESG factors integration strategy (Renneboog et al., 2008). Concurrently, the strategies of negative and positive selection constitute the so-called narrow approach to socially responsible investing (SRI), whereas engagement strategies and the integration of ESG factors are classified as socially responsible investing in a broad sense (Mikołajek-Gocejna, 2018). The aforementioned criteria for SRI strategies are employed on a global scale,

Table 4.4 Seven criteria for socially responsible investment strategies in the European market

No.	*SRI Investment Criteria*	*Description*	*Aggregate Annual Growth Rates: 2017 vs. 2015 (%)*
1.	Sustainability Themed Investments	Selection of investments based on a chosen issue from the area of sustainable development (e.g. renewable energy sources)	1
2.	Best-in-Class Investments	Selection of investments in the best-in-class, i.e. in companies that are leaders in their industries, considering social responsibility, environmental protection and corporate governance	9
3.	Norms-based Screening Investments	Investing based on considered and confirmed international norms and standards by a given entity	−21
4.	Exclusion of Investment Portfolio	Negative selection, exclusion of investment portfolio in certain companies, industries or countries	−3
5.	ESG Criteria Integration	Integration of ESG criteria in financial analysis and investment decision	27
6.	Shareholder Engagement	Engagement of owners and shareholders of potential investment in sustainable development	7
7.	Impact Investment	Investments in companies, organisations or funds with the intention of generating social and ecological impact along with obtaining a financial return on investment (including microfinance loans, investments in local communities, social enterprises and start-ups)	5

Source Based on Eurosif (2019, pp. 16–17)

though there may be some variations at the regional level, arising from the diverse definitions of this investment category across different countries, as previously mentioned. However, it appears that investors are inclined to offer greater recognition to companies that demonstrate a commitment to environmental and social responsibility, as opposed to excluding them based on specific products or practices (Berry & Junkus, 2013).

Despite this, on the European capital market, socially responsible investments that take into account the aforementioned exclusions, i.e. negative selection and shareholder engagement, enjoy the greatest success in terms of value, even though the aggregated returns of the former have declined, as shown in Table 4.4. The integration of ESG factors and the consideration of norms and standards also remain significant, while investments aimed at sustainable development, best in class or impact investments attract significantly fewer financial assets—the latest aggregated data, from 2017, are presented in Table 4.5. It is important to note that the European Commission is currently engaged in the development of novel non-financial reporting guidelines that align with the ESRS standards, particularly with regard to the disclosure of sustainable finance information. Consequently, alterations to the criteria for SRI investment strategy can be anticipated. It is essential that these changes are aligned with market practices and the requirements of EU directives (Eurosif, 2022). Furthermore, it is imperative to emphasise that the Polish SRI investment market exhibits the lowest level of such investments in comparison to other European countries (see, Table 4.5).

Research on socially responsible investing is multidisciplinary in nature and predominantly focused on developed markets, especially those of North America and Europe. The role of ESG factors in the development of socially responsible investing and the SRI investment market appears to be of crucial importance (Widyawati, 2020). A systematic literature review conducted by Abhayawansa and Mooneeapen (2022) has identified four key areas of research in the field of SRI investment. The areas, as outlined by researchers, are as follows: firstly, investor behaviour in relation to ESG investing; secondly, ESG investment strategies; thirdly, the results and characteristics of funds and portfolios focused on ESG factors; and fourthly, ESG ratings. Additionally, a rapidly evolving research direction pertains to the evaluation of investment portfolio exposure to climate change risk (Matos, 2020).

Importantly, key SRI assets on the global stage are not limited to company shares evaluated through the prism of ESG criteria. The key assets also include investment funds that invest in a socially responsible manner, as well as a broader range of sustainable and responsible investment instruments (Riedl & Smeets, 2017). Consequently, the selection of investment products and tools frequently mirrors the values and convictions of investors. Furthermore, analysis of investment portfolios through the lens of ESG factors has been demonstrated to enhance their quality (Fritz & von Schnurbein, 2019).

Table 4.5 Criteria for SRI investment strategies in selected European countries in individual investment strategy categories in 2017 (in million EUR)

European Countries	*Best in Class (Best-in-Class) (in million EUR)*	*Sustainable Development (Sustainability Themed) (in million EUR)*	*Norms-Based Screening (Norms-based Screening) (in million EUR)*	*ESG Factors Integration (ESG Integration) (in million EUR)*	*Shareholder Engagement (Engagement and Voting) (in million EUR)*	*Exclusions (Exclusions) (in million EUR)*	*Impact Investing (Impact Investing) (in million EUR)*	*Total (in million EUR)*
Austria	14,023	992	9871	3695	12,358	76,543	1030	118,512
Belgium	15,570	8101	31,654	97,428	18,502	249,014	1151	421,420
Denmark	100	65	50,080	16,527	23,820	211,048	0	301,640
France	295,178	20,620	1,845,679	920,055	23,897	768,128	1894	387,541
Germany	22,068	9184	50,789	49,612	9284	148,711	5232	171,610
Italy	58,137	52,861	105,842	70,425	135,729	144,954	51,960	192,458
Netherlands	83,449	7125	631,721	627,477	724,809	724,704	1391	280,066
Poland	0	0	6841	2500	5431	7181	0	21,953
Spain	10,364	12,665	11,327	67,995	11,750	176,742	9171	300,014
Sweden	25,419	1966	305,833	297,182	874,724	720,292	6422	223,188
Switzerland	40,889	18,775	64,435	77,069	77,925	234,877	15,041	264,291
UK	2036	16,463	28,391	200,787	2,854,400	219,534	15,284	713,835
Total	**585,733**	**148,817**	**314,463**	**423,782**	**4,855,429**	**104,148**	**108,576**	**234,938**

Source Based on Eurosif (2019, p. 83)

The advent of financial technologies and the evolution of digital assets, such as cryptocurrencies, tokens and NFTs, have expanded their scope and paved the way for those that incorporate environmental considerations and support sustainable development (Alharbi et al., 2025). A notable accomplishment in this regard is the emergence of green cryptocurrencies, which are designed to address the ecological challenges associated with cryptocurrency mining and transactions. Green cryptocurrencies utilise environmentally friendly consensus mechanisms to mitigate ecological threats, thereby responding to the mounting demand for investments that consider environmental factors (Anwer et al., 2023). Moreover, the research findings of Anwer et al. (2023) indicate that SRI indices and cryptocurrency indices exhibit co-movements during periods of crisis, such as the pandemic. However, under normal market conditions, these indices remain predominantly independent. This finding suggests that the two asset classes may act as mutual hedges.

Converging conclusions were arrived at by Alharbi et al. (2025), who indicated a moderate level of return and volatility transmission between green cryptocurrencies and ESG stocks. In accordance with the prevailing theoretical framework, cryptocurrencies function as recipients of spillover effects with regard to returns and volatility, with stocks serving as the primary transmitters of such effects. The findings thus indicate that a crisis in one market has the potential to readily propagate to other markets, thereby instigating a chain reaction that poses a threat to the overall stability of the system. Furthermore, a high level of systemic linkages can also be attributed to the influence of socially responsible investing. The authors of the studies posit that the Paris Agreement, which aims to limit climate change and promote sustainable development through responsible investing, has increased the demand for green cryptocurrencies.

In light of the financial market innovations discussed above, investors now have access to a broad range of investment options that are socially, environmentally and governance responsible. These options enable the construction of diversified and well-balanced investment portfolios. These opportunities are available to both individual and institutional investors. In countries such as the United States and other Western economies, leading SRI funds are present in every major asset class, such as stocks, bonds, or investment funds (Camilleri, 2020). Consequently, the number of investors who recognise the potential to enhance the value of their investments while contributing to the realisation of social and environmental objectives is increasing.

It is evident that investors play a pivotal role in promoting ESG criteria. This assertion is supported by extant research, which has demonstrated the integration of social and environmental factors in investment decision-making processes (Sultana et al., 2018), risk management (van Duuren et al., 2016), and optimisation of the investment process (Cappucci, 2018). Nevertheless, certain studies have indicated the presence of potential risks associated with an excessive focus on ESG criteria in investment decisions. These issues encompass the potential for failure to identify pivotal elements of business and financial models (Schoenmaker & Schramade, 2019), as well as inconsistencies in business justifications for investments, inadequate data quality, and an absence of uniform standards and definitions (Friede, 2019).

In consequence of the risks previously referenced, there has been an escalation of tensions surrounding ESG in recent years, particularly in the United States. It is evident that prominent investment banks, including Morgan Stanley, Bank of America, Wells Fargo, Goldman Sachs and Citi, have withdrawn from the Net-Zero Banking Alliance—a United Nations initiative that aims to achieve zero greenhouse gas emissions by 2050 (Bloomberg, 2025). Research conducted by Morningstar indicates that sustainable funds in the United States experienced their inaugural annual capital outflow in 2023, with a total withdrawal of $13 billion from ESG-focused investments (Statkiewicz, 2024). Notwithstanding this trend, larger ESG funds exhibited financial resilience, attaining a median return for investors of 24.4%, outperforming the S&P 500 index in the same year. In the context of the mounting anti-ESG movement, companies are finding themselves compelled to navigate an increasingly volatile environment characterised by discordant expectations. On the one hand, there is pressure to 'stay out of politics', while on the other, there is an expectation that companies will engage in addressing prevalent social challenges (Winston, 2024). Edmans (2023b) proclaimed the 'end of ESG' and advanced the argument that ESG should not be the recipient of 'special treatment'. From this standpoint, the integration of environmental, social and governance considerations into all investment strategies is imperative for achieving long-term value creation, and this should not be regarded as a niche category. ESG considerations are no more exceptional than other intangible factors, such as management quality or innovation. Consequently, a holistic evaluation of companies is essential, as opposed to a myopic focus on ESG factors.

In accordance with this postulate, investors are progressively analysing assets on the basis of non-financial data and taking into account environmental aspects, such as carbon dioxide emissions, social factors, including employee satisfaction, and governance issues, for example, board structure (Matos, 2020). Their objective is twofold: firstly, to restrict investment in ventures that pose a significant ESG risk; and secondly, to encourage companies to adopt more sustainable practices, even in the absence of explicit regulatory requirements or policy directives from the incumbent administration.

4.4 Analysis of the Market for Socially Responsible Investing in Poland

Despite the relatively favourable economic conditions that have persisted following the 2007–2009 financial crisis, the Polish market for socially responsible investing remains in the early stages of development (Lulewicz-Sas & Kilon, 2014b; Remlein, 2017; Kravchuk, 2022). The phenomenon under discussion can be attributed to a multitude of factors, including social, economic, political and legislative considerations. A salient factor contributing to this issue is the absence of local regulations and rules that incorporate ESG factors into the investment policies of funds and asset managers. Despite the introduction of a regulation by the Ministry of Finance in 2009 (Ministry of Finance, 2009), which stipulated that companies listed on the Warsaw Stock Exchange must include a detailed description of their corporate governance activities in their annual reports, and the initiation of the Code of Good Practice by the Warsaw Stock Exchange (WSE, 2016), which is supported by a comprehensive and regularly updated website that is rich in information, these actions appear to be insufficient to popularise the idea of socially responsible investing. The European Sustainability Reporting Standards (ESRS), the subject of Chap. 8, are anticipated to effect a substantial transformation in this domain.

In response to these expectations, the Warsaw Stock Exchange (WSE) published a guide for companies on ESG reporting in accordance with the EU CSRD directive and the aforementioned ESRS reporting guidelines in October 2023. This guide was developed in collaboration with Steward Redqueen and with the support of the European Bank for Reconstruction and Development (EBRD). The objective of the initiative was to provide support to companies listed on the WSE in reporting ESG results in a manner that aligns with the requirements of investors, assists them in preparing for impending regulatory obligations, and fosters favourable conditions for the advancement of sustainable finance in Poland (WSE, 2023). This document proved to be a significant facilitation not only in implementing EU non-financial reporting guidelines, but above all in popularising the consideration of ESG aspects in investment decisions made on the Polish market.

In Europe, the United Kingdom is a leading nation in the field of socially responsible investments. Since 2000, an amendment to the pension law has required capital trustees, particularly pension funds, to include in their annual reports a statement indicating the extent to which their investment decisions consider social, environmental and ethical factors (The Pension Regulator, 2024). Since 2019, trustees have also been required to explain how they integrate financially material ESG considerations into their investment selection, retention and realisation decisions, as well as their stewardship activities. In Poland, socially responsible investing is a relatively recent practice, and as such, numerous challenges remain regarding its development and the promotion of awareness about the social, environmental and ethical implications of investment decisions.

According to the most recent data available from Eurosif, the scale of SRI investments in Poland in 2017 reached 22 billion euros (Eurosif, 2019). As illustrated in Table 4.6, the SRI investment strategies present on the Polish capital market in 2015 and 2017 were dominated by investments guided by the exclusion of selected industries or companies and the consideration of norms and standards of operation. The present study explores the absence of recognition in our country of the increasingly popular global trend of Impact Investing, i.e. investing that has a positive impact on the social environment and the environment.

The level of SRI investing in Poland is significantly lower than in other European Union countries (see, Table 4.5 above). Eurosif (2019) identifies a paucity of demand for socially and environmentally responsible investments as a contributing factor to this phenomenon. This is attributable to an absence of awareness regarding the nature of such investments, their relative effectiveness and efficiency when contrasted with conventional investment strategies within capital markets. Furthermore, there is an absence of SRI investment leaders in Poland, who would be responsible for building a portfolio based on ecological and social projects.

The first pioneering study on the extent to which investors in Poland consider social and environmental factors in their investment decisions was conducted by the Warsaw Stock Exchange and Deloitte in 2012. The study

Table 4.6 The market for SRI investments in Poland in 2015 and 2017 in individual categories of investment strategies

SRI Investments in Poland (in million EUR)	*2015*	*2017*
Thematic investments in sustainable development	3762	0
Best in class	2717	0
Consideration of norms and standards	2769	6841
Exclusions	2769	7181
Integration of ESG factors	0	2500
Shareholder engagement	0	5431
Impact Investing	34	0

Source Eurosif (2019, p. 103)

revealed that a significant majority of respondents recognised the potential impact of environmental and social factors on companies' financial performance. Concurrently, a mere 26% of survey respondents expressed awareness of the existence of ethical funds within the Polish market. These funds specialise in investing in companies that prioritise sustainable and socially responsible operations. The vast majority (94%) of investors participating in the study were aware of the existence of the RESPECT Index on the Warsaw Stock Exchange. Despite the fact that 81% of respondents admitted that they do not analyse the composition of the index, an increasing number of investors are declaring that they take ESG criteria into account in their decision-making processes (Deloitte, 2012).

A number of institutions have been identified as providing support for the development of the SRI investment sector and the inclusion of ESG aspects in business in Poland. These include the Institute for Responsible Finance (Institute for Responsible Finance, n.d.), the Polish ESG Association (Polish ESG Association, n.d.), the ESG Committee of the Polish Chamber of Commerce (Polish Chamber of Commerce, n.d.) and the Sustainable Finance Platform established by the Ministry of Finance of the Republic of Poland (Ministry of Finance, n.d.). Its membership comprises key public administration institutions and the Polish capital market, which support the development of the Polish SRI market. The following institutions and organisations are involved in this project: the European Bank for Reconstruction and Development, the Association of Individual Investors, the Ministry of Climate and Environment, the Polish Association of Listed Companies, the

Chamber of Brokerage Houses, the National Fund for Environmental Protection and Water Management, the Financial Supervision Authority, the Warsaw Stock Exchange, the Polish Development Fund, the Association of Polish Banks, the Polish Private Equity and Venture Capital Association, the Ministry of State Assets, the Polish Insurance Chamber, the European Investment Bank, the Chamber of Fund and Asset Management, the Bank Gospodarstwa Krajowego, the Ministry of Finance, the National Bank of Poland and the UN Global Compact Network Poland.

According to Kłobukowska (2019), who has identified the elements that distinguish SRI investing as an innovation in the Polish financial market, the foundation of the socially responsible investment market in Poland should be seen in corporate governance—an area whose significance was elevated following the implementation of EU law after Poland's accession to the European Union in 2004. It is an obligation incumbent upon public companies listed on the Warsaw Stock Exchange to ensure that they provide transparent information regarding their corporate governance policy in their annual financial reports. The socially responsible investment market in Poland was included in the Eurosif report for the first time in 2010. In 2009, the market value was estimated at approximately 1 billion euros, constituting approximately 0.3% of the total value of assets under management (Eurosif, 2011). As previously referenced, the aforementioned organisation estimated the size of the Polish SRI market at 22 billion euros in 2017, indicating a growing trend.

4.5 Summary and Conclusions

This chapter provides an overview of the development and significance of socially responsible investing and ESG investing in the global, European and Polish markets. The study discusses the evolution of the concept of SRI, integrated with ESG criteria, into a significant element of investment strategies with two objectives: the generation of financial profits and the exertion of a positive impact on society and the environment. In European markets, socially responsible investing (SRI) is gaining popularity, with investors increasingly incorporating environmental, social and corporate governance aspects into their investment decisions.

However, an analysis of the Polish SRI investment market indicates that Poland lags behind other European countries in terms of the scale and advancement of these investments. Despite growing awareness and several positive initiatives, this market in Poland is still in its early stages of development, due to various social and economic regulations. The absence of widely accepted reporting standards and a paucity of knowledge regarding the benefits of SRI represent significant barriers to the development of this market.

The conclusions drawn from the analysis indicate the necessity for further development and promotion of SRI investing in the Polish market, particularly in the context of new regulations, such as the European Sustainability Reporting Standards (ESRS). The implementation of these measures has the potential to enhance transparency and credibility in the realm of ESG information, thereby fostering investor trust and catalysing the growth of SRI investments.

In summary, socially responsible investing and ESG investing are playing an increasingly important role in both global and European markets. Despite the fact that their development in Poland remains relatively limited at present, there is substantial potential for acceleration, provided that appropriate regulatory frameworks and educational initiatives are put in place. In the long term, sustainability-oriented investing could become a key component of investment strategies within the Polish capital market.

References

Abhayawansa, S., & Mooneeapen, O. (2022). Directions for future research to steer environmental, social and governance (ESG) investing to support sustainability: A systematic literature review. *Handbook of accounting and sustainability* (pp. 318–341).

Adamska, A., Dąbrowski, T. J., & Grygiel-Tomaszewska, A. (2015). Społecznie odpowiedzialne inwestowanie w Polsce na tle sytuacji w wybranych krajach Unii Europejskiej. *Nauki O Finansach*, *2*(23), 73–95.

Aldowaish, A., Kokuryo, J., Almazyad, O., & Goi, H. C. (2022). Environmental, social, and governance integration into the business model: Literature review and research agenda. *Sustainability*, *14*(5), 2959. https://doi.org/10.3390/su14052959

Alharbi, S. S., Naveed, M., Ali, S., & Moussa, F. (2025). Sailing towards sustainability: Connectedness between ESG stocks and green cryptocurrencies. *International Review of Economics & Finance*, *98*, 103848. https://doi.org/10.1016/j.iref.2025.103848

Anwer, Z., Farid, S., Khan, A., & Benlagha, N. (2023). Cryptocurrencies versus environmentally sustainable assets: Does a perfect hedge exist? *International Review of Economics & Finance*, *85*, 418–431. https://doi.org/10.1016/j.iref.2023.02.005

Berry, T. C., & Junkus, J. C. (2013). Socially responsible investing: An investor perspective. *Journal of Business Ethics*, *112*(4), 707–720. https://doi.org/10.1007/s10551-012-1567-0

Bloomberg. (2025, January 2). *Morgan Stanley follows Citi, BofA in quitting climate group*. Retrieved January 8, 2025, from https://www.bloomberg.com/news/articles/2025-01-02/morgan-stanley-leaves-net-zero-alliance-for-banks

Camilleri, M. A. (2020). The market for socially responsible investing: A review of the developments. *Social Responsibility Journal*, *17*(3), 412–428. https://doi.org/10.1108/SRJ-06-2019-0194

Capital Institute. (2023). *8 Principles of regenerative economy*. Retrieved August 20, 2024 from https://capitalinstitute.org/8-principles-regenerative-economy/

Cappucci, M. (2018). The ESG integration paradox. *Journal of Applied Corporate Finance*, *30*(2), 22–28. https://doi.org/10.1111/jacf.12296

Czerwonka, M. (2013). *Inwestowanie Społecznie Odpowiedzialne*. Wydawnictwo Difin.

Deloitte. (2012). *Decyzje inwestycyjne a odpowiedzialny biznes. Raport z badania*. Listopad 2012. Retrieved April 3, 2024, from https://www.gpw.pl/pub/files/PDF/RESPECT_Raport_11.2012.pdf

Edmans, A. (2023b). The end of ESG. *Financial Management*, *52*(1), 3–17. https://doi.org/10.1111/fima.12413

European Commission. (2020a). *Taxonomy: Final report of the Technical Expert Group on Sustainable Finance w 2020*. Retrieved July 21, 2024, from https://finance.ec.europa.eu/system/files/2020-03/200309-sustainable-finance-teg-final-report-taxonomy-annexes_en.pdf

European Commission. (2020b). *EU taxonomy for sustainable activities*. Retrieved July 20, 2024, from https://finance.ec.europa.eu/sustainable-finance/tools-and-standards/eu-taxonomy-sustainable-activities

European Commission. (2021). *Zrównoważone finansowanie w UE*. Retrieved July 20, 2024, from https://poland.representation.ec.europa.eu/news/zrownowazone-finansowanie-w-ue-2021-07-06

European Commission. (2023a). *Commission Delegated Regulation (EU) 2023/2772 of 31 July 2023 supplementing Directive 2013/34/EU of the European Parliament and of the Council as regards sustainability reporting standards*. Retrieved from https://eur-lex.europa.eu/eli/reg_del/2023/2772/oj

European Commission. (2023b). *Daily news 31/07/2023*. Retrieved August 2, 2024, from https://ec.europa.eu/commission/presscorner/detail/it/mex_23_4044

European Parliament and Council. (2019). Regulation (EU) 2019/2088 of 27 November 2019 on sustainability-related disclosures in the financial services sector. *Official Journal of the European Union*, *317*, 1–16. https://eur-lex.europa.eu/eli/reg/2019/2088/oj/eng

European Parliament and Council of the European Union. (2019). *Regulation (EU) 2019/2088 of 27 November 2019 on sustainability-related disclosures in the financial services sector*. Retrieved from https://eur-lex.europa.eu/legal-content/EN/TXT/?uri=CELEX:32019R2088

Eurosif. (2011). *Report. European SRI study 2010*. Bruksela. Retrieved March 12, 2024, from https://www.eurosif.org

Eurosif. (2018). *European SRI study 2018* (pp. 16–17). Eurosif. Retrieved May 12, 2024, from https://www.eurosif.org/wp-content/uploads/2021/10/European-SRI-2018-Study.pdf

Eurosif. (2019). *Report. European SRI study 2018*. Bruksela. Retrieved March 12, 2024, from https://www.eurosif.org

Eurosif. (2022). *EU sustainable finance & SFDR: Making the framework fit for purpose Eurosif policy recommendations for Article 8 & 9 product labels*. Retrieved November 19, 2024, from https://www.eurosif.org/wp-content/uploads/2022/06/Eurosif-Report-June-22-SFDR-Policy-Recommendations.pdf

Friede, G. (2019). Why don't we see more action? A metasynthesis of the investor impediments to integrate environmental, social, and governance factors. *Business Strategy and the Environment*, *28*(6), 1260–1282. https://doi.org/10.1002/bse.2346

Fritz, T. M., & von Schnurbein, G. (2019). Beyond socially responsible investing: Effects of mission-driven portfolio selection. *Sustainability*, *11*(23), 23. https://doi.org/10.3390/su11236812

GIIN. (2019). *Core characteristics of impact investing*. Retrieved August 20, 2024, from https://thegiin.org/characteristics/

GIIN. (2023). *What you need to know about impact investing*. Retrieved August 20, 2024, from https://thegiin.org/impact-investing/need-to-know/

Global Sustainable Investment Alliance. (2020). *Global sustainable investment review 2020*. Retrieved June 30, 2024, from https://www.gsi-alliance.org/wp-content/uploads/2021/08/GSIR-20201.pdf

GRI. (2023). *European commission signals ESRS alignment with GRI*. Retrieved August 4, 2023, from https://www.globalreporting.org/news/news-center/european-commissionsignals-esrs-alignment-with-gri/

Institute for Responsible Finance. (n.d.). *Strona główna*. Retrieved August 4, 2024, from https://iof.org.pl/

International Finance Corporation (IFC). (2012). *IFC performance standards on environmental and social sustainability*. Retrieved July 22, 2024, from https://www.ifc.org/content/dam/ifc/doc/mgrt/ifc-performance-standards.pdf

International Finance Corporation (IFC). (2023). *Building a better future: 2023 annual report—Financials*. Retrieved January 26, 2025, from https://www.ifc.org/en/our-impact/annual-report

Kłobukowska, J. (2019). *Społecznie odpowiedzialne inwestowanie na rynku kapitałowym w Polsce.* Stan i perspektywy rozwoju. Wydawnictwo naukowe Uniwersytetu Mikołaja Kopernika.

Kravchuk, I. (2022). Performance of equity fund investment strategies in Poland. *Sustainability, 14*(20), 20. https://doi.org/10.3390/su142013078

Leite, P., & Cortez, M. C. (2014). Style and performance of international socially responsible funds in Europe. *Research in International Business and Finance, 30*, 248–267. https://doi.org/10.1016/j.ribaf.2013.09.007

Li, R. (2022). Literature Review of ESG Investment. In *Proceedings of the 2022 5th International Conference on Humanities Education and Social Sciences (ICHESS 2022)* (2964–2972). *Advances in Social Science, Education and Humanities Research.* https://doi.org/10.2991/978-2-494069-89-3_340

Lulewicz-Sas, A., & Kilon, J. (2014b). The effectiveness of SRI funds in Poland. *Procedia—Social and Behavioral Sciences, 156*, 194–197. https://doi.org/10.1016/j.sbspro.2014.11

Matczak, K., Przybył, J., & Wojciechowski, J. (2019). Czynniki środowiskowe w analizie ESG. *Kwartalnik Kolegium Ekonomiczno-Spolecznego. Studia I Prace, 4*(40).

Matos, P. (2020). ESG and responsible institutional investing around the world: A critical review. *CFA Institute Research Foundation Literature Reviews.* https://doi.org/10.2139/ssrn.3668998

Mikołajek-Gocejna, M. (2018). Europejski rynek inwestycji społecznie odpowiedzialnych. *Marketing I Rynek, 11*, 277–289.

Ministry of Finance. (2009). *Rozporządzenie Ministra Finansów z dnia 25 września 2009 r. w sprawie szczegółowych zasad sporządzania przez jednostki inne niż banki, zakłady ubezpieczeń i zakłady reasekuracji sprawozdań finansowych* (Dz. U. 2009 nr 169 poz. 1327). Retrieved August 12, 2024 from https://isap.sejm.gov.pl/isap.nsf/DocDetails.xsp?id=WDU20091691327

Ministry of Finance. (n.d.). *Startuje Polska Platforma Zrównoważonych Finansów.* Retrieved August 4, 2024, from https://www.gov.pl/web/finanse/startuje-polska-platforma-zrownowazonych-finansow

Nagel, S., Hiss, S., Woschnack, D., & Teufel, B. (2017). Between efficiency and resilience: The classification of companies according to their sustainability performance. *Historical Social Research, 42*(1), 189–210. https://doi.org/10.12759/hsr.42.2017.1.189-210

NYSE. (2023). *NYSE best practices for sustainability reporting.* Retrieved April 30, 2024, from https://www.nyse.com/esg-guidance

Polish Chamber of Commerce. (n.d.). *Komitet KIG ds. ESG.* Retrieved August 4, 2024, from https://kig.pl/esg-i-zrownowazony-rozwoj/komitet-kig-ds-esg/

Polish ESG Association. (n.d.). *Strona główna.* Retrieved August 4, 2024, from https://polskiestowarzyszenieesg.pl/

Principles for Responsible Investment. (2023a). *Signatory Update. January–March 2023.* Retrieved June 29, 2024, from https://www.unpri.org/download?ac=18691

Principles for Responsible Investment. (2023b). *What is responsible investment?*. Retrieved June 29, 2024, from https://www.unpri.org/introductory-guides-to-responsible-investment/what-isrespoWhatnsible-investment/4780.article

Principles for Responsible Investment. (2024). *About stewardship.* Retrieved May 29, 2024, from https://www.unpri.org/stewardship/about-stewardship/6268.article

Regenerators. (2023). *Invest in a regenerative economy.* Retrieved August 20, 2024, from https://theregenerators.org/action-areas/consume-with-consideration/create-locally-focused-circular-economies/invest-in-a-regenerative-economy/

Remlein, M. (2017). Strategie społecznie odpowiedzialnego inwestowania w polityce inwestycyjnej polskich przedsiębiorstw. *Finanse, Rynki Finansowe, Ubezpieczenia, 88*(1), 541–551.

Renneboog, L., Ter Horst, J., & Zhang, C. (2008). Socially responsible investments: Institutional aspects, performance, and investor behavior. *Journal of Banking and Finance, 32*(9), 1723–1742. https://doi.org/10.1016/j.jbankfin.2007.12.039

Riedl, A., & Smeets, P. (2017). Why do investors hold socially responsible mutual funds? *The Journal of Finance, 72*(6), 2505–2550. https://doi.org/10.1111/jofi.12547

Sandberg, J., Juravle, C., Hedesström, T. M., & Hamilton, I. (2009). The heterogeneity of socially responsible investment. *Journal of Business Ethics, 87*(4), 519–533. https://doi.org/10.1007/s10551-008-9956-0

Schoenmaker, D., & Schramade, W. (2019). Investing for long-term value creation. *Journal of Sustainable Finance & Investment, 9*(4), 356–377. https://doi.org/10.1080/20430795.2019.1625012

Stankiewicz, A. (2024, January 17). *U.S. sustainable funds register first annual outflows in 2023: Mediocre performance weighed on investor sentiment last year.* Morningstar. Retrieved November 28, 2024, from https://www.morningstar.com/sustainable-investing/us-sustainable-funds-register-first-annual-outflows-2023

Sultana, S., Zulkifli, N., & Zainal, D. (2018). Environmental, social and governance (ESG) and investment decision in Bangladesh. *Sustainability, 10*(6), 1831. https://doi.org/10.3390/su10061831

Sustainalytics. (2025). *Sustainalytics: ESG research, ratings & data.* Retrieved March 22, 2025, from https://www.sustainalytics.com/

The Pensions Regulator. (2024, July 30). *Market oversight: Review of trustee compliance with environmental, social and governance duties.* The Pensions Regulator. Retrieved September 15, 2025, from https://www.thepensionsregulator.gov.uk/en/document-library/research-and-analysis/market-oversight-esg#:~:text=submit%20to%20us.-,SIPs,evaluating%20their%20asset%20managers'%20performance

Thomson Reuters. (2025). *Clarifying the complex*. Retrieved March 22, 2025, from https://www.thomsonreuters.com/en.html

Trinks, A., Scholtens, B., Mulder, M., & Dam, L. (2018). Fossil fuel divestment and portfolio performance. *Ecological Economics, 146*, 740–748. https://doi.org/10.1016/j.ecolecon.2017.11.036

UN. (2004). *Who cares wins. Connecting financial markets to a changing world*. Retrieved January 9, 2025, from https://documents1.worldbank.org/curated/fr/444801491483640669/pdf/113850-BRI-IFC-Breif-whocares-PUBLIC.pdf

United Nations Sustainable Stock Exchanges Initiative. (2024a). *About the SSE*. Retrieved July 20, 2024, from https://sseinitiative.org/about/

United Nations Sustainable Stock Exchanges Initiative. (2024b). *ESG disclosure*. Retrieved July 20, 2024, from https://sseinitiative.org/esg-disclosure

van Duuren, E., Plantinga, A., & Scholtens, B. (2016). ESG integration and the investment management process: Fundamental investing reinvented. *Journal of Business Ethics, 138*(3), 525–533. https://doi.org/10.1007/s10551-015-2610-8

Widyawati, L. (2020). A systematic literature review of socially responsible investment and environmental social governance metrics. *Business Strategy and the Environment, 29*(2), 2. https://doi.org/10.1002/bse.2393

Winston, A. (2024). 2024 was a bad year for sustainability. *Harvard Business Review*. Retrieved December 27, 2024, from https://hbr.org/2024/12/2024-was-a-bad-year-for-sustainability

World Bank. (2025a). *ESG data portal*. Retrieved April 22, 2025, from https://esgdata.worldbank.org/

World Bank. (2025b). *Environmental and social standards*. Retrieved April 22, 2025, from https://projects.worldbank.org/en/projects-operations/environmental-and-social-framework/brief/environmental-and-social-standards

WSE. (2016). *Dobre Praktyki Spółek Notowanych na GPW 2021*. Retrieved December 3, 2024, from https://www.gpw.pl/pub/GPW/files/PDF/GPW_1015_17_DOBRE_PRAKTYKI_v2.pdf

WSE. (2023). *Wytyczne do raportowania ESG Przewodnik dla spółek. Październik 2023*. Retrieved November 14, 2023, from https://www.gpw.pl/pub/GPW/ESG/Wytyczne_do_raportowania_ESG.pdf

CHAPTER 5

Leading Financial Instruments for ESG Investments in Poland and Worldwide

5.1 Introduction

The present chapter focuses on key financial instruments for ESG investments, both in Poland and worldwide. The initial discussion focuses on the global market for ESG financial instruments, emphasising their dynamic evolution and increasing recognition within the investment sector. A wide range of sustainable investment instruments is presented, including green bonds, social bonds and ESG-linked bank products. The purpose of these instruments is to support projects that are beneficial to the environment and society. The present study focuses on the requirements for the issuance of green bonds and their growing popularity, especially in Europe.

The latter part of the chapter examines the Polish ESG investment market, analysing available instruments and challenges related to their implementation. Examples of responsible investments in banking products, real estate, investment funds and debt financial instruments are presented, highlighting their growing importance in the context of sustainable development. This analysis also includes a reflection on the current state of the ESG investment market in Poland and the prospects for its further development, with an emphasis on the need for intensification of activities in this area.

K. Łudzińska, *International ESG Perspectives*,
https://doi.org/10.1007/978-3-032-11666-6_5

5.2 Leading ESG Instruments: Characteristics and Investment Assumptions

ESG criteria are gaining increasing recognition in the investment world, as evidenced by the dynamic growth of funds allocated to sustainable investment funds—from 5 billion USD in 2018 to almost 70 billion USD in 2021 (Pérez et al., 2022). A pivotal instrument in this domain is purpose-driven financing, encompassing sustainable financing or green financing, which is designed to mobilise capital for the execution of projects that yield environmental and societal benefits. This encompasses, inter alia, investments in renewable energy sources, energy efficiency measures, sustainable construction practices and biodiversity conservation initiatives. From a social perspective, green financing may be considered to encompass a variety of areas, including municipal housing projects, in addition to educational and medical infrastructure. For companies, securing financing to meet various operational and development needs, such as through loans or bond issuance, is also essential. As illustrated in Table 5.1, a conceptual framework has been developed for the classification of sustainable financial solutions. This framework distinguishes between the purpose-driven and general-purpose use of funds.

In recent years, there has been a notable proliferation of innovative instruments within the domain of sustainable financing. This encompasses loans, mergers and acquisitions, and capital market products that are

Table 5.1 Overview of sustainable financial solutions

Financial solutions	*Purpose-driven financing of social or environmental projects E.g. renewable energy, municipal construction, medical care, etc.*	*General financing focused on ESG outcomes E.g. GHG emission reduction in the production process, reduction of workplace accidents, etc.*
Bonds	• Green Bonds • Social Bonds	• Sustainability-Linked Bonds
Loans	• Green Loans • Social Loans	• Sustainability-Linked Loans • ESG Rating-Linked Loans
Other Financial Tools	• Green/Social • Factoring	• Sustainability-Linked/ESG Factoring • ESG-Hedging

Source Based on Krawczyńska-Kaczmarek (2024)

Table 5.2 Main categories of sustainable financing instruments

Financial instrument	*Purpose*
Green bonds and loans	Funds from them are allocated to climate and ecological initiatives
Sustainable development bonds	Profits are allocated to projects combining ecological and social aspects
Transformation bonds issued by high carbon footprint organisations	Supporting decarbonisation processes
Social bonds	Improving social welfare, generating positive changes in local communities
Sustainability-linked bonds and loans, the terms of which are adjusted to the sustainable development goals of the issuing entity	Promoting the ecological and social responsibility of organisations
Loans supporting clean energy projects, including	Financing clean energy projects, including the purchase of low-emission technologies and energy storage in the grid

Source Based on McKinsey and Company (2022)

dedicated to ESG principles. Nevertheless, the heterogeneity of the concept, in conjunction with the absence of universally accepted definitions, can pose challenges to consistent impact measurement. The primary categories of these instruments are outlined in Table 5.2, encompassing instruments issued by both corporate entities and local governments.

The growing engagement of financial markets in promoting sustainable development can be attributed to the availability of a wide range of instruments. The total value of sustainable bonds issued worldwide, including green, social and sustainability-linked bonds, reached 965 billion dollars in 2021, representing an increase of 80% compared to the previous year (McKinsey & Company, 2022). Meanwhile, the value of sustainable syndicated loans in 2021 reached 683 billion US dollars, marking an increase of over 200% compared to 2020 (McKinsey & Company, 2022). Sustainable bonds currently account for approximately 12% of the total global bond market, while sustainable loans represent almost 13% of the global loan market. A particularly marked increase in emissions was observed in 2020. This phenomenon can be attributed, at least in part, to the rapid growth in the provision of loans associated with sustainable development, which increased threefold between 2020 and 2021, and the surge in green loans, which rose by 71% during the same period (McKinsey & Company, 2022).

The leading debt instruments dedicated to financing ESG investments worldwide are *GSS + bonds*, the acronym of which is derived from the following words: Green, Social and Sustainable. According to the Climate Bond Initiative report (CBI, Climate Bonds Initiative, 2023a), the cumulative global volume reached 3.9 trillion USD in the first quarter of 2023 (Fig. 5.1). As illustrated in Table 5.3, the most notable categories of GSS + bonds are green, social, sustainability, sustainability-linked (SLB) and transition bonds. However, it is the green bonds that represent the instrument with the largest capitalisation. The ensuing discourse shall direct its

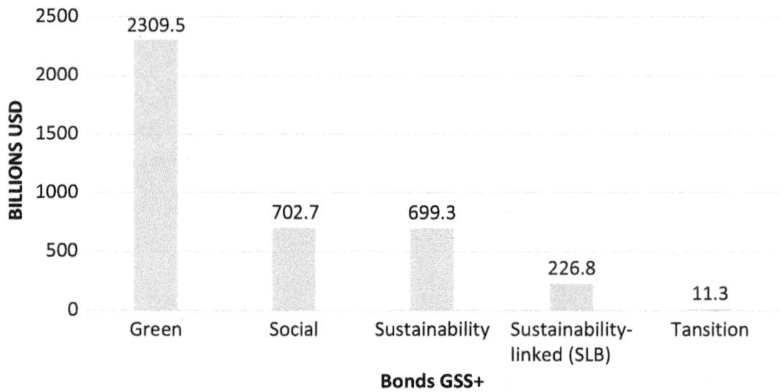

Fig. 5.1 Cumulative volume of GSS+ debt instruments at the end of the first quarter of 2023. *Source* Based on data from the Climate Bonds Initiative (2023b)

Table 5.3 GSS + debt instruments in the first quarter of 2023 and cumulatively since 2006

GSS + Bonds	*Q1 2023*		*Cumulative since 2006*	
	USD billion	*% share*	*USD billion*	*% share*
Green	122.9	60	2309.5	58
Social	30.6	15	702.7	18
Sustainability	29.6	14	699.3	18
SLB	21.4	10	226.8	6
Transition	0.2	1	11.3	0
Total	**204.7**	**100**	**3949.6**	**100**

Source Based on Climate Bonds Initiative (2023b)

attention towards an exposition of the salient characteristics of these pivotal green financial instruments. These instruments are to be employed as a case study, with the objective of providing a comprehensive illustration of the broader evolution of sustainable investment tools.

The fundamental distinction between green bonds and conventional bonds is predicated on the former's explicit stipulation of the allocation of funds procured through their issuance. These funds are earmarked exclusively for initiatives pertaining to sustainable development or environmental conservation. These have been defined in detail in the form of market-valued, non-binding guidelines developed by the International Capital Market Association (ICMA) and the Climate Bonds Initiative (CBI). The Green Bond Principles (GBP) are a set of guidelines that delineate the optimal practices for the issuance of green bonds. The GBP were first published in June 2018, and subsequently updated in June 2021 (ICMA, 2021).

For bonds to be recognised as green on the international financial market, they must undergo a certification process, for which the International Capital Market Association (ICMA) is responsible. The Green Bonds Principles (GBP) provide issuers with assistance in the financing of environmentally sustainable projects that support the economy in achieving net-zero greenhouse gas emissions and protect the environment. It is recommended that issuers adopt a transparent issuance process and disclose information that investors, banks, sub-issuers, agents and other entities can use to understand the characteristics of a given green bond. The Global Banking Principles (GBP) encompass four fundamental components: the utilisation of proceeds, the project evaluation and selection process, the management of proceeds and the reporting process (ICMA, 2022). The green bond, as a financial instrument, is predicated on the allocation of the proceeds from issuance to green projects. It is imperative that this allocation is reflected in the legal documentation of each bond series that is issued. The aforementioned projects may include, but are not limited to, the following: renewable energy, energy efficiency, biodiversity protection, pollution prevention and control (ICMA, 2022).

In 2007, the European Investment Bank (EIB) pioneered the introduction of green bonds, initially designated as Climate Awareness Bonds (Sertore, 2022). Subsequent to this initiative, the disbursement of proceeds from green bond issuance to ecological projects has been meticulously monitored and comprehensively reported. The popularity of green bonds is growing. The green bond market, both globally and within the European Union, exhibited an average annual growth rate of 50%

between 2015 and 2020, accounting for 3 to 3.5% of total bond issuance (Climate Bonds Initiative, 2021). In Europe alone, the total value of green issuances in 2020 was approximately PLN 1747 billion (Ministry of Finance, Ministry of Finance of the Republic of Poland, 2021). The Climate Bonds Initiative, an organisation which fulfils the role of monitoring the GSS+ bond market, has presented a list of its largest global issuers in 2023 (see, Table 5.4). Despite forecasts indicating the perpetuation of this market's growth, analysts advocate for the accelerated development of the high-quality green bond market to achieve the objectives outlined in the Paris Agreement (EU Briefing, 2022).

In response to the mounting interest in the field of sustainable financing, the European Commission has devised a strategy for the issuance of green bonds under the EU Next Generation programme. The objective of this initiative is to generate funds amounting to €250 billion (European Commission, 2021). The Next Generation EU framework for green bonds provides investors with clear guidance on the allocation and use of funds, as well as robust reporting mechanisms. The framework under discussion can be distilled into four key aspects: the initial distribution of financial resources, the process of determining suitable investment opportunities, the management of the financial resources that have been allocated, and the transparency surrounding the environmental impact of these investments. It is important to note that the guidelines adopted by the European Commission are fully aligned with the Green Bond Principles (GBP) established by the International Capital Market Association (ICMA, 2022).

Table 5.4 The ten largest issuers of green bonds in the first half of 2023

Issuer	*Country*	*Volume (in billion USD)*
Germany	Germany	15.0
EIB	International entity	13.2
Italy	Italy	13.0
United Kingdom	United Kingdom	9.8
KFW	Germany	7.3
European Union	International entity	6.5
Austria	Austria	6.4
Intesa Sanpaolo SpA	Italy	5.6
Gaci First Investment Co PIF	Saudi Arabia	5.5
Bank of China	China	4.4

Source Based on Climate Bonds Initiative (2023a)

In the subsequent phase, the European Parliament and Council Regulation No. 2023/2631 was adopted, thereby establishing uniform regulations for European green bonds (EuGB) and the disclosure of information concerning environmentally sustainable bonds (European Parliament and Council, 2023). The regulation was initiated on 20 December 2023 and formally implemented on 9 January 2024 within the EU member states. It was incorporated into the national legal framework of Poland on 21 December 2023. The primary objectives of the regulation are threefold: firstly, to standardise the requirements for issuers of green bonds; secondly, to prevent fragmentation of regulations in European Union countries; and thirdly, to define the criteria for allocating bond revenues to finance environmentally sustainable activities in accordance with the EU Taxonomy. Moreover, the regulation introduces a system of registry and supervision over external controllers of green bonds; and also counteracts greenwashing, i.e. falsely declaring bond compliance with environmental objectives (European Parliament and Council, 2023). The regulation in question is applicable to a broad spectrum of issuers, encompassing financial institutions, commercial enterprises, local governments and states. In order to be designated a 'European Green Bond', issuers are required to meet a series of detailed requirements with regard to the utilisation of funds and the manner in which they are reported.

Poland has been identified as a leader in the field of green bond issuance within the European market. As early as 2016, the Polish Ministry of Treasury undertook the inaugural issuance of Polish green bonds, thereby establishing Poland as a global leader in the domain of sovereign green bond offerings (Skuza & Modzelewska, 2020). This event signified a pivotal moment in the global financial landscape, as it marked the inaugural instance in which a national government, in this case the Polish government, had issued green bonds with the explicit purpose of financing projects that would have a demonstrable and beneficial impact on the environment. This initiative has garnered international recognition, as evidenced by the awarding of the Climate Bonds Award to Poland in 2017 by the Climate Bonds Initiative for executing the world's first sovereign green bond issuance (PAP, 2017).

The development of the global green bond market has contributed to an increase in trading of these financial instruments (Lipowicz, 2023). In response to these trends, specialist indices for green bonds were initiated in 2014 to assist investors in making informed investment decisions. The advent of these indices served to reduce information gaps, thereby offering investors valuable indications regarding the profitability of various issuances and enabling more accurate comparisons. Among the pioneering indices from 2014, one can mention the Bank of America Merrill Lynch Green Bond Index, which was developed to monitor bonds financing ecological projects and pro-ecological initiatives (Next Finance, 2014), and the Bloomberg Barclays MSCI Global Green Bond Index, which provides a comprehensive overview of the global fixed income green bond market (Bloomberg Barclays, 2021). Other notable indices that merit mention include the S&P Green Bond Index, the Bloomberg MSCI Global Green Bond Index and the Solactive Green Bond Index.

In addition to green bonds, social bonds are also worthy of note. These initiatives are designed to raise funds for both existing and new projects that demonstrate a positive social impact. The principles of social bonds, which bear a resemblance to green bonds, were developed in 2017 by ICMA with the aim of providing support to issuers in financing projects that deliver social benefits. The issuance of financial instruments in accordance with the stipulated standards set forth by the SBP is expected to facilitate the provision of transparent social references, in conjunction with the generation of investment opportunities. The principles of social bonds, updated in June 2023, are voluntary guidelines that recommend issuers a clear process and disclosure of information that investors, banks, subissuers, rating agencies and other entities can use to understand the characteristics of a given social bond (ICMA, 2023).

As with green bonds, social bonds can be issued by governments and central banks to fund a variety of projects with a positive social impact, such as the construction of affordable housing or the expansion of access to healthcare. In 2015, the Instituto de Crédito Oficial (ICO) introduced the first official social bond, with the objective of providing support to small and medium-sized enterprises operating in economically disadvantaged regions of Spain, whilst concurrently promoting the protection and creation of new employment opportunities (Goldman & Sachs, 2023). In 2020, in the midst of the global COVID-19 pandemic, the European Commission initiated the SURE initiative (Support to Mitigate Unemployment Risks in an Emergency) as a response to the economic and social challenges engendered by the virus. As part of this initiative, a social bond issuance amounting to 17 billion euros was undertaken, with the objective of directly covering costs associated with financing national crisis response strategies in the context of the social crisis engendered by the pandemic. The European Commission was assisted in this issuance by financial institutions such as Barclays (IRL), BNP Paribas, Deutsche Bank, Nomura and UniCredit. The funds thus accumulated were subsequently redistributed to beneficiary countries in the form of loans, with the stated aim of helping them cover costs directly related primarily to job preservation (European Commission, 2020).

In conclusion, it should be emphasised that instruments financing ESG investments today constitute a key mechanism in shaping the sustainable economy of the future. These instruments empower investors to allocate capital to projects that yield financial returns while concomitantly contributing to the achievement of social and environmental objectives. The mounting significance of these factors is indicative of a transformative shift within the capital market, characterised by the progressive integration of ESG criteria and the concomitant augmentation in the magnitude of allocated financial assets.

5.3 Key Instruments of Socially Responsible Investments in the Polish Market: Current State and Development Prospects

Despite the fact that ESG investments are not developing as dynamically in Poland as in other European markets, they are also attracting interest. The instruments offered within these investments provide investors with a wide

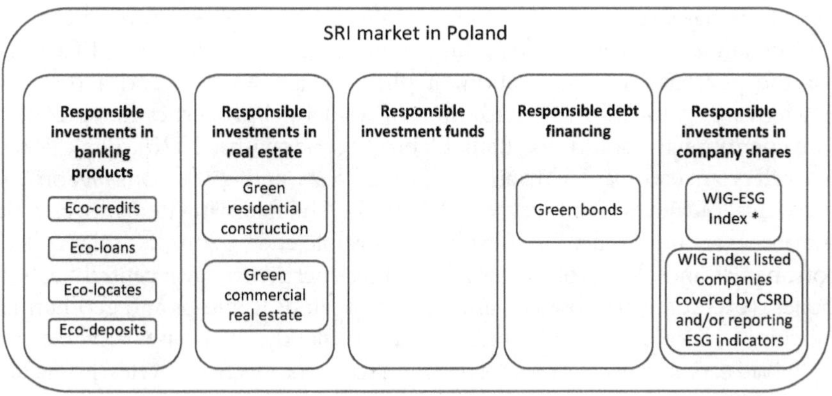

Fig. 5.2 SRI market in Poland—framework diagram. *Listed until 31.07.2024

range of opportunities, allowing for the placement of funds in sustainable or green assets, in line with their return expectations and engagement in social and environmental issues.

In the context of the Polish market, investors have the option to select sustainable and socially responsible investments from several primary categories, including banking products, real estate, investment funds, debt instruments and company shares. A thorough examination of the ESG indices of the Warsaw Stock Exchange is presented in Sect. 6.3. Figure 5.2 provides a graphical representation of the framework of the Polish SRI market, offering an overview of the key tools available to SRI investors in the Polish market.

5.3.1 Responsible Investments in Banking Products

Responsible investments in banking products encompass a range of financial instruments, including loans, credits, deposits and savings accounts. Financial institutions offering such products consider not only economic criteria but also social and environmental factors. In Poland, a significant number of banking institutions provide financial instruments, termed ‘eco-loans’ or ‘eco-credits’, to individual customers seeking to finance projects that fall within the domain of environmental sustainability. These projects encompass a wide range of initiatives, including energy efficiency measures, the utilisation of renewable energy sources, the installation of photovoltaic systems and heat pump technology, among others.

Bank Ochrony Środowiska (Environmental Protection Bank) is a prominent financial institution in this sector, offering a range of environmentally-oriented financial products, including green loans, ‘clean air’ credit, ECOloan for the purchase and installation of photovoltaic systems, and a thermo-modernisation loan for the renovation of residential properties that incorporate energy-saving solutions (Bank Ochrony Środowiska, 2025). Bank Pekao SA offers an eco-loan with an APR of 13.82% and a 0% commission for ecological purposes (Bank Pekao S.A., 2025). The following items are eligible for purchase and installation subsidies: renewable energy sources (solar collectors, panels and photovoltaic cells, including energy storage); central heating boilers (excluding coal boilers) and eco-pea coal; heat pumps and geothermal heating; windows, doors and materials for insulating the house, roof; electric or hybrid cars and electric motorcycles and scooters, electric bicycles; home bio sewage treatment plants; ventilation with heat recovery; home water treatment stations from own intakes and rainwater recovery systems. It is evident that a plethora of financial institutions proffer analogous offerings of eco-loans and eco-credits to individual customers. Among these institutions are: Bank PKO BP S.A (Bank Pekao BP S.A., 2025), Santander Bank Polska (Santander Bank Polska, 2025), and Alior Bank, which offers 'Ekoraty' credit for the financing of photovoltaic installations, heat pumps, home sewage treatment plants, and other environmentally friendly, individual purchases (Alior Bank, 2025).

Furthermore, enterprises have the option of obtaining loans that have environmental benefits. Bank City Handlowy, in collaboration with Bank Gospodarstwa Krajowego, has been offering loans that prioritise environmental sustainability. These *eco-loans* are made possible through the financial support of the European Funds for the Modern Economy (2021–2027), specifically under the 3.1 Action. *Ecological loan*. This is a grant that provides support for micro-, small and medium-sized enterprises, as well as small, mid-cap and mid-cap enterprises. It facilitates co-financing of investments in infrastructure and technologies that increase energy efficiency or use more ecological energy sources (Bank City Handlowy, 2025). An exemplar of such an investment is the ESG-linked loan, which in 2019 was obtained by the Energa Group, as the first company in Poland to do so. A loan amounting to PLN 2 billion, with a duration of five years, was granted for the implementation of sustainable development goals. The loan was financed by a banking consortium comprising Santander Bank Polska S.A. (acting as coordinator), Bank Gospodarstwa Krajowego, PKO Bank Polski S.A., CaixaBank S.A. Branch in Poland, and MUFG Bank N.V. (Energa Group, Energa, 2019). The funds were primarily allocated to the development of renewable energy generation capacity (so-called RES) and the further modernisation of power transmission infrastructure.

5.3.2 Responsible Property Investments

Responsible property investments include new green construction projects, encompassing both residential and commercial properties, such as shopping centres, distribution centres and office buildings. These projects place a strong emphasis on energy savings, utilities and the control of CO_2 emissions during construction and property management.

Also, SRI investments in real estate focus on existing building infrastructure and revitalisation projects in post-industrial areas, including the construction of affordable housing. Furthermore, responsible investors ensure that construction investment projects are based on contracts that respect workers' rights and good business practices (Think Co., 2022). Banks support such investments by offering green mortgages to individual customers. One such bank is mBank, which offers loans to finance the purchase or construction of houses or flats in blocks or single-family buildings with low energy consumption (mBank, 2025). Among construction companies on the Polish market, Echo Investment stands out with its ESG strategy, Echo-Archicom 2030. This strategy includes reducing CO_2 emissions in construction investments and in its own offices; introducing processes that limit the carbon footprint; achieving zero emissions by 2030; protecting urban greenery; and counteracting 'urban sprawl' (i.e. operating in already urbanised areas). The company also aims to supply all construction sites with energy obtained from renewable energy sources (RES) by 2026 (Echo Investment, 2023).

The Polish Green Building Council (PLGBC) is one of Poland's leading non-governmental organisations promoting green building projects, whether individual or commercial. Since 2008, the PLGBC has been working to transform buildings, cities and their surroundings so that they are planned, designed, constructed, used, modernised, demolished and processed in a manner that aligns with sustainable development goals (PLGBC, 2025a). The Polish association is part of a global community of 77 green building associations within the World Green Building Council. As of September 2025, the PLGBC had 255 members in Poland (PLGBC, 2025b). Of these, 39% were architects, designers, service providers and property managers; 24% were development companies, investors and contractors; 25% were manufacturers; and 11% were various institutions and local governments. The association runs many local and national projects (e.g. 'Buildings are like people'), as well as participating in international initiatives (e.g. 'Building Life' for the European Green Deal). These projects aim to promote good practices and stimulate market changes relating to climate, health, resources and sustainable development.

5.3.3 Responsible Investment Funds

Responsible investment funds differ from 'traditional' funds in that they consider how the investment's profits are generated (as discussed in Chap. 4 on SRI investing worldwide). In the Polish context, SRI funds are those that meet two criteria simultaneously (Gierałtowska, 2017): first, their investment policy states that they invest in ethical and ecological ventures, companies with high social responsibility standards, and other projects or companies whose activity is widely recognised as responsible; and second, the names of the funds contain elements of the aforementioned investment policy (i.e. the funds are labelled as green, ethical, responsible, SRI, ecological or healthcare-related, etc.).

Until 2017, no socially responsible investment (SRI) funds were operating on the Polish capital market (Gierałtowska, 2017), and their presence remains limited to this day. As of September 2025, 11 domestic investment fund companies (TFI) were offering funds aligned with environmental, social and governance (ESG) criteria, most of which originated from foreign markets. The funds currently available in Poland include: Allianz PIMCO ESG Income, Allianz PIMCO Global Bond ESG, UNIQA European Equity ESG, inPZU Sustainable Water Economy Equity, inPZU Green Energy Equity, inPZU Green Bonds, PKO Green Transformation Bonds, Generali Ecological Equity, PKO Ecology and Social Responsibility Global Equity and NN Global Sustainable Equity (My Funds, 2025). Despite this growing selection, the Polish capital market still lacks strictly ethical funds (Czerwonka, 2023).

Established in 1989 in cooperation with local governments, the National Fund for Environmental Protection and Water Management is the only public fund allocating resources for the protection of the natural environment and water resources (National Fund for Environmental Protection and Water Management, 2025). Green investments are also supported by the Polish Development Fund (PFR), which, in January 2023, presented its new strategy to support the construction of a low-emission economy in Poland: the PFR Green Hub. PFR's activities include investing 250 million PLN in four investment funds focused on green investments: General Atlantic (investing in ClimateTech); Eurozeo Smart City (investing in smart city projects); Contrarian Ventures (investing in early-stage start-ups); and Montis Capital (investing in Polish green companies) (Investor Zone, 2023; PFR Ventures, 2024).

5.3.4 *Responsible Debt Financing*

Responsible debt financing is the practice of borrowing funds while incorporating sustainable development criteria into the financing process. One of the most popular tools is the green bond, which was introduced in Sect. 4.2. In 2016, Poland became the first country in the world to issue green treasury bonds, worth 750 million euros. The first issue of green corporate bonds took place in 2019 (Ministry of Finance of the Republic of Poland, 2021).

Despite such initiatives, the market is not developing intensively. According to an analysis by the Ministry of Finance, Poland has a significantly smaller value of aggregated green bond issues than Western European or Scandinavian countries. However, it leads ahead of countries with a less developed capital market and thus has great potential in the area of future corporate and municipal green bond issues (Ministry of Finance of the Republic of Poland, 2021). As of 15 August 2023, the Climate Bonds Initiative reported that the size of green bond issues in Poland was 7.1 billion USD (Climate Bonds Initiative, 2023b).

A 2021 KPMG report prepared for the Ministry of Finance of the Republic of Poland presents an analysis of the possibilities for the further development of Poland's green bond market in connection with the Capital Market Development Strategy (SRRK), highlighting actions in the area of sustainable financing (KPMG., 2021). The Ministry of Finance plays a leading role in implementing the strategy in cooperation with the European Bank for Reconstruction and Development (EBRD), using funds from the European Commission's Structural Reform Support Programme. Local governments have embraced sustainable financing, with Grudziądz becoming the first Polish city to issue green bonds. The Municipal Water and Sewage Treatment Plant Ltd. was directly involved in this step, obtaining a certificate enabling the financing and refinancing of bonds totalling 63.2 million PLN in 2021 (Milewska, 2022). Throughout the issuance process, the city collaborated with DNB Bank Polska, which purchased these bonds for its portfolio. Following in Grudziądz's footsteps, Łódź issued green bonds worth 50 million PLN from a total issue of 418 million PLN (Lipowicz, 2023). There is a growing consensus that local governments have significant potential to increase debt issuance through green bonds to finance environmentally sustainable local investments. This market is expected to continue expanding in the coming years.

The first corporate green bonds also debuted on the Polish capital market. According to data from the Warsaw Stock Exchange at the end of 2021, the Polish corporate green bond market consisted of ten issuers (Institute of Responsible Finance, Instytut Odpowiedzialnych Finansów, 2022). Green bonds have therefore become an attractive financing tool for sustainable investments, including for Polish companies (Gemra, 2021). The first such initiative by a company took place in 2020 with the Polsat Cyfrowy Group.

Since then, many other companies, including New Energy Investments and PKN Orlen, have followed suit (Ślażyńska-Kluczek, 2022).

The Warsaw Stock Exchange offers corporate green bonds via the Catalyst market within its dedicated 'Warsaw Sustainable Segment'. This segment is intended for issuers and investors interested in debt instruments financing sustainable development projects. Catalyst enables companies to raise capital effectively through bond issuance, while offering investors a wide range of options. To qualify for this segment, issuers must provide a statement confirming that the securities they issue support the financing of sustainable development activities (WSE Catalyst, 2025). Currently, nine issuers offer 26 bonds on the WSE Catalyst corporate green bond market (2025), as shown in Table 5.5. In 2023, eleven green bonds were issued by eight different issuers (Łudzińska, 2024), representing an increase of almost 140%.

By issuing green bonds, issuers can raise additional funds and build a positive image in the eyes of investors (Ślażyńska-Kluczek, 2022). It is a method of raising capital and an opportunity to demonstrate commitment to sustainable development. However, it is important to note that financing through green bonds comes with certain obligations, such as preparing detailed reports, monitoring investment compliance with green financing criteria and obtaining opinions from independent experts.

Responsible investment in company shares involves considering not only traditional financial factors, but also environmental, social and governance criteria. These include environmental protection, climate change, workers' rights and human rights. Companies that excel in these areas often feature in stock exchange social responsibility indices. Similarly, the Warsaw Stock Exchange first included such companies in the RESPECT index and subsequently in the WIG-ESG (see, Chap. 6 for more on this).

In summary, the analysis of the SRI investment market in Poland refers to the key conclusions of the Chamber of Fund and Asset Managers' report on the state of the investment fund market in Poland in 2022 (Chamber of Fund and Asset Managers, 2022). Over the last decade, there has been a significant increase in the value of accumulated fund assets, driven by trends in global capital markets. This growth peaked in September 2021, when the net sum of assets exceeded 314 billion zlotys. However, the economic situation began to deteriorate in the following months. This was due to the acceleration of inflation, the slowdown in economic growth and the aggressive monetary policy of global central banks, resulting in declines in the stock and bond markets.

Table 5.5 Corporate Green Bonds—Warsaw Sustainable Segment on the Warsaw Stock Exchange (1 March 2025)

Number of issuers	*Issuer*	*Name of green bond*	*Segment/ trading place*	*Currency*
1	ANWIM	ANW1126	GPW ASO	PLN
2	BOŚ SA	BOS1228	GPW ASO	PLN
3	CYFROWY POLSAT	CPS0130	GPW ASO	PLN
4	EUROPEAN BANK	E151129	GPW RR	PLN
		EIB0227	GPW RR	PIN
		EIB0243	GPW RR	PLN
		EIB0429	GPW RR	PLN
		EIB1134	GPW RR	PLN
5	GHELAMCO INVEST	GHE0128	GPW RR	PIN
		GHE0226	GPW ASO	GBP
		GHE0327	WSE ASO	GBP
		GHE0728	WSE ASO	PIN
		GHE1027	WSE RR	GBP
		GHE1127	WSE ASO	GBP
		GHE1128	WSE ASO	GBP
		GHE1227	WSE ASO	EUR
6	PEKAO	PE01127	WSE RR	EUR
7	PKO MORTGAGE BANK	PHP0625	WSE RR	EUR
8	PKO BP	PK00927	WSE RR	EUR
9	POLENERGIA	PEP1029	WSE ASO	GBP
10	ORLEN	PKN12.25	WSE ASO	GBP
		PKN0528	WSE RR	EUR
11	R.POWER SA	RP11029	WSE ASO	PIN
		RP21029	WSE ASO	PIN
		RPW1029	WSE ASO	PIN
12	TAURON POLSKA ENERGIA	TPE1025	WSE ASO	GBP

Acronyms WSE ASO—Warsaw Stock Exchange Alternative Trading System; WSE RR—Warsaw Stock Exchange Regulated Market; WSE BS—Warsaw Stock Exchange Bond Spot Market
Source Based on WSE Catalyst data (WSE Catalyst, 2025)

This negative trend was further exacerbated by the armed conflict between Russia and Ukraine. Consequently, 2022 saw a 11.8% decrease in the value of accumulated funds, reaching 266.3 billion zlotys. This represents 87% of the entire market (Chamber of Fund and Asset Managers, 2022).

In addition, the NN Responsible Investment Index fund, which is managed by NN Investment Partners TFI (an investment fund management company) and has assets totalling 1.244 billion zlotys, is one of the largest equity funds in Poland, ranking just behind the 'traditional' Allianz and PKO Innovation and Global Technology funds (Chamber of Fund and Asset Managers, 2022, p. 25). Therefore, it is noteworthy that the 2022 report from the Chamber of Fund and Asset Managers seems to overlook key aspects related to ESG initiatives and SRI investment strategies. It lacks an analysis of the efficiency and strategies of socially responsible funds operating on the Polish market. This is somewhat surprising, given that the Chamber is involved in consultations on changes to EU regulations affecting the operations of investment fund management companies and investment firms. Work on modifying regulations, especially in the context of ESG aspects, is ongoing.

In 2022, the European Securities and Markets Authority (ESMA) began consulting on guidelines relating to the use of the terms 'ESG' and 'sustainable' in fund names (ESMA, 2022). The 'Guidelines on the use of terms related to ESG or sustainable development in fund nomenclature' were published on 21 August 2024 and came into effect on 21 November 2024 (ESMA., 2024). These guidelines aim to identify instances where fund names incorporating terms related to ESG or sustainable development are deemed unfair, unclear, or misleading. ESMA emphasises that a fund's name is a key source of information for investors and a crucial marketing tool. As it is often the first detail investors encounter, it can significantly influence their decisions, even though they are expected to look beyond it and carefully examine the fund's disclosures (ESMA., 2024).

5.4 Summary and Conclusions

This chapter explores the evolution and significance of financial instruments linked to ESG investing in global markets and in Poland. Instruments such as green bonds and social bonds are becoming an increasingly popular means of financing projects that benefit investors, the environment and society. In response to rising investor awareness of the need for sustainable development, the global market for these instruments is growing.

Although the development of ESG investments is not as dynamic in Poland as in other European countries, there are already instruments gaining importance in this area. The Polish sustainable investment market offers opportunities in segments such as banking products, real estate, investment funds and debt financial instruments, including green bonds. Pioneering examples from the Polish market demonstrate that ESG investments can bring financial benefits and positively impact social development and environmental protection.

The analyses highlight the need to further develop the ESG investment market in Poland, which shows great potential. Efforts to promote sustainable investments and raise awareness of them among investors and issuers must be intensified. At the same time, the growing commitment of financial institutions and companies to ESG offers hope for the dynamic future development of this market, which will play a key role in establishing a sustainable Polish economy.

References

Bank, A. (2025, August 14). Retrieved from https://www.aliorbank.pl/klienci-indywidualni/kredyty-i-pozyczki/kredyty-ratalne/ekoraty.html

Bank City Handlowy. (2025, August 14). Retrieved from https://www.citibank.pl/poland/corporate/polish/fundusze-unijne/kredyt-ekologiczny.htm

Bank Ochrony Środowiska (2025, March 14). Retrieved from https://www.bosbank.pl/klient-indywidualny/pozyczki-i-kredyty/eko-kredyty?gad_source=1&gclid=Cj0KCQjwytS-BhCKARIsAMGJyzo5Cl1tjy4WwRCaY-HwMgniPDb9pNZ9TrJMMHMwIX_Kt2FGnh2GEQIaAltcEALw_wcB&gclsrc=aw.ds

Bank Pekao, S. A. (2023). Retrieved August 14, 2024, from https://www.pekao.com.pl/klient-indywidualny/pozyczanie-gotowki/eko-pozyczka.html

Bank Pekao, S. A. (2025, March 14). Retrieved from https://www.pekao.com.pl/klient-indywidualny/pozyczanie-gotowki/eko-pozyczka.html

Bloomberg Barclays. (2021). *Bloomberg barclays MSCI global green bond index.* Retrieved August 14, 2024, from http://www.msci.com/documents/10199/242721/Barclays_MSCI_Green_Bond_Index.pdf/6e4d942a-0ce4-4e70-9aff-d7643e1bde96

Chamber of Fund and Asset Managers. (2022). *Raport roczny o rynku funduszy inwestycyjnych w Polsce w 2022 roku.* Retrieved from https://www.izfa.pl/raporty#pozostale-raporty

Climate Bonds Initiative. (2021). *2021 already a record year for green finance with over $350bn issued!* Retrieved August 14, 2024, from https://www.climatebonds.net/2021/11/2021already-record-year-green-finance-over-350bn-issued

Climate Bonds Initiative. (2023a). *Sustainable debt market summary H1 2023.* Retrieved November 18, 2024, from https://www.climatebonds.net/data-insights/publications/h1-market-report-2023

Climate Bonds Initiative. (2023b). *Sustainable debt market summary Q1 2023.* May 2023. Retrieved November 19, 2024, from https://www.climatebonds.net/data-insights/publications/q1-2023-market-update-sustainable-debt-shows-recovery

Czerwonka, M. (2023, May 23). *Podstawowe założenia inwestowania etycznego*. Obserwator Finansowy. Retrieved November 19, 2024, from https://www.obserwatorfinansowy.pl/bez–kategorii/rotator/podstawowe-zalozenia-inwestowania-etycznego/

Echo Investment. (2023). *Strategia ESG Echo-archicom 2030*. Retrieved March 15, 2025, from https://www.echo.com.pl/preview,1748,strategia-esg-echo-archicom-2030.pdf

Energa, G. (2019). Retrieved August 14, 2025, from https://media.energa.pl/pr/462341/energa-pozyskalapierwszy-w-polsce-kredyt-odpowiedzialny-spolecznie-ma

ESMA. (2022). *ESMA launches a consultation on guidelines for the use of ESG or sustainability-related terms in funds' names*. Retrieved August 22, 2024, from https://www.esma.europa.eu/press-news/esma-news/esma-launches-consultation-guidelines-useesg-or-sustainability-related-terms

ESMA. (2024). *Guidelines_ on funds' names using ESG or sustainability-related terms*. Retrieved March 8, 2025, from https://www.esma.europa.eu/sites/default/files/2024-08/ESMA34-1592494965-657_Guidelines_on_funds_names_using_ESG_or_sustainability_related_terms.pdf

European Commission. (2020). *European Commission issues first emission of EU SURE social bonds*. Retrieved August 16, 2024 from https://ec.europa.eu/commission/presscorner/detail/en/ip_20_1954

European Commission. (2021). *Questions and answers: Next generation EU green bond framework and funding plan update*. Retrieved August 1, 2024, from https://ec.europa.eu/commission/presscorner/detail/hu/QANDA_21_4567

European Parliament and Council. (2023). *Regulation (EU) 2023/2631 of the European parliament and of the council of 22 november 2023 on European green bonds and optional disclosures for bonds marketed as environmentally sustainable and for sustainability-linked bonds*. Retrieved from http://data.europa.eu/eli/reg/2023/2631/oj

EU Briefing. (2022). *European green bonds a standard for Europe, open to the world*. Retrieved August 1, 2024, from https://www.europarl.europa.eu/RegData/etudes/BRIE/2022/698870/EPRS_BRI(2022)698870_EN.pdf

Gemra, K. (2021). Świadomość funkcjonowania green bonds na polskim rynku obligacji korporacyjnych. *Kwartalnik Nauk O Przedsiębiorstwie*, *4*, 30–38. https://doi.org/10.33119/KNoP.2021.61.4.3

Gierałtowska, U. (2017). Inwestowanie odpowiedzialne społecznie – Nowy trend na rynku kapitałowym. *Finanse, Rynki Finansowe, Ubezpieczenia*, *6*(90), 23–36. https://doi.org/10.18276/frfu.2017.90-02

Goldman & Sachs. (2023). *Investing for inclusive growth*. Social Bond Market Insight for Investors. Retrieved from https://www.gsam.com/content/gsam/uk/en/advisers/resources/investment-ideas/social-bonds.html

ICMA. (2021). *The sustainability disclosure regime of the European Union*. International Capital Market Association. Retrieved August 29, 2024, from https://www.icmagroup.org/assets/documents/Sustainable-finance/The-Sustainability-Disclosure-Regime-of-the-European-Union-ICMA-September-2021-220921.pdf

ICMA. (2022). *Bond index serving mapping*. Retrieved August 1, 2024, from https://www.icmagroup.org/assets/documents/Sustainable-finance/2022-updates/GSS-Bond-Index-Supporting-Paper_June-2022-280622.pdf

ICMA. (2023). *Social bond principles voluntary process guidelines for issuing social bonds*. Retrieved August 14, 2024, from https://www.icmagroup.org/sustainable-finance/the-principles-guidelines-and-handbooks/social-bond-principles-sbp/

Instytut Odpowiedzialnych Finansów. (2022). *Zielone Finanse w Polsce 2022. Rola giełd w rozwoju rynku zielonych obligacji*. Retrieved August 16, 2024 from https://iof.org.pl/wp-content/uploads/2022/06/Raport_Zielone_Finanse_2022.pdf

Investor Zone. (2023). *PFR Zielone Inwestycje*. Retrieved March 2, 2025, from https://strefainwestorow.pl/w-zielonej-strefie/klimat/pfr-zielone-inwestycje

KPMG. (2021). *Perspektywy rozwoju rynku zielonych obligacji w Polsce*. Retrieved August 15, 2024, from https://assets.kpmg.com/content/dam/kpmg/pl/pdf/2021/12/pl-Raport-KPMG-na-zlecenie-MF-Perspektywy-rozwoju-rynku-zielonych-obligacji-w-Polsce.pdf

Krawczyńska-Kaczmarek, M. (2024). Finansowanie w formule Sustainability Linked katalizatorem zrównoważonej transformacji w realnej gospodarce. In W. L. Kotecki (Ed.), *Zielone Finanse W Polsce* (pp. 50–59). Instytut Odpowiedzialnych Finansów. https://ungc.org.pl/wp-content/uploads/2024/06/Zielone_finanse_w_Polsce_2024.pdf

Lipowicz, M. (2023). Rola i miejsce zielonych obligacji w finansowaniu zrównoważonego rozwoju. *Studies in Risk and Sustainable Development. Ryzyko i Zrównoważony Rozwój. Studia Uniwersytetu Ekonomicznego W Katowicach*, *397*, 1–21. https://doi.org/10.22367/srsd.2023.397.6

Łudzińska, K. (2024). *Od Społecznej Odpowiedzialności Do ESG W Zarządzaniu. Wybrane Aspekty*. Wydawnictwa Uniwersytetu Warszawskiego Sekcja Wydawnicza Wydziału Zarządzania UW. https://doi.org/10.7172/978-83-235-6498-0.swwz.22

mBank. (2025). Retrieved March 14, 2025, from https://www.mbank.pl/indywidualny/kredyty/kredyty-hipoteczne/eko/

McKinsey & Company. (2022). *Banking on a sustainable path*. Global Banking Annual Review 2022. Retrieved August 20, 2024, from https://www.mckinsey.com/industries/financial-services/our-insights/global-banking-annual-review#/

Milewska, A. (2022). Green bonds as an opportunity to rationalise local-government finances/Zielone obligacje jako szansa racjonalizacji finansów samorządowych. *Economic and Regional Studies, 15*(3), 323–333. https://doi.org/10.2478/ers2022-0022

Ministry of Finance of the Republic of Poland. (2021). *Raport: Perspektywy rozwoju rynku zielonych obligacji w Polsce 2021*. Retrieved August 29, 2024, from https://www.gov.pl/web/finanse/raport-perspektywyrozwoju-rynku-zielonych-obligacji-w-polsce

My Funds. (2025). *Moje Fundusze*. Retrieved September 14, 2025, from https://mojefundusze.pl/

National Fund for Environmental Protection and Water Management. (2025, March 2). *Narodowy Fundusz Ochrony Środowiska i Gospodarki Wodnej*. Retrieved from https://www.gov.pl/web/nfosigw/

Next Finance. (2014). *BofA merrill lynch global research launches green bond index*. Retrieved August 14, 2023, from https://www.next-finance.net/BofA-Merrill-Lynch-Global-Research

PAP. (2017, March 7). *Polska nagrodzona w Londynie za rządową emisję zielonych obligacji*. PAP MediaRoom. https://pap-mediaroom.pl/polska-nagrodzona-w-londynie-za-rzadowa-emisje-zielonych-obligacji

Pérez, L., Hunt, V., Samandari, H., Nuttall, R., & Biniek, K. (2022). *Does ESG really matter—and why?* McKinsey Quarterly. Retrieved August 21, 2024, from https://www.mckinsey.com/~/media/mckinsey/businessfunctions/sustainability/ourinsights/doesesgreallymatterandwhy/does-esg-really-matter-and-why-vf.pdf

PKO BP S.A. (2025, March 14). Retrieved from https://www.pkobp.pl/klient-indywidualny/kredyty-pozyczki/ekopozyczka?srsltid=AfmBOopy0iEmIFPTB2mfb-FQQd0xa70P7MU777uDdqFSuWitn2DfP0m6/

PFR Ventures. (2024). *PFR green hub*. Retrieved March 2, 2025, from https://pfrventures.pl/program-dla-vc/podsumowanie-green-hub

PLGBC. (2025a, March 15). *Raport roczny 2024*. Retrieved from https://indd.adobe.com/view/5d1dbf06-89c8-4529-b6d5-ce6de65eff49

PLGBC. (2025b, September 15). *Polish green building council*. Retrieved from https://plgbc.org.pl/

Santander Bank Polska. (2025). Retrieved August 14, 2025, from https://www.santander.pl/santander-leasing/pozyczka/pozyczka-na-instalacje-fotowoltaiczne

Sertore, S. (2022, July 19). *15 years of EIB green bonds: Leading sustainable investment from niche to mainstream*. European Investment Bank. Retrieved August 15, 2024, from https://www.eib.org/en/stories/15-years-green-bond

Skuza, S., & Modzelewska, A. (2020). Zielone finanse publiczne w Polsce. Stan obecny i autorskie propozycje zmian. *Zeszyty Prawnicze BAS, 1*, 9–29.

Ślażyńska-Kluczek, D. (2022). Zielone obligacje jako metoda finansowania projektów inwestycyjnych. *Kwartalnik Nauk O Przedsiębiorstwie, 63*(1), 33–44.

Think Co. (2022). *Odpowiedzialne inwestycje. ESG na rynku nieruchomości.* Retrieved August 14, 2024, from https://thinkco.pl/raport-odpowiedzialne-inwestycje/

WSE Catalyst. (2025, March 1). *Warsaw sustainable segment.* Retrieved from https://gpwcatalyst.pl/notowania-obligacji-warsaw-sustainable-segment

CHAPTER 6

ESG Indices on the Polish Capital Market: 15 Years of Experience and Lessons Learned

6.1 Introduction

This chapter presents the evolution and significance of ESG indices on the Polish capital market, focusing on the experiences gathered over 15 years of their operation. By analysing two indices of the Warsaw Stock Exchange, the RESPECT Index—the first SRI (Socially Responsible Investing) index in Central and Eastern Europe, and its successor WIG-ESG, their composition, methodology, and investment efficiency are discussed. Particular attention is paid to the impact of these indices on the Polish capital market, including investment decisions and responsible investment strategy.

The chapter also reviews and characterises ESG indices on global exchanges, with particular attention to their investment efficiency. This broader perspective introduces a global context that enables comparison between Polish experiences and international standards and outcomes.

A review of experiences and conclusions from 15 years of ESG index practice provides valuable insight into their role as tools for evaluating sustainable development and their effects on corporate financial performance. The chapter also highlights key lessons that can inform the development of ESG indices and support the growth of responsible investing in Poland.

K. Łudzińska, *International ESG Perspectives*,
https://doi.org/10.1007/978-3-032-11666-6_6

6.2 ESG Indices Worldwide: Characteristics and Investment Efficiency

The field of socially responsible investments in company shares is evolving in two distinct yet interconnected directions. On the one hand, the global capital market offers a wide range of investment portfolios and funds, including fiduciary structured products, which allocate capital to entities primarily engaged in socially responsible and ecological products and services. These include companies engaged in the production or contribution to the production of renewable energy sources, the collection and recycling of waste, including packaging waste, and the development of new bio- and ecotechnologies. Conversely, the market for investment in companies offering traditional products and services, whilst concurrently incorporating ESG criteria within their operations and management strategy, is undergoing active development. In the latter scenario, ESG stock indices have been demonstrated to facilitate investment decision-making processes.

ESG indices, also referred to as SRI (Socially Responsible Investing) indices, social responsibility indices or sustainable development indices, comprise companies that voluntarily undergo audits assessing their pro-social and pro-environmental activities. These companies are typically distinguished by sound management practices and transparency. The development of ESG indices can be attributed to the mounting demand from the capital market for standardised instruments to evaluate investments in the shares of companies that demonstrate a commitment to social responsibility. Such indices evaluate firm-level performance not only in environmental, social and managerial aspects, but also financial results. It is evident that the comprehensive approach adopted by the aforementioned entities serves as a valuable guide for investors, facilitating the conscientious and informed decision-making process across multiple dimensions, including economic, ecological and social considerations.

Companies with the highest ESG ratings within their respective sector are included in ESG indices, making them a good investment option (MSCI, 2019). Most of the companies included in ESG indices are attractive as equity investments or as bond issuers. Participation in ESG indices can improve financial performance, lower the cost of capital and reduce potential financial risk (Chen & Xie, 2022). Moreover, investments in ESG indices gradually motivate companies to implement more sustainable operational practices and contribute to the development of legal and regulatory provisions (Apergis et al., 2022).

In addition, such tools are valuable for both individual and institutional investors as they enable the analysis of those aspects of a company's operations that are not traditionally found in its financial report. Many companies have recognised this market need and voluntarily seek inclusion in ESG indices, often committing significant resources in the qualification and monitoring process. Prior to being included in the index, firms are required to disclose extensive information necessary for evaluating their performance against ESG criteria.

The development of ESG indices is undertaken by specialised agencies and organisations that are engaged in analysis and assessment in the domain of sustainable development. The most prominent of these entities, along with their corresponding ESG indices, are presented in Table 6.1. Currently, over 500 ESG indices are listed in Europe alone, and their regularly updated list can be found on the Euronext websites (Euronext, 2025). The first and oldest social responsibility index in the world is the MSCI KLD 400 Social Index, launched in the United States on January 1, 1990, under the name KLD 400 Social Domini Index (Łudzińska, 2009a, 2009b) and currently listed as FTSE Russell's KLD's Domini 400 Social Index. Another of the most established SRI indices that evaluates CSR and sustainable development is the Dow Jones Sustainability Index (Łudzińska, 2013). Companies included in the Dow Jones indices are analysed by S&P Dow Jones Indices (also listed in Table 6.1). Among the leading ESG indices on global markets, the S&P ESG Index Family and MSCI ESG Indexes on the American market, FTSE4Good Index Series on the British market, and Stoxx EURO Sustainability Indexes on European markets should certainly be mentioned.

Among other, market-recognised ESG indices not listed in Table 6.1, are the Bloomberg indices (Bloomberg, 2024), the Calvert Social Index (Calvert Research and Management, 2024), and those developed by Thomson Reuters or LSEG (formerly Refinitive) (LSEG, 2024).

The process of including a company in an ESG index is complex, and the methodological framework for the FTSE4Good Index Series, presented in Table 6.2, illustrates this complexity. In its selection process, FTSE4Good uses the general ESG rating and the FTSE Russell data model. The ratings and data cover over 7200 securities from 47 different markets. They consist of an overall score, which is then used to adjust weights in the FTSE4Good index series. This score is then divided into various so-called pillars and topics, which are based on over 300 individual assessment indicators. These are used to individually assess each company's ESG risk exposure.

Table 6.1 Selected leading ESG indices in the world

Organisation	*Description*	*Main ESG indices**
S&P Dow Jones Indices	An international company that creates, manages, and licenses various stock indices worldwide. It is one of the most well-known and respected index companies in the financial markets. The company was formed as a result of the merger of Standard & Poor's (S&P) and Dow Jones & Company's index activities. The Dow Jones Sustainability Index is the most well-known and one of the first SRI indices in the world	**Main ESG indices:** S&P ESG • ESG Select Equal Weight • Dow Jones Sustainability Indices • DJSI Diversified • S&P Sustainability Screened **Climate ESG indices:** • Paris-Aligned & Climate Transition (PACT) • Carbon Efficient • S&P Global 1200 Fossil Fuel Free • Carbon Budget **Thematic ESG indices:** • Paris-Aligned & Climate Transition (PACT) • Carbon Efficient • S&P Global 1200 Fossil Fuel Free • Carbon Budget

(continued)

Table 6.1 (continued)

Organisation	*Description*	*Main ESG indices**
MSCI Inc. (Morgan Stanley Capital International)	A global firm specialising in tools for investors, such as indices, portfolio analytics, risk management tools and other services. It is one of the most recognised firms in the investment field worldwide, and its indices are widely used by investors, fund managers and other financial institutions. MSCI is particularly known for its wide range of ESG indices	**ESG Screen Indices**: (indices with exclusions related to specific business engagement issues or limiting exposure to entities emitting the most carbon dioxide): • MSCI ESG Screened • MSCI ex Controversial Weapons • MSCI ex Tobacco Involvement • MSCI USA Catholic Values • MSCI Islamic **ESG Integrate Indices** (indices representing diversified strategies integrating ESG data with widely traded indices): • MSCI SRI • MSCI KLD 400 • MSCI ESG Leaders • MSCI ESG Focus • MSCI ESG Universal • MSCI USA ESG Select **ESG Target Indices** (indices designed to target a selected ESG area): • MSCI Sustainable Impact • MSCI Women's Leadership • MSCI Japan Human and Physical Investment

(continued)

Table 6.1 (continued)

Organisation	*Description*	*Main ESG indices**
FTSE Russell	A global provider of indices and analytical data, whose products are used by investors worldwide. The company was established in 2015 following the merger of the London Stock Exchange Group (LSEG), FTSE Group and Russell Investments, and offers, among others, FTSE4Good indices	**Climate Indices:** • FTSE Green Revenues • FTSE ex Fossil Fuels • FTSE EU Climate Benchmarks • FTSE Environmental Markets • FTSE EPRA Nareit Green Real Estate • Russell Green America • FTSE TPI Climate Transition • FTSE JPX Net Zero Japan • FTSE Global Climate • FTSE Smart Sustainability **ESG Indices:** • FTSE Global Choice • Russell US ESG • FTSE4Good • FTSE UK ESG Risk-Adjusted • FTSE Blossom Japan • FTSE ESG • FTSE Ping and China ESG • FTSE ESG Emerging Markets • FTSE ESG Low Carbon Select • FTSE Women on Boards Leadership

(continued)

Table 6.1 (continued)

Organisation	*Description*	*Main ESG indices**
STOXX Ltd.	A global index provider, which is part of the Qontigo group, a joint venture between Deutsche Börse Group and General Atlantic. The company offers a wide range of indices used by investors worldwide	**Key ESG indices:** • STOXX® ASIA/PACIFIC 600 ESG BROAD MARKET • EURO STOXX 50® ESG • STOXX® EUROPE 600 ESG-X • STOXX® USA 500 ESG-X • STOXX® GLOBAL ESG LEADERS • STOXX® GLOBAL ESG ENVIRONMENTAL LEADERS • STOXX® GLOBAL ESG SOCIAL LEADERS • STOXX® GLOBAL ESG GOVERNANCE LEADERS • EURO STOXX® ESG TARGET • EURO STOXX® ESG TARGET TE **ESG Leaders indices:** • EURO STOXX® ESG Leaders 50 • STOXX® Europe ESG Leaders 50 • STOXX® Asia/Pacific ESG Leaders 50 • STOXX® North America ESG Leader 50

(continued)

Table 6.1 (continued)

Organisation	*Description*	*Main ESG indices**
		Climate indices: • EURO STOXX® 50 LOW CARBON • STOXX® EUROPE 600 LOW CARBON • EURO STOXX® CLIMATE TRANSITION BENCHMARK • EURO STOXX® PARIS-ALIGNED BENCHMARK • STOXX® EUROPE 600 CLIMATE TRANSITION BENCHMARK • STOXX® EUROPE 600 PARIS-ALIGNED BENCHMARK • EURO STOXX 50® ESG **ISS STOXX® biodiversity indices:** • ISS STOXX® ASIA/PACIFIC AC BIODIVERSITY • ISS STOXX® DEVELOPED EUROPE BIODIVERSITY • ISS STOXX® DEVELOPED WORLD BIODIVERSITY • ISS STOXX® EMERGING MARKETS BIODIVERSITY • ISS STOXX® EUROPE 600 BIODIVERSITY • ISS STOXX® US BIODIVERSITY • ISS STOXX® WORLD AC BIODIVERSITY • ISS STOXX® WORLD AC BIODIVERSITY LEADERS

(continued)

Table 6.1 (continued)

Organisation	*Description*	*Main ESG indices**
		Other ESG indices: • STOXX® GLOBAL ESG SELECT KPIS INDEX • EURO STOXX® ESG-X Select Dividend 30 • STOXX® Europe ESG-X Select Dividend 30 • STOXX® Asia/Pacific ESG-X Select Dividend 30 • STOXX® North America ESG-X Select Dividend 40 • iSTOXX® Global ESG Select 100 • iSTOXX® Global ESG Select 50 • iSTOXX® Europe ESG Select 30
NASDAQ	NASDAQ offers a complete family of environmental indices, tracking the growing clean energy sector, also known as 'green' indices. The indices include companies working to increase economic development based on carbon dioxide emission reduction	**NASDAQ green index families:** • Nasdaq OMX Solar • Nasdaq OMX Global Water • Nasdaq OMX U.S. Water • Nasdaq OMX Wind • Nasdaq OMX Green Economy

*Selected indices are equity indices, which track the quotations of equity companies. The list does not include fixed income indices, i.e. the bond market (government, corporate and others). Status of the study: 1.12.2024

Source Based on information on the websites of index providers—FTSE Russell (2025); MSCI Inc. (2025); Nasdaq (2025); S&P Dow Jones Indices (2025); STOXX Ltd (2025)

The index creation process consists of three main stages, initiated by a review of the base index components considering their market capitalisation. In the case of the FTSE4Good index, the base indices are FTSE Developed Index and FTSE All-Share Index.

The process of inclusion in the FTSE4Good Index Series, presented in Table 6.2, is not universal and does not apply to all companies or ESG indices. Each institution develops its own specific methodology for selecting companies for their indices. The ongoing advancement of technology has led an increasing number of companies to adopt advanced artificial intelligence (AI) tools to optimise and automate decision-making processes related to index selection (Jagyasi & Raut, 2022). AI enables faster data analysis, pattern identification and more precise forecasting, significantly increasing the efficiency and accuracy of the entire process. The choice of the appropriate AI model for index construction depends on the nature, quality and quantity of available data (Croom et al., 2018).

Previous research on ESG indices highlights their importance and effectiveness in evaluating corporate performance. Adeneye and Ahmend (Adeneye & Ahmed, 2015) in an analysis of 500 UK companies observed a clear, positive correlation between return on invested capital and corporate social responsibility, confirmed by inclusion in the SRI index. Companies' reputation usually improves significantly after joining social responsibility indices, resulting in a significant increase in their share value (Blajer-Gołębiewska, 2014). Such a trend results from the rigorous procedures required for inclusion in SRI indices, which compel companies to meet demanding criteria. As a result, even the announcement of a forthcoming inclusion, prior to its actual implementation, can lead to an increase in return on investment indicators.

The preparatory process leading to inclusion in the ESG index prompts companies to adapt their practices with the procedures and criteria required for entry (Slager et al., 2010). Research conducted by Ramchander et al. (2012), on the financial performance of companies in the Domini Social 400 Index, confirmed that inclusion in the index leads to an increase in the company's share value, while negatively impacting the share prices of competitors. Strategies based on social responsibility enable companies to have better access to capital, by reducing costs and establishing more durable relationships with stakeholders, and also increase transparency, which reduces information asymmetry (Cheng et al., 2014). This situation encourages many global companies to join SRI indices. As Camilleri

Table 6.2 Framework process of ESG index construction on the example of the FTSE4Good index

Process stage	*Criterion*	*Action description*
Stage 1	Selection of companies—index components	In the first stage, companies are selected from the base index to be included in the ESG index. The selection criteria have been carefully developed to reflect the best ESG risk management practices. To qualify for the FTSE4Good Index Series, companies must achieve a minimum ESG score of 3.3 out of 5.0 for developed markets and 2.9 for emerging markets. Similar criteria are used to remove a company from the index: if the score falls below 2.9 (for developed markets) or 2.4 (for emerging markets). This process ensures that only companies demonstrating the best ESG management practices are included in the index
Stage 2	Exclusion of companies based on controversy and business activity	Exclusion of companies based on controversy and business activity** | In the second stage, companies involved in controversial activities or operating in ethically questionable industries are excluded. To ensure the indices comply with the highest standards of social responsibility, companies associated with the production of tobacco, weapons systems and controversial types of weapons, such as cluster ammunition, anti-personnel mines, depleted uranium-based weapons, chemical, biological and nuclear weapons, are excluded. Coal producers also do not qualify for inclusion in the index. If a company already part of the index becomes involved in controversial activities, it may be removed
Stage 3	Publication and re-review of the index composition	In the third stage, the index composition undergoes regular publication and review, which takes place twice a year—in June and December. If a company receives a rating below the set minimum threshold, it is granted a 12-month period to improve its position before it is finally excluded from the index. This mechanism not only motivates companies to improve their corporate practices but also contributes to the stability and transparency of the index, promoting companies' adaptation to the required standards

Source Based on FTSE Russell (2023)

(2020) noted, they act as a certificate of credibility for companies wishing to demonstrate that their actions yield tangible, positive results.

Research findings indicate that investors take ESG results into account in the investment decision-making process, arguing that ESG issues, such as climate change, health and safety regulations in the workplace, and stakeholder protection, affect the risk and return on invested capital (Giese et al., 2019). Thus, ESG ratings have become a significant element of investment decision-making, also through ESG indices. At the same time, research indicates the existence of strong links between return rates and the volatility of ESG indices, with European and North American indices mainly generating spillover effects, and indices from the Asia-Pacific region and India primarily receiving them, as suggested by Wan et al. (2024). In their opinion, portfolios that minimise the interdependence of return rates are more effective in hedging against risk, while portfolios that minimise the interdependence of volatility generate higher return rates. These conclusions provide valuable guidance for investors and support regulators in their efforts to maintain financial stability.

ESG indices also serve an additional function as a complementary investment indicator, analysing the results of listed companies (Joliet & Titova, 2018). Research conducted by van Duuren et al. (2016) reveals that managers of conventional investment funds also take ESG results into account in their investment decisions. ESG indices are also frequently utilised by investors to evaluate not only company performance, but also their programmes, policies and even entire industries in terms of sustainable development (Lassala et al., 2021). Consequently, there has been an observed rise in the number of investors, analysts and research firms who specialise in the collection and analysis of ESG data, in addition to the monitoring of corporate practices (Dumas & Louche, 2016). A significant proportion of these entities possess sophisticated ESG databases, which they utilise to furnish their clientele with analyses, recommendations, benchmarks and social-environmental engagement strategies. These catalogues present a comprehensive overview of ethical investment funds, delineating their strategic approaches, selection criteria and voting policies (Leite & Cortez, 2014). By acting in this manner, they provide assistance to responsible investors in the process of making informed investment decisions.

In conclusion, ESG indices can therefore be regarded as key instruments for assessing and measuring corporate engagement in sustainable development. These tools enable investors to efficiently identify companies that demonstrate a capacity to respond effectively to social, environmental and governance challenges. Furthermore, the ESG indices provide a crucial reference point for benchmarking and comparative analyses within individual industries and sectors. Their presence serves to emphasise the necessity of integrating ESG criteria into investment strategies, thereby reflecting both the mounting social expectations regarding business responsibility and the growing prevalence of such criteria in the investment landscape.

6.3 ESG Indices on the Warsaw Stock Exchange: From Inception to Closure and Performance Assessment

6.3.1 *RESPECT Index: The First SRI Index in Central and Eastern Europe—Composition, Methodology, and Performance Evaluation*

The Warsaw Stock Exchange (WSE) is widely regarded as the preeminent financial centre in Central and Eastern Europe. At present, 402 companies are listed on the WSE, with a total capitalisation of 2 203 295,31 million zlotys.[1] The Exchange plays a pivotal role in shaping the capital market in Poland, proactively promoting responsible business principles and introducing regulations with the objective of increasing transparency and sustainable development. As early as 2002, the WSE introduced the first regulations on corporate governance, which have been functioning as the Code of Good Practice for listed companies since 2007. The most recent update to the Code was in 2021, and it is still undergoing development (WSE, 2021). Furthermore, in 2009, the WSE initiated the RESPECT index, the first socially responsible companies' index in Central and Eastern Europe, constituting a pioneering development in the region. This was followed by the introduction of the WIG ESG index in 2019, which highlighted the Exchange's commitment to promoting sustainable business practices.

The RESPECT Index debuted on the main market of the Warsaw Stock Exchange on 19th November 2009. Its name was created as an acronym of English terms: *responsibility*, *ecology*, *sustainability*, *participation*, *environment*, *community* and *transparency* (Wiśniewski, 2010). Thus, the English term *respect* was adopted, which in Polish carries the same meaning—*respekt.*

[1] As of 10.09.2025; WSE (2025). *GPW Statistics.* Retrieved March 15, 2025, from https://www.gpw.pl/statystyki-gpw.

The index methodology was developed by the Warsaw Stock Exchange in cooperation with Forbes, Kulczyk Investments and Deloitte Poland. According to the WSE resolution of 18th November 2009, the first edition of the index included 16 companies listed on the WSE, excluding the NewConnect market, foreign companies and those listed on a dual listing basis. From its inception until its closure in 2019, the RESPECT Index underwent 12 composition updates.

The aim of the RESPECT Index was to identify companies managed in a responsible and sustainable manner while remaining attractive from an investment perspective. In practice, this meant selecting firms that, like those included in other stock market indices, demonstrated liquidity, high-quality reporting, strong investor relations and sound corporate governance. By incorporating these elements into its qualifying criteria, the RESPECT Index served as a genuine benchmark for professional investors (WSE, 2009).

Between 2009 and 2013, the composition of the index varied and was based on the social responsibility rating of audited companies. Application for inclusion in the index was voluntary, and until 2013, the first six editions involved submitting a completed RESPECT rating survey and expressing readiness to provide additional information to the authorised auditor, Deloitte. Only Polish companies listed on the main WSE market could apply for inclusion in the index. From the 7th edition on 17 December 2013, foreign companies listed on the WSE were considered for the first time (WSE, 2013). Furthermore, from the 7th edition onwards, not all companies on the main floor were included in the verification process, as had previously been the case, but only those included in the WIG20, mWIG40 or sWIG80 indices.

The Index Committee revised the list of companies included in the index based on the RESPECT Rating conducted. The Index Committee was authorised to make extraordinary adjustments, consisting of removing or adding a company to the index-covered list (Łudzińska, 2013a). The Steering Committee, composed of representatives of the authors of the index's methodology and the Scientific Council (a group of independent experts), supervised the ongoing operationalisation of the index. In the first two editions of the RESPECT Index, companies were evaluated for inclusion once a year. From the third edition (announced on 14 July 2011) to the sixth edition (announced on 24 January 2013), the index composition was revised twice a year on a semi-annual basis. From the 7th edition onwards, the index returned to an annual revision schedule, with updates made on the last Friday of November. This rule remained in effect until the final index composition was announced on 12 December 2018.

The RESPECT rating survey was based on the international sustainability reporting standard set by the Global Reporting Initiative (GRI). Although the GRI guidelines are intended to standardise non-financial reporting rather than qualify companies for stock indices, they formed the basis for the creation of the inaugural RESPECT survey, which was adapted to the specifics of the Polish market. The survey focused on the principles of sustainable development, considering three key areas: the economy, the environment and society. The 'strategy and management' domain has also been incorporated, in line with the contemporary approach that incorporates the 'G' criterion (governance) as part of ESG considerations. Corporate governance practices were assessed by the Warsaw Stock Exchange team in collaboration with the Association of Stock Exchange Issuers.

The first RESPECT Rating survey comprised 45 closed-ended questions, enabling a precise assessment of the extent to which specific practices and processes had been implemented within the company (Łudzińska, 2013). Each question had an assigned point value (from 1 to 3) and a weight considering its importance in the economic, social, or environmental areas. Information obtained from the surveys was additionally verified based on documents provided by the companies. The data then underwent automated statistical correlation and regression analysis, identifying potential relationships between responsible management and the achievement of specific results by companies.

The RESPECT Index was an income index, taking into account income from dividends and subscription rights (Łudzińska, 2009b). The base value was set at 1000 points, while the base capitalisation was consistent with the announcement of the first RESPECT Rating. The base date for calculating the index was set at 31 December 2008. In the initial period, from 2009 to 2012, the RESPECT Index value was recalculated twice a day, with an accuracy of 0.01 point and made publicly available on the Warsaw Stock Exchange websites. The share of companies in the RESPECT Index portfolio was limited to 10%. If the number of index participants was less than 20, the share of one company in the stock portfolio was limited to 25%. Unlike other ESG indices, such as the Dow Jones Sustainability Indexes, the RESPECT Index did not impose sector restrictions at that time.

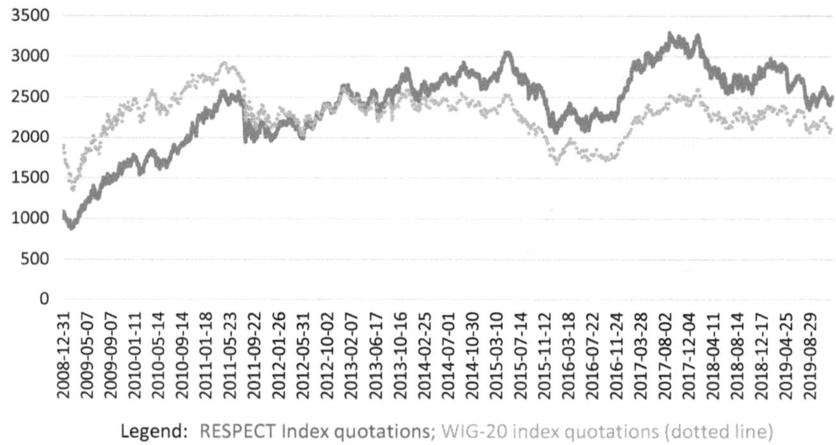

Fig. 6.1 RESPECT Index vs. WIG-20 Index Quotations (2009–2019). *Source* Own study based on historical quotations of the RESPECT Index and WIG-20 Warsaw Stock Exchange (WSE, 2024c)

As mentioned above, the qualification procedure changed with the announcement of the 7th edition of the RESPECT Index in 2013 and remained in effect until the 12th edition was announced on 12 December 2018. Companies were assigned to specific rating classes based on the number of points received, as determined by the collected and analysed questionnaires. Those that received the highest scores were qualified for inclusion in the RESPECT Index. The RESPECT rating questionnaire has once again been updated in line with the non-financial reporting standards of the Global Reporting Initiative. That revision was based on the ESG concept because it explicitly encompasses three key areas: social responsibility, environmental protection and corporate governance.

Over the course of 10 years of its presence on the Warsaw Stock Exchange, the number of RESPECT Index participants almost doubled from the initial 16 to 31. Only eight companies were part of the index throughout its existence: Azoty Group, EL Construction, Handlowy Bank (Citi Handlowy), ING Bank Śląski, KGHM, Lotos, PGNiG (Polish Oil and Gas Company) and Orange Poland. Some companies, such as PKN Orlen, Apator, Santander BP SA, or Bank Ochrony Środowiska were not included in certain years, and often appeared in the index under a different name due to mergers and acquisitions and ownership changes. One such company was Santander Bank Polska, which continued its presence in the RESPECT Index after taking over BZWBK Bank, which in turn had been listed in the RESPECT portfolio since 2013 (7th edition) after taking over Kredyt Bank. The most dynamic increase in index participants occurred in the last three years of its existence (2017–2019).

The RESPECT Index continued to serve as an income index, but from the 7th edition, i.e., from 17 December 2013, it began to be calculated continuously, with minute frequency. The opening value of the index was published at the start of the session, provided that the share prices allowed for the valuation of at least 65% of the index portfolio in a given session (WSE, 2024a). The closing value of the index was published on the WSE websites and made available to interested entities and news agencies after the end of the session. The companies' shares in the index (weights) represented the number of shares in free float, reduced by the number of shares introduced to exchange trading. They were rounded to full thousands. The shares of the largest companies in the index were limited to 25% when the index had fewer than 20 participants and to 10% when the number of index participants was higher than 20 companies (WSE, 2024a).

As illustrated in Fig. 6.1, the aggregated, historical quotations of the RESPECT Index from its inauguration on 19 November 2009 to its last quotation on 30 December 2018 are presented, in comparison with the results of the leading index of the Warsaw Stock Exchange (WIG-20), which includes the top 20 companies. In the initial period, its quotations were lower compared to the WIG-20 index quotations. However, beginning in 2013, this trend underwent a reversal, with the RESPECT index demonstrating enhanced performance. According to data from the Warsaw Stock Exchange (WSE), the RESPECT index demonstrated a higher return rate in comparison to the WIG index, which represents the average market rate. From November 2009 to December 2018, i.e. over a period of nine years of the index's existence, there was an increase in value of 70%. Concurrently, the broad market WIG index exhibited an increase of 47%, while the WIG20 experienced a decline of 4% (WSE, 2018).

In the context of the Polish capital market, the RESPECT index was the subject of extensive research. The efficacy of investment strategies based on its quotations was analysed in comparison with investments directed by key base indices, including WIG, WIG-20, WIG-40 and WIG 80.

Research on the long-term impact of sustainable investing in Poland clearly indicated that the first Polish ESG index achieved better results than conventional indices published by WSE (e.g.: Cegliński, 2015; Janik & Bartkowiak, 2015; Jedynak, 2012). The RESPECT Index demonstrated above-average profitability and relatively low investment risk, primarily until 2012 (Czerwińska, 2012; Laskowska, 2018). However, following 2015, the superior performance of the RESPECT Index became undetectable, and the risk associated with it was commensurate with or greater than the risk of investing in other index portfolios (Golaszewska-Kaczan et al., 2016). Zieliński (2015) demonstrated that, in the majority of sectors, companies from the RESPECT Index portfolio attained a valuation that was higher than that of other companies. However, the disparities in valuation were too insignificant to be considered a factor influenced by CSR.

In a study conducted by Lulewicz-Sas (2014), the performance of the RESPECT Index was compared with that of the WIG-20 index over the first five years of RESPECT trading on the Warsaw Stock Exchange. The study demonstrated that companies included in the RESPECT Index achieved higher returns than those included in the WIG 20 index, despite both indices exhibiting a comparable level of risk at divergent stages of the market cycle. In each of the years examined, shares of RESPECT Index companies offered investors a higher risk premium compared to the market, regardless of prevailing conditions. In periods of rising market trends, the risk premium for RESPECT-listed shares was found to be almost double that of WIG-20 companies. Conversely, in periods of market downturns, RESPECT company shares exhibited enhanced resilience, demonstrating reduced vulnerability to sudden and significant decreases in value. This behaviour is indicative of a greater degree of financial stability. Moreover, the author's previous study examined the outcomes of the RESPECT Index and the corporations encompassed by it during the years 2009–2014. The analysis revealed that corporations comprising the RESPECT Index exhibited higher returns on invested capital and dividend rates in comparison to those included in the WIG and WIG-20 indices (Łudzińska, 2017).

The high returns of the RESPECT Index during its first five years on the market were noteworthy. According to Cegliński (2015), this performance was primarily driven by the spectacular increases in the share prices of two constituent companies: KGHM and PKN Orlen. Adopting Cegliński's assumptions, Zaremba (2023) analysed the 9-year results of the index, in the years 2011–2019, against other indices and showed that investing in RESPECT was not more profitable than investing in WIG, mWIG40 or sWIG80, but at the same time recorded higher returns compared to the WIG20 index.

Concurrently, the research conducted by Białkowski and Sławik (2021) examined the price implications associated with alterations in the composition of the RESPECT Index over the entire 10-year period of its existence, encompassing the years 2009 to 2019. The findings of the research indicate a significant negative response in the share prices of companies that were included or excluded from the index. The analysis revealed that both inclusion and exclusion in relation to the RESPECT Index resulted in a lower level of returns. The effect was short-lived, yet statistically significant, suggesting that events such as the addition or removal from the RESPECT index, in conjunction with the subsequent announcement of both events, create opportunities for the sale of shares in companies covered by the index. Moreover, the research suggests that investors on the Warsaw Stock Exchange tend to sell shares of socially responsible companies, at least in the short term. This finding is somewhat unexpected, and the authors attribute it to the short-term nature of the investor reaction analysed in the study.

An interesting study was conducted by Sikacz and Wołczek (2017), who did not focus on investment performance, but rather on the evaluation of companies included in the RESPECT Index in terms of ESG factors. The data for the analysis came from the ASSET4 ESG and Thomson Reuters Eikon databases. The aim of the analysis was to check whether companies from the RESPECT index actually fully meet the criteria of environmental, social and corporate governance management. The research findings revealed notable discrepancies in the ESG ratings of the analysed companies. ESG scores derived from the ASSET4 ESG database were generally more favourable than those obtained through other sources. Notably, some companies with relatively low ESG ratings were included in the 10th edition of the RESPECT Index, raising concerns among the researchers about the transparency and rigour of the index's company selection process. At the same time, the findings of Sikacz & Wołczek (2017) appear to align with the challenge discussed in Sect. 2.6, namely, the lack of consistency in ESG ratings for the same companies when assessed by different rating agencies, as highlighted by Berg, Kölbel and Rigobon (2022).

In summary, the RESPECT Index, as the inaugural ESG index in Central and Eastern Europe, has become a symbol of innovation and the integration of corporate social responsibility principles within the Polish capital market. This index was introduced in late 2009, during the global financial crisis, yet it gained recognition and proved to be a success on the capital market. The instrument exhibited a consistent tendency to generate higher returns in comparison to traditional benchmark indices, thereby underscoring the investment appeal of socially responsible companies. Concurrently, it disseminated the concept of social responsibility and sustainable development among the broadly defined stakeholders of the Polish capital market. Despite the RESPECT Index's robust performance over the past decade, the Warsaw Stock Exchange has decided to reconsider its strategy. The WSE Management Board issued Resolution No. 804/2019 on 12 August 2019, thereby introducing a new social investment index, the WIG-ESG Index, which replaced the RESPECT Index with effect from 3 September, 2019.

6.3.2 WIG-ESG: A New Standard for Responsible Investing on the Warsaw Stock Exchange—Assumptions and Initial Conclusions

The WIG-ESG index, which was listed on the Warsaw Stock Exchange from 3 September 2019 to 28 June 2024, comprised all companies included in the WIG20 and mWIG40 indices. Consequently, the largest companies listed on the WSE were automatically included, regardless of whether and to what extent they operated in accordance with ESG criteria. This represented a significant departure from the underlying principles of the RESPECT Index. The WIG-ESG was calculated based on the value of a portfolio comprising shares of companies that adhere to the principles of socially responsible business, particularly in the areas of environmental, social, economic and corporate governance issues (WSE, 2019).

The index's introduction can be seen as a response on the part of the Warsaw Stock Exchange management to the growing interest in responsible investing and the inclusion of ESG criteria by investors. A study undertaken by PwC in 2021 confirmed that ESG aspects have a significant impact on the valuation of companies on the Polish market (PwC, 2021). While half of the surveyed investors acknowledged the relevance of ESG factors, though not considering them decisive, nearly 30% indicated a willingness to lower their valuation or withdraw from an investment if ESG risks were deemed too high. However, it is noteworthy that brokerage analysts did not customarily incorporate ESG considerations into their investment recommendations, a factor that is likely to have contributed to the decision to discontinue the WIG-ESG index.

Moreover, there was and still is no uniform approach to information sources and investment evaluation criteria in the field of ESG on the Polish market. Currently, investors draw on a variety of information sources, yet they make relatively limited use of non-financial reports published by companies (PwC, 2021). The WIG-ESG index was intended to serve as a guideline for assessing the ESG performance of the largest companies listed on the Warsaw Stock Exchange. The first investment fund to adopt the WIG-ESG index as its benchmark was NN Investment Partners TFI (ETF.com.pl, 2024). In its investment strategy, the fund uses ESG factor analysis, shareholder engagement and exclusions. It does not invest in companies producing tobacco, deriving a significant part of their revenues from coal mining, extracting oil from oil sands, producing controversial weapons and trading weapons with entities subject to embargo (NN TFI, 2024).

The base value of the WIG-ESG index was set at 10,000.00 points on 28 December 2018. The WIG-ESG was an income index, meaning that its calculation accounted not only for share price movements but also for income from dividends and other corporate actions. The share of one company in the index was limited to 10%, while the total share of companies, each of which exceeded 5%, was limited to 40% (WSE Benchmark, 2024a). The WIG-ESG index included 23 components of the last 12th edition of the RESPECT Index. Seven companies managing ESG risk well (long-term components of the RESPECT Index), i.e. Apator, ZEW Cogeneration, Bank for Environmental Protection, Forte Furniture Factory, Trakcja PRKiI, PCC Rokita, did not enter the WIG-ESG index, as they were not components of WIG20 or mWIG40 (Zaremba, 2023). The WIG-ESG Index consistently comprised 60 companies and, like the RESPECT Index, did not impose any sector restrictions.

The evaluation of companies in terms of ESG factors included in the WIG-ESG index was no longer the responsibility of the WSE team and Deloitte as an independent auditor, but Sustainalytics, and after its merger with Morningstar in April 2020—Morningstar Sustainalytics (Morningstar, 2020). Morningstar Sustainalytics is one of the world's leading providers of ESG research and ratings. The company provides data, analysis, and tools that help investors make decisions using ESG factors. Morningstar Sustainalytics evaluates companies based on their ESG performance, focusing on identifying and analysing those aspects that may affect the company's ability to maintain profitability and manage risk (Sustainalytics, 2024). The company developed a ranking of WIG20 and mWIG40 companies based on their consideration of ESG factors. In this ranking, companies could score between 0 and 100 points, with lower scores indicating stronger adherence to ESG evaluation criteria (Rogowski & Lipski, 2022). Entities were ranked according to the mentioned points and classified into five groups. Depending on the assignment to a specific group, the number of free-floating shares of a given index participant was limited to 0% (for companies from the first group) or up to 40% (for companies from the fifth group) (Rogowski & Lipski, 2022).

However, as previously mentioned, the primary criteria for determining a company's position in the WIG-ESG Index, similarly to the WIG20 and mWIG40 indices, remained market capitalisation and share turnover value. While this approach was designed to favour the largest companies, it also had the effect of reducing the weighting of companies from the WIG20 and mWIG40 indices with low ESG ratings by up to 30% in the WIG-ESG Index compared to their weighting in the WIG Index (WSE Benchmark, 2024b). Consequently, substantial corporations with sub-standard ESG ratings would maintain a substantial influence on the index, though to a lesser extent than if they were not subject to an evaluation of their social, environmental and corporate governance dimensions. It should be noted that the composition of the WIG20 and WIG40 indices was subject to alteration following each quarterly adjustment, which in turn resulted in a change in the composition of the WIG-ESG index. In the three-year period subsequent to the index's inception and preceding its revision in March 2022, a total of 15 companies experienced a replacement within the index portfolio (Zaremba, 2023). Consequently, there have been calls to revise the inclusion criteria of the WIG-ESG Index in order to promote companies that demonstrate strong ESG performance and to exclude those making minimal efforts in this area (Zaremba, 2023).

According to a study by the Warsaw Stock Exchange conducted in 2022 among investors on the impact of ESG factors on investment decisions, the WIG-ESG index was known to over 90% of respondents and became a significant information indicator for professional stock market investors (WSE, 2022). The transition from the RESPECT Index to the WIG-ESG was therefore smooth and well received by the market. The main differences between the new WIG-ESG index and its predecessor, the RESPECT Index, are presented in Table 6.3.

With regard to investment efficiency, the WIG-ESG index has been shown to outperform other leading indices of the Warsaw Stock Exchange, particularly in comparison with the base WIG20 and mWIG40 indices (WSE Benchmark, 2023). In the short term, the index offered the highest potential gains, while over the medium term of three years, it

Table 6.3 Key assumptions of the RESPECT and WIG-ESG indices listed on the Warsaw Stock Exchange

Description	*RESPECT Index*	*WIG-ESG*
First listing date	19 November 2009	3 September 2019
Last listing date	30 December 2019	-
Base index value	1000 points	10,000 points
Criteria for selecting companies for the index	Companies with the highest liquidity included in the WIG index (until 2012) and companies included in the WIG20, mWIG40 and sWIG80 indices (from 2013 to 2019) listed on the Warsaw Stock Exchange; inclusion in the index based on voluntary company submissions by completing an ESG survey and providing other documents	All companies listed on the Warsaw Stock Exchange included in the WIG20 and mWIG40 indices, regardless of sector or ESG results quality
Sector exclusions	No	No
Entity assessing companies in terms of ESG factors	Warsaw Stock Exchange and Deloitte, as an independent auditor	Morningstar Sustainalytics, an international provider of ESG risk assessment solutions

Source Based on WSE Benchmark (2024b) and WSE (2013, 2024a)

allowed investors to minimise losses. The compilation of aggregated, historical WIG-ESG index quotations, from its first quotation on 3rd September 2019 to the last day (28th June 2024), and the aggregated results of the WIG-20 index of the Warsaw Stock Exchange in the same period, also confirms its good performance (Fig. 6.2). However, the WIG-ESG demonstrated clear volatility in comparison to the WIG-20 quotations, which exhibited greater stability during the period under analysis. A decline in both indices was recorded in the spring of 2020, which was likely related to the outbreak of the pandemic of Coronavirus Disease 2019 (Covid-19). In the final year prior to closure, the WIG-ESG index exhibited a discernible upward trend.

It is worth noting that the WIG-ESG index, which automatically includes large and medium-sized companies listed on the Warsaw Stock Exchange, did not directly reflect the actual level of their engagement with ESG factors. While this approach is not exclusive to the WIG-ESG Index, it contrasts with

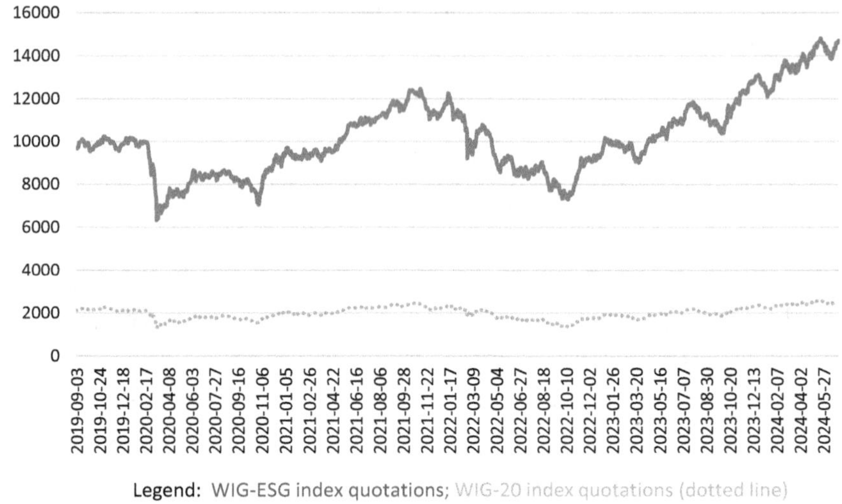

Fig. 6.2 WIG-ESG vs. WIG-20 Index Quotations (03.09.2019–28.06.2024). *Source* Based on historical data from WIG-ESG Index and WIG-20 Index (WSE, 2024b)

international standards for constructing ESG indices and socially responsible investment portfolios, which frequently prioritise more rigorous ESG performance criteria in the selection process. The majority of indices prioritise authentic corporate actions pertaining to sustainable development and social responsibility, as opposed to their sectoral specifics or market capitalisation. These results in decisions to include companies in indices based on a wide range of criteria that reflect the pursuit of promoting responsibility in the social, environmental and governance areas. Consequently, the methodology employed for evaluating companies within the WIG-ESG index, considering ESG criteria, may give rise to certain concerns.

The modification of the WIG-ESG Index methodology proposed by Zaremba (2023), which included not only the possibility of incorporating smaller companies (such as those from the sWIG80, in line with the RESPECT Index model) but also the introduction of exclusion criteria based on ESG scores, was not adopted. However, following public consultations held from 21 February to 10 March 2024, the Warsaw Stock Exchange decided to discontinue the listing of the WIG-ESG Index as of 28 June 2024

(Bank.pl., 2024). Consequently, there is currently no ESG-focused index listed on the Warsaw Stock Exchange. The official reason provided by the index administrator was 'lack of interest in the index on the part of the entities applying [...] and high costs of developing the index' (WSE Benchmark, WSE Benchmark, 2024c). Concurrently, the Warsaw Stock Exchange has issued an official statement asserting its commitment to the introduction of products that incorporate ESG factors and the objectives of energy transformation. However, as of 1 September 2025, no further information has been disclosed regarding this matter.

The decision to discontinue the WIG-ESG Index came as a surprise to the market and was made without significant media attention. Only a few expressions of surprise and disappointment appeared in industry media and on individual social media profiles. The Warsaw Stock Exchange administration did not publicise the decision widely, nor did it initiate a broader discussion beyond the formal public consultations. This muted response further suggests that the WIG-ESG Index lacked substantial market interest. As a result, the Exchange's management deemed its continued maintenance unjustified.

However, it is worthwhile to consider the underlying reasons for this decision. A salient factor that emerged from the preceding discussion pertained to the dearth of adequate investor education concerning the intricacies of sustainable development. This knowledge gap is a significant contributing factor to the limited demand for the WIG-ESG index, which ultimately led to its discontinuation. A notable problem was also identified as the lack of consideration of ESG results in asset management recommendations (PwC, 2021). Another contributing factor may have been the methodology used to select companies for inclusion in the index. As previously mentioned, companies were included automatically based on their membership in the WIG20 and mWIG40 indices, rather than on the basis of their actual ESG performance. A failure to demonstrate a commitment to sustainable development merely resulted in a lower ranking position, rather than exclusion from the index. Consequently, the WIG-ESG index proved incapable of adequately reflecting the real impact of companies on environmental, social and governance issues, despite the fact that some constituents did demonstrate meaningful achievements in these areas. The market swiftly recognised these limitations, and consequently, the index composition was not widely utilised as a meaningful indicator in ESG-related investment decision-making.

The WIG-ESG index was listed for a period of less than five years, and its liquidation may prove to be premature in the long term, especially in the context of EU regulations on non-financial reporting. The CSRD directive stipulates the requirement for listed companies with a workforce of at least 10 employees to disclose ESG factors from 2029 onwards (European Parliament & Council, 2022, 2025). In order to maintain its competitive position, it is essential that the Warsaw Stock Exchange adapts to these evolving expectations and, ideally, develops new tools to support informed investment in companies that are environmentally, socially and corporately responsible.

6.4 Summary and Conclusions

ESG indices on the Polish capital market, particularly the RESPECT Index and its successor WIG-ESG, played a pivotal role in promoting responsible investing and sustainable development in Poland. Over the course of 15 years, the Polish capital market underwent significant changes, which led to an increase in investor awareness of ESG criteria. These changes also influenced the perception of companies engaged in these initiatives.

The RESPECT index, a pioneering ESG index in Central and Eastern Europe, has emerged as a symbol of innovation on the Warsaw Stock Exchange, underscoring the significance of corporate social responsibility. The decade-long record demonstrated that allocating capital to enterprises that align with ESG principles can yield investment returns that surpass the mean average, particularly during the initial years of the index's implementation. However, subsequent years indicated the necessity for the enhancement of assessment tools and the qualification of companies for ESG indices, with a view to ensuring full reflection of their actual commitment to sustainable development.

The introduction of the WIG-ESG index in 2019, as a new standard of responsible investing on the Warsaw Stock Exchange, was a continuation and development of the idea initiated by the RESPECT index. Although WIG-ESG introduced a more automated and integrated assessment methodology, covering all companies from the WIG20 and mWIG40 indices, the challenges associated with clear and consistent assessment of ESG criteria remained relevant. The decision to discontinue its publication in June 2024, although it was a surprise for market participants, was accepted with understanding. The index did not meet the expectations placed in it by both the Exchange and its stakeholders, especially investors. In the era of sustainable development challenges and the obligation of non-financial reporting, it is expected that the Warsaw Stock Exchange, wanting to remain a leader in the region, will propose other tools to support the market in considering ESG aspects in the actions of companies listed on the Warsaw Stock Exchange.

A comparison of Polish ESG indices with global standards and experiences demonstrates that, although Poland has yet to make significant advances in this area, the progress made over the last 15 years is noteworthy. The study's key conclusions indicate a necessity for the continued development and enhancement of tools to support ESG data quality and benchmarking. Additionally, there is a call to raise awareness among investors and companies regarding the significance of the reporting mechanisms. It is imperative that ESG is integrated with decision-making processes in the capital market to achieve the sustainable development goals set for companies in Poland.

References

Adeneye, Y. B., & Ahmed, M. (2015). Corporate social responsibility and company performance. *Journal of Business Studies Quarterly*, *7*(1), 151–166.

Apergis, N., Poufinas, T., & Antonopoulos, A. (2022). ESG scores and cost of debt. *Energy Economics*, *112*, 106186. https://doi.org/10.1016/j.eneco.2022.106186

Bank.pl. (2024, February 21). GPW Benchmark przestanie publikować Indeks WIG-ESG z powodu braku zainteresowania rynku. Bank.pl. Retrieved Mar ch 3, 2025, from https://bank.pl/gpw-benchmark-przestanie-publikowac-indeks-wig-esg-z-powodu-braku-zainteresowania-rynku/

Benchmark, W. S. E. (2023, January). *Stopy zwrotu—styczeń 2023* [PDF]. Retrieved February 2, 2024, from https://gpwbenchmark.pl/pub/BENCHMARK/files/PDF/statystyki/2023_01_stopy_zwrotu.pdf

Benchmark, W. S. E. (2024b). *Opisy indeksów*. Retrieved August 28, 2024, from https://gpwbenchmark.pl/opisy-indeksow

Berg, F., Kölbel, J. K., & Rigobon, R. (2022). Aggregate confusion: The divergence of ESG ratings. *Review of Finance*, *26*(6), 1315–1344. https://doi.org/10.1093/rof/rfac033

Białkowski, J., & Sławik, A. (2021). Do investors respond to changes in the composition of sustainability indices? *Bank I Kredyt*, *52*(4), 319–338. https://hdl.handle.net/10092/103557

Blajer-Gołębiewska, A. (2014). Do stock exchange indices based on reputational factors matter? *International Journal of Academic Research*, *6*(4), 251–257.

Bloomberg. (2024). *ESG and Climate Indices Resources*. Retrieved July 28, 2024, from https://www.bloomberg.com/professional/product/indices/esg-and-climate-indices-resources/#sasb

Calvert Research and Management. (2024). *Calvert Indexes*. Retrieved July 28, 2024, from https://www.calvert.com/calvert-indexes.php

Camilleri, M. A. (2020). The market for socially responsible investing: A review of the developments. *Social Responsibility Journal*, *17*(3), 412–428. https://doi.org/10.1108/SRJ-06-2019-0194

Cegliński, P. (2015). 5 lat funkcjonowania respect index. Ocena i perspektywy. In W. M. Buszko, D. Krupa, & A. Drews (Eds.), *Perspektywa—Wyzwania Współczesnej Gospodarki* (239–254). Wydawnictwo Naukowe Uniwersytetu Mikołaja Kopernika.

Chen, Z., & Xie, G. (2022). ESG disclosure and financial performance: Moderating role of ESG investors. *International Review of Financial Analysis*, *83*, 102291. https://doi.org/10.1016/j.irfa.2022.102291

Cheng, B., Iannou, I., & Serafeim, G. (2014). Corporate social responsibility and access to finance. *Strategic Management Journal*, *35*(1), 1–23.

Croom, S., Vidal, N., Spetic, W., Marshall, D., & McCarthy, L. (2018). Impact of social sustainability orientation and supply chain practices on operational performance. *International Journal of Operations and Production Management*, *38*(12), 2344–2366. https://doi.org/10.1108/IJOPM-03-2017-0180

Czerwińska, T. (2012). Efektywność inwestycji społecznie odpowiedzialnych na rynku akcji. *Problemy Zarządzania*, *10*(4/39), 129–140.

Dumas, C., & Louche, C. (2016). Collective beliefs on responsible investment. *Business and Society*, *55*(3), 427–457. https://doi.org/10.1177/0007650315575327

ETF.com.pl. (2024). NN Indeks Odpowiedzialnego Inwestowania. Retrieved December 20, 2024, from https://etf.com.pl/fundusze-indeksowe/fundusze-akcji-polska/nn-indeks-odpowiedzialnego-inwestowania/

Euronext. (2025). *ESG Indices: Full List*. Retrieved February 2, 2025, from https://live.euronext.com/en/products/indices/esg-indices

European Parliament, & Council. (2025). Directive (EU) 2025/794 of 14 April 2025 amending Directive (EU) 2022/2464 and Directive (EU) 2024/1760 as regards the dates for the application of certain sustainability reporting and due diligence requirements (Text with EEA relevance). Official Journal of the European Union, L, 16 April 2025. https://eur-lex.europa.eu/eli/dir/2025/794/oj

European Parliament and Council. (2022). Directive (EU) 2022/2464 of the European Parliament and of the Council of 14 December 2022 amending Regulation (EU) No 537/2014, Directive 2004/109/EC, Directive 2006/43/EC and Directive 2013/34/EU, as regards corporate sustainability reporting (Text with EEA relevance). Retrieved from: https://eur-lex.europa.eu/eli/dir/2022/2464/oj. Accessed March 12, 2024.

Giese, G., Lee, L.-E., Melas, D., Nagy, Z., & Nishikawa, L. (2019). Foundations of ESG investing: How ESG affects equity valuation, risk, and performance.

Journal of Portfolio Management, *45*(5), 69–83. https://doi.org/10.3905/jpm.2019.45.5.069

Golaszewska-Kaczan, U., Kilon, J., & Marcinkiewicz, J. (2016). An assessment of the attractiveness of investments in the shares of socially responsible businesses based on the RESPECT Index, Annales. *Ethics in Economic Life*, *19*(3), 113–127.

Jagyasi, D., & Raut, A. (2022). *A study of approach for investors to identify risks and opportunities based on machine learning algorithm (2022). Proceedings of the International Conference on Innovative Computing & Communication (ICICC) 2022*. https://doi.org/10.2139/ssrn.4361058

Janik, B., & Bartkowiak, M. (2015). The comparison of socially responsible indices in Central and Eastern Europe. *International Journal of Environmental Technology and Management*, *18*(2), 153–169.

Jedynak, T. (2012). Efektywność strategii inwestycji w akcje spółek społecznie odpowiedzialnych na przykładzie Respect Index. *Zeszyty Naukowe Polskiego Towarzystwa Ekonomicznego*, *12*, 161–172.

Joliet, R., & Titova, Y. (2018). Equity SRI funds vacillate between ethics and money: An analysis of the funds' stock holding decisions. *Journal of Banking and Finance*, *97*, 70–86. https://doi.org/10.1016/j.jbankfin.2018.09.011

Laskowska, A. (2018). Stock market indices as a measurment tool for profitability of corporate social responsibility activities. *Copernican Journal of Finance and Accounting*, *7*(4), 71–86.

Lassala, C., Orero-Blat, M., & Ribeiro-Navarrete, S. (2021). The financial performance of listed companies in pursuit of the Sustainable Development Goals (SDG). *Economic Research-Ekonomska Istrazivanja*, *34*(1), 427–449.

Leite, P., & Cortez, M. C. (2014). Style and performance of international socially responsible funds in Europe. *Research in International Business and Finance*, *30*, 248–267. https://doi.org/10.1016/j.ribaf.2013.09.007

LSEG (2024). *ESG Index*. Retrieved July 28, 2024, from https://www.lseg.com/en/ftse-russell/indices/esg-index

Łudzińska, K. (2009a). Społeczna odpowiedzialność przedsiębiorstw i jej wpływ na budowę wartości. In W. S. A (Ed.), *Migracja Kapitału W Globalnej Gospodarce* (366–392). Wydawnictwo Difin.

Łudzińska, K. (2009b). Indeksy zrównoważonego rozwoju przedsiębiorstw. *Kwartalnik Nauk O Przedsiębiorstwie*, *4*, 63–70.

Łudzińska, K. (2013). Indeksy zrównoważonego rozwoju a wycena przedsiębiorstw przez rynki kapitałowe. *W A. Szablewski (Red.), Zmienność Rynków a Wartość Przedsiębiorstw*, 239–249.

Łudzińska, K. (2017). Społeczna odpowiedzialność a wartość przedsiębiorstw na rynku kapitałowym. *Problemy Zarządzania*, *15*(1/66), 207–220.

Lulewicz-Sas, A. (2014). Społecznie odpowiedzialne inwestowanie narzędziem koncepcji społecznie odpowiedzialnego biznesu. *Ekonomia I Zarządzanie*, *6*(1), 142–157. https://doi.org/10.12846/j.em.2014.01.08

Morningstar. (2020, April 21). *Morningstar to acquire Sustainalytics and expand access to ESG research, data and analytics for investors worldwide*. Retrieved July 21, 2024, from https://newsroom.morningstar.com/newsroom/news-archive/press-release-details/2020/Morningstar-to-Acquire-Sustainalytics-and-Expand-Access-to-ESG-ResearchData-and-Analytics-for-Investors-Worldwide/default.aspx

MSCI. (2019). MSCI ESG Leaders Indexes methodology. Retrieved November 24, 2024, from https://www.msci.com/eqb/methodology/meth_docs/MSCI_ESG_Leaders_Methodology_Feb2019.pdf

MSCI Inc. (2025). *ESG Indexes*. Retrieved February 2, 2025, from https://www.msci.com/our-solutions/indexes/esg-indexes

Nasdaq. (2025). *Green Equity Indexes*. Retrieved February 2, 2025, from https://www.nasdaq.com/solutions/green-equity-indexes

PwC. (2021). Raport: ESG—Miecz Damoklesa, czy szansa na strategiczną zmianę? Retrieved April 20, 2024, from https://www.pwc.pl/pl/pdf-nf/2021/ESG_Miecz_Damoklesa_raport_PwC_2021.pdf

Ramchander, S., Schwebach, R. G., & Staking, K. (2012). The informational relevance of corporate social responsibility: Evidence from SD 400 index reconstructions. *Strategic Management Journal*, *33*, 303–314. https://doi.org/10.1002/smj.952

Rogowski, W., & Lipski, M. (2022). Znaczenie informacji niefinansowej w świetle wymogów zrównoważonego rozwoju oraz turbulentnego otoczenia. *Kwartalnik Nauk O Przedsiębiorstwie*, *64*(2), 2. https://doi.org/10.33119/KNoP.2022.64.2.3; Rok, B. (2007). Biznes społecznie odpowiedzialny – teoria i praktyka. W J. Hausner (red.), *Ekonomia społeczna a rozwój* (157–172). MSAP.

Russell, F. T. S. E. (2023). Index overview: FTSE4Good Index Series. Pioneering global ESG indexes. Retrieved July 29, 2024, from https://research.ftserussell.com/products/downloads/ftse4good-brochure.pdf

Russell, F. T. S. E. (2025). *Sustainable Investment Indices*. Retrieved February 2, 2025, from https://www.ftserussell.com/index/category/sustainable-investment

S&P Dow Jones Indices. (2025). *ESG Indices*. Retrieved February 2, 2025, from https://www.spglobal.com/spdji/en/index-family/esg/

Sikacz, H., & Wołczek, P. (2017). Analiza ESG spółek z indeksu RESPECT—Podsumowanie badań. *Zeszyty Naukowe Szkoły Głównej Gospodarstwa Wiejskiego w Warszawie. Polityki Europejskie, Finanse I Marketing*, *18*(67). https://doi.org/10.22630/PEFIM.2017.18.67.32

Slager, R., Gond, J.-P., & Moon, J. (2010). What gets measured gets managed? The impact of SRI indices in responsible corporate behaviour. *Academy of Management Annual Meeting Proceeding*, *1*, 1–6. https://doi.org/10.5465/ambpp.2010.54493472

STOXX Ltd. (2025). *Sustainability Indices.* Retrieved February 2, 2025, from https://www.stoxx.com/discovery-search?category=theme&superType=esg&sustainability&indexFamily=standard

Sustainalytics. (2024). *Sustainalytics.* Retrieved July 21, 2024, from https://www.sustainalytics.com/

TFI, N. N. (2024). ESG—Nasze podejście. Retrieved December 20, 2024, from https://www.nntfi.pl/esg

van Duuren, E., Plantinga, A., & Scholtens, B. (2016). ESG Integration and the investment management process: Fundamental investing reinvented. *Journal of Business Ethics, 138*(3), 525–533. https://doi.org/10.1007/s10551-015-2610-8

Wan, J., Yin, L., & Wu, Y. (2024). Return and volatility connectedness across global ESG stock indexes: Evidence from the time-frequency domain analysis. *International Review of Economics and Finance, 89*, 397–428. https://doi.org/10.1016/j.iref.2023.10.038

Wiśniewski, T. K. (2010). Indeks RESPECTIndex jako inicjatywa Giełdy Papierów Wartościowych w procesie tworzenia zasad CSR na polskim rynku kapitałowym. *Zeszyty Naukowe: Polityki Europejskie, Finanse I Marketing, 4(53)*, 301–311.

WSE. (2009). *Opis projektu RESPECT Index.* Retrieved June 16, 2024, from https://www.gpw.pl/pub/files/PDF/opis_indeksow/Respect/RESPECT.pdf

WSE. (2013). *RESPECT Index.* Warsaw Stock Exchange. Retrieved September 10, 2025, from https://www.gpw.pl/aktualnosc?cmn_id=52040&title=RESPECT+Index

WSE. (2018). Nowy skład RESPECT Indeks [New composition of the RESPECT Index]. Retrieved February 12, 2023, from https://www.gpw.pl/aktualnosc?cmn_id=107753&title=Nowy+sk%C5%82ad+RESPECT+Index

WSE. (2019). Giełda uruchamia indeks WIG-ESG [The Exchange launches the WIG-ESG Index]. Retrieved February 20, 2023, from https://www.gpw.pl/pl-ri-komunikatyprasowe?ph_main_01_start=show&cmn_id=108700&title=GPW+uruchamia+indeks+WIG-ESG

WSE. (2021). Kodeks dobrych praktyk [Code of Best Practice]. Retrieved February 8, 2025, from https://www.gpw.pl/dobre-praktyki2021

WSE. (2022). Komunikat prasowy z dn. 22.07.2022: Inwestorzy stawiają na ESG [Press release of 22.07.2022: Investors focus on ESG]. Retrieved July 23, 2023, from https://www.gpw.pl/pl-ri-komunikaty-prasowe?ph_main_01_start=show&cmn_id=112787&title=Inwestorzy+stawiaj%C4%85+na+ESG

WSE. (2024a). *Archiwum notowań.* Retrieved June 16, 2024, from https://www.gpw.pl/archiwum-notowan

WSE. (2024b). Archiwum notowań. Retrieved November 20, 2024, from https://www.gpw.pl/archiwum-notowan?show_x=Poka%C5%BC+wyniki&type=1&instrument=WIG-ESG&date=

WSE. (2024c). Archiwum notowań. Retrieved November 21, 2024, from https://www.gpw.pl/archiwum-notowan?fetch=0&type=1&instrument=RESPECT&date=&show_x=Poka%C5%BC+wyniki

WSE. (2025). *Statystyki GPW*. Retrieved March 15, 2025, from https://www.gpw.pl/statystyki-gpw

WSE Benchmark. (2024a). Karta indeksu—NN Indeks Odpowiedzialnego Inwestowania (ISIN: PL9999998955). Retrieved December 8, 2024, from https://gpwbenchmark.pl/karta-indeksu?isin=PL9999998955

WSE Benchmark. (2024c). Zmiana Metody Indeksów Giełdowych: Dokument Konsultacyjny. GPW Benchmark. Retrieved November 25, 2024, from https://gpwbenchmark.pl/pub/BENCHMARK/files/PDF/materialy/Dokument_konsultacyjny_2.2024.pdf

Zaremba, U. (2023). Strong ESG risk management as a way to improve organisational resilience in times of crisis: An analysis of WIG-ESG index constituents. *Financial Sciences. Nauki O Finansach*, *28*(1), 1. https://journals.ue.wroc.pl/fins/article/view/139 (Pozyskano z).

Zieliński, M. (2015). Wpływ realizacji koncepcji CSR na wycenę spółek akcyjnych. *Prace Naukowe Uniwersytetu Ekonomicznego We Wrocławiu*, *401*, 642–650.

CHAPTER 7

The Effectiveness of Socially Responsible Investment in Poland and Globally: A Research-Based Perspective

7.1 Introduction

This chapter examines the efficiency of socially responsible investing (SRI), analysing academic research and market practices. It outlines various methods of assessing the impact of environmental, social and governance (ESG) factors on investment performance, drawing on global capital markets and the Polish context. Despite the growing popularity of SRI and the expanding body of research on the subject, empirical findings remain inconclusive.

The first part of the chapter reviews key studies on global markets, in which positive, neutral and negative relationships have been identified between the application of ESG criteria and financial results. It then turns to analysing SRI efficiency in Poland, where the market is still in its infancy. Studies of the Polish market produce varied results in terms of both the financial performance of SRI portfolios and investors' attitudes towards this form of investment. Key challenges in Poland include the limited availability of assets that meet ESG criteria and a general lack of investor awareness of their importance.

The section analyses the ongoing debate concerning the actual impact of investments aligned with sustainable development principles on financial performance in the context of both international markets and the specific conditions of the Polish market.

K. Łudzińska, *International ESG Perspectives*,
https://doi.org/10.1007/978-3-032-11666-6_7

7.2 Efficiency of SRI Investment on Leading Capital Markets

Socially responsible investing (SRI) has become a prominent focus of scholarly research worldwide. Although much of the literature emphasises comparisons between the financial performance of SRI and that of traditional investments, the efficiency of SRI remains a subject of ongoing debate in academic and business circles.

The study of the relationship between environmental and social outcomes—collectively known as corporate social performance (CSP)—and corporate financial performance (CFP) began in the 1970s. Since then, scientists, experts, investors and various organisations have produced over 2000 empirical studies and numerous literature reviews examining this relationship (Friede et al., 2015). However, even the most comprehensive literature reviews analyse only a fraction of existing primary studies, making it difficult to generalise conclusions. Consequently, knowledge regarding the financial impact of incorporating environmental, social and governance (ESG) criteria remains fragmented and inconclusive.

Moskowitz (1972) was one of the earliest researchers to examine the financial efficiency of socially responsible investment and argue that it could yield financial benefits. Based on data from 14 leading companies in the United States, he found that those acting responsibly could expect better financial results. Subsequent studies by Diltz (1995), Russo and Fouts (1997) and King and Lenox (2002) confirmed a positive correlation between higher rates of return on investment and the responsible environmental behaviour of corporations. Guerard (1997) demonstrated that social audits of investment opportunities can lead to higher returns on invested capital. Feldman et al. (1997) estimated that companies that improve their environmental policies and practices could potentially achieve a 5% higher return on invested capital than those that do not.

Russell and Brockman (2011) demonstrated that socially responsible companies tend to generate higher returns on capital while exhibiting lower investment risk and a reduced likelihood of financial loss. Brzeszczyński and McIntosh (2014) examined the performance of British socially responsible equity portfolios included in the 'Global 100 Most Sustainable Corporations in the World' list, which is published annually in the UK by the non-governmental organisation Corporate Knights (Corporate Knights, 2022). Their research confirmed that, between 2000 and 2010, SRI portfolios generated higher average returns than comparable stock indices. Specifically, the annual average excess return (including dividends) was 5.26% relative to the FTSE 100 index and 5.69% relative to the FTSE4Good index. However, these return differentials were not statistically significant when assessed over the entire 11-year period, in individual years, or across shorter intervals.

Meanwhile, in their international study based on 103 fiduciary funds of socially responsible investing from Germany, the United Kingdom and the United States, Bauer et al. (2005) found no significant differences in risk-adjusted returns between ethical and traditional investment funds during the period 1990–2001. Statman (2000) compared the performance indicators of the KLD Domini Social 400 Index, the oldest SRI index in the world, and the S&P 500 Index, finding no statistically significant difference in returns over the period 1990–1998. Ten years later, Ramchander et al. (2012) examined the financial performance of companies included in the same index. They found that inclusion in the index was associated with a positive market reaction, reflected in an increase in share price, while exclusion from the index led to a decline in share price.

The MSCI KLD 400 Social Index currently forms part of the MSCI ESG Indexes family of sustainable investment benchmarks. It includes companies with high Environmental, Social and Governance ratings, while excluding those deemed to have a negative environmental or social impact. Its designated comparative benchmark is the MSCI USA IMI Index, which comprises companies that have not been screened for ESG criteria (MSCI, 2025). Table 7.1 shows the performance of both indices. While the MSCI USA IMI Index tends to perform better in the short term, the performance differences over longer periods of three years or more are statistically negligible.

Geczy, Stambauch and Levin's (2005) research into the investment decisions of institutional investors revealed a reverse trend: by selecting SRI funds over traditional funds, investors could potentially incur an annual loss of 3.7%. However, this potential underperformance was not attributed to socially responsible investing per se, but rather to the selection of individual funds and their respective performance. The researchers observed that investors who selected funds included in SRI indices performed similarly to those who opted for traditional funds, with both groups experiencing an average annual loss of around 0.5%. Significantly greater losses arise when investors adopt active investment styles such as value investing, since the range of available SRI funds within these styles is considerably more limited. Schroeder (2007) examined the effectiveness of SRI investing by analysing

Table 7.1 Results of MSCI KLD Social Index and MSCI USA IMI Index as of 28 February 2025

Net capital return rate of MSCI KLD 400 Social Index and MSCI USAIMI Index

	1 month	*3 months*	*1 year*	*Year to Date (YTD)*	*Annually*			
					3 years	*5 years*	*10 years*	*Since 31.08.2010*
MSCI KLD Social Index	−2.62	−4.24	12.94	−1.06	10.21	15.54	12.14	13.94
MSCI USA IMI Index	−1.91	−2.00	17.15	1.10	11.17	15.78	11.89	13.99

Source Based on MSCI. (2025)

the performance of 29 corporate social responsibility indices rather than the returns of individual SRI funds. The results indicated that these indices did not exhibit significantly different risk-adjusted returns compared to their respective benchmarks. Furthermore, several of the SRI indices demonstrated slightly higher levels of risk than their respective benchmarks.

Subsequent research by Fritz and von Schnurbein (2019) produced mixed results regarding investment portfolios screened for ESG factors. They identified both negative effects and instances where no such effects were observed. They argue that ESG screening reduces reputational risk and improves return on investment, particularly with regard to corporate governance issues among ESG criteria. Similarly, Brooks and Oikonomou (2018) argue that there is a consensus in the literature, supported by meta-analyses (including Friede et al., 2015; Revelli & Viviani, 2015), which states that portfolios controlled for social and environmental factors do not perform better or worse than conventional portfolios with similar characteristics. They believe there are several reasons for this. Firstly, the positive effects of environmental and social actions at the company level (i.e. value-increasing or risk-reducing) are almost simultaneously offset by the negative effects of suboptimal diversification in SRI portfolios, leading to a neutral overall result. Secondly, relatively few corporate performance studies take into account transaction costs, fund management fees, or other incidental expenses, despite such considerations being standard in investment portfolio research. These costs, which may be higher for SRI portfolios, can potentially offset the positive effects observed in corporate analyses focused on social and environmental performance.

Despite many years of multidimensional research on the financial performance of socially responsible investments, the conclusions remain inconclusive. At the same time, the SRI investment market has seen an increasing number of stakeholders, including agencies, non-governmental organisations and research firms involved in monitoring corporate actions and practices relating to environmental protection, social responsibility and corporate governance. Consequently, SRI portfolios are routinely evaluated by specialised entities to assess and verify their environmental, social and corporate governance credibility (Camilleri, 2020). A growing body of evidence suggests that investors do not necessarily have to sacrifice high financial returns when investing in socially responsible or environmentally sustainable assets. Empirical findings challenge the assertion that screening for environmental, social and governance factors results in poorer corporate financial performance (Salaber, 2013; Trinks & Scholtens, 2017).

Financial motives appear to play a secondary role in decisions related to socially responsible investments (Riedl & Smeets, 2017), with social and environmental preferences emerging as the primary drivers. Socially responsible investors tend to expect lower returns from SRI funds than from conventional funds, suggesting a readiness to forego potential financial gains in order to align their investments with environmental and social values. Hartzmark and Sussman (2019) present evidence that, in the American mutual fund market, investors value sustainable development more highly than the maximum expected rate of return on capital. Their analysis shows that classifying funds as having low sustainable development results in net outflows of over 12 billion US dollars, whereas classifying them as having high sustainable development leads to net inflows of over 24 billion US dollars. Available data suggests that sustainable development is perceived as a positive indicator of future performance. However, it does not conclusively demonstrate that funds with high levels of sustainability outperform those with lower levels in financial terms. Researchers interpret these findings as being consistent with the significant role that non-financial motives, such as environmental and social considerations, play in shaping investors' decisions.

Akin conclusions were drawn by Bauer, Ruof and Smeetz (2021), who conducted a study among members of a US pension fund that gives its participants a meaningful say in sustainable investment policy. Their findings suggest that two-thirds of shareholders in the pension fund favour increasing engagement with companies that are aligned with sustainable development goals, even when they anticipate potential negative financial consequences. Fama and French (2007) describe this phenomenon as a 'taste for assets', viewing investments as consumer goods that reflect personal values and preferences as well as financial instruments.

A similar trend can be observed in investment strategies that take an approach opposite to that of SRI investments. These strategies focus on sectors that are usually excluded by ethical screening, such as alcohol, tobacco and weapons manufacturing. Studies examining the effectiveness of investing in 'sin stocks' suggest that moral pressure on investors, rather than lower financial returns, is the main reason for avoiding these sectors (e.g. Hong & Kacperczyk, 2009; Kim & Venkatachalam, 2011). Duliniec and Tomaszewski (2016) demonstrate that, in the long run, investments in assets considered unethical yield a higher return on invested capital than traditional investments or those considered ethical. Similarly, Bolton and Kacperczyk (2021) examine the impact of carbon dioxide emission levels on investment returns in the US stock market. Their analysis shows that shares in companies with higher total carbon dioxide emissions tend to deliver higher investment returns, as measured by publicly available stock market indicators such as the price-to-book value ratio (P/BV). However, the authors were unable to attribute the return premium associated with higher carbon dioxide emissions to differences in unexpected profitability or other established risk factors. Nevertheless, they found that institutional investors are applying exclusionary screening of investments based on direct emission intensity—measured as the ratio of total CO_2 emissions to sales volume—in several key sectors, and are already demanding compensation for their exposure to carbon dioxide emission risk.

There is considerable evidence to suggest that the relationship between ESG performance and financial returns on socially responsible investment is non-linear, which may at least partially explain why previous research results have been inconclusive. Barnett and Salomon (2006) conducted an innovative analysis which demonstrated that SRI funds applying either a very high or very low number of environmental, social and governance criteria significantly outperformed those applying a moderate number of such screens. The emerging picture shows that there is a non-monotonic, U-shaped relationship between the degree of engagement with social, environmental and governance aspects, and financial performance. The lowest risk-adjusted results are seen in funds focusing on a few ESG dimensions. According to the authors, this approach is justified—funds with a limited range of ESG criteria can effectively diversify most of the unrewarded risk, while funds with a wide range of ESG criteria benefit from the positive effects of social and environmental actions. Conversely, funds with an average number of ESG criteria are in the least favourable position as they do not achieve significant success at either end of the spectrum, resulting in comparatively weaker financial performance than their competitors.

Kotsantonis et al. (2016) organised data on the financial performance of SRI investments and debunked common but erroneous beliefs about this strategy. They presented their conclusions in the form of six myths, which they analysed and refuted in detail. The first myth concerns the belief that ESG programmes reduce capital returns and long-term value for shareholders. In reality, however, companies that apply these standards gain a strategic advantage by offering higher returns and lower risk. The subsequent myths that the authors debunk include the beliefs that ESG is already fully integrated with mainstream investment management and that companies have no control over the types of shareholders who invest in their stock. The authors highlight the increasing availability and credibility of ESG data, which, contrary to the myth, play a key role in fundamental analysis. They also emphasise that ESG contributes to risk minimisation, operational efficiency growth and opening new markets. They argue that the integration of ESG factors is not inconsistent with fiduciary duties, as confirmed by the 2015 amendment to ERISA guidelines in the USA, which recognised the positive impact of ESG on companies' financial performance (U.S. Department of Labor, 1974).

In summarising the results of empirical studies on the impact of environmental, social and governance criteria on financial performance, several key observations made by Brooks and Oikonomou (2018) are worth highlighting. ESG reporting is often associated with improved performance in environmental, social and governance dimensions, as well as financial outcomes. A positive, statistically significant, albeit economically small, relationship has been observed between socially and environmentally responsible actions and corporate financial performance. The risk-adjusted results of SRI funds and indices almost coincide with those of their conventional counterparts. Investment strategies based on negative screening incur certain financial costs. A clear negative relationship is also observed between ESG performance and financial risk in different asset classes and markets. Furthermore, there is an asymmetry in the financial consequences of social and environmental actions: the negative financial effects of social irresponsibility often outweigh the financial benefits of refraining from socially responsible actions. Nevertheless, the relationship between social and environmental performance and financial outcomes remains unclear. However, evidence suggests that ESG-related actions and outcomes play a significant role in key corporate decisions, such as executive compensation and mergers and acquisitions.

Therefore, although the effectiveness of SRI investing is still being debated, it is attracting increasing attention from academics and investors. A growing body of evidence suggests that responsible investments can generate financial returns, as well as meaningful social, environmental and governance benefits. These issues are particularly relevant today, given the growing social and environmental demands and the rapidly evolving market conditions (see, Chap. 1). Looking ahead, global challenges such as climate change and social inequalities may further reinforce the role of SRI strategies, establishing them as an integral part of responsible corporate management.

7.3 Effectiveness of SRI Investing in the Polish Market

As mentioned in the previous chapter, the Polish SRI investment market is still in its infancy and, consequently, relatively few research results in this area have been published to date. Research on SRI investing in Poland can be divided into three main categories. The first focuses on analysing the effectiveness of SRI investing on the Warsaw Stock Exchange by comparing the performance of stock indices over different time periods. The second strand examines the effectiveness of ESG fund investments compared to the performance of conventional funds. The third strand explores the attitudes of investors and broader Polish society towards socially responsible investing.

Czerwińska (2009) was the pioneer of the first stream of research on the Polish SRI market, analysing the implementation of the concept of socially responsible investing by Polish pension funds. Pension funds are unique among other investment funds due to their socio-economic nature. As they aim to accumulate and multiply the capital entrusted to them by clients over many years, they cannot ignore social challenges and expectations (Czerwińska, 2009). The effects of their investment strategies impact the quality of life of society, the ultimate beneficiary of these funds. According to Czerwińska, pension funds should consider ethical, ecological and social aspects in the investment process, in addition to financial criteria. Polish Open Pension Funds (OFE) operate within strict regulations that present challenges in terms of implementing SRI strategies. The specifics of the Polish market and the restriction that OFEs can invest no more than 5% of their assets abroad (Ministry of Finance, 2000) make it difficult to integrate SRI investment strategies. Nevertheless, there is a need for greater engagement in SRI investing. Implementing this approach requires cooperation between various capital market entities, supervisory bodies and pension system beneficiaries.

In a subsequent study, Czerwińska (2012) examined the relationship between social responsibility and investment effectiveness on the Warsaw Stock Exchange. She analysed the distribution of returns and the risk of investing in companies included in the RESPECT index (see, Chap. 6 for more information) in relation to other investment benchmarks, namely other indices and sub-indices of the stock exchange (including WIG, WIG20, mWIG80 and WIG-Banks, among others). Returns were analysed from November 2009, when the RESPECT index was first listed, to

March 2012. The results of the study clearly indicated that the return on the RESPECT index during the review period was significantly higher than the returns on the WIG, WIG20, mWIG40 and WIG80 indices. Among the sector indices, only the returns on WIG-DEVELOPERS, WIG-FOOD and WIG-CHEMISTRY were significantly higher. Furthermore, during a market downturn, the RESPECT index showed the least decrease in value compared to the other analysed indices.

These findings were further supported by analyses from Wolska and Czerwonka (2013), who also demonstrated that RESPECT outperformed the main Warsaw Stock Exchange index (WIG). Their study reported positive profitability and return on investment, even when risk was taken into account. The performance of the RESPECT index suggests that selecting companies based on ESG factors and transparency can lead to favourable investment outcomes.

Further research examined the effectiveness of socially responsible investing in securities. Czerwińska and Kaźmierkiewicz (2015) evaluated the ESG rating of publicly listed companies on the Warsaw Stock Exchange, investigating whether firms that demonstrate greater transparency in non-financial disclosures exhibit lower stock return volatility—an indicator of reduced investment risk. Over the three-year period analysed (2010–2013), companies with a higher ESG rating demonstrated stronger financial performance, including above-average returns, lower volatility and smaller forecasting error. The study concluded that corporate social responsibility enhances corporate transparency and may significantly reduce information asymmetry in the capital market. Furthermore, statistically significant differences in return standard deviations were observed between investment portfolios, suggesting potential benefits from diversifying investments based on ESG ratings. However, Czerwińska and Kaźmierkiewicz cautioned against overinterpreting the findings due to the limited timeframe of the study, which restricts the generalisability of its conclusions. Nevertheless, a positive correlation was evident between ESG data transparency and lower investment risk.

Gierałtowska (2017) conducted a noteworthy comparative analysis of the performance of the RESPECT Index and a selection of international indices comprising socially responsible companies, including: DJSI World, FTSE4GOOD Global, MSCI KLD 400 Social and other Polish indices (WIG and WIG20). The results of Gierałtowska's study indicate that the performance of the analysed indices varied. Inclusion in a socially responsible index does not guarantee that investing in a company will produce the expected returns. Nevertheless, the findings emphasise that integrating ESG factors into financial analysis is a growing trend that is likely to become increasingly significant in the future.

However, subsequent studies produced markedly different results, suggesting that corporate social responsibility considerations do not significantly impact investment decisions in the Polish capital market. Kłysik-Uryszek (2020) analysed the performance of companies included in the RESPECT Index to determine whether they were characterised by lower investment risk and higher profitability. The study also examined whether investors perceived these companies as being more stable and profitable than other companies listed on the Warsaw Stock Exchange. The study revealed that companies not engaged in CSR activities achieved higher returns at lower investment risk than those implementing a CSR strategy. This suggests that portfolios composed of companies not pursuing CSR were more profitable than those focused on socially responsible firms. These findings contradict earlier studies by Czerwińska (2012) and Czerwińska and Kaźmierkiewicz (2015), which indicated a positive relationship between CSR practices and investment performance.

A few years later, research was conducted to examine the effectiveness of investing in shares of companies included in the WIG-ESG Index, the successor to the RESPECT Index. The results were entirely different. Mikołajek-Gocejna (2022) conducted a pioneering analysis of the systematic risk associated with shares listed on the WIG-ESG Index between 2019 and 2022, covering the period of the Covid-19 pandemic. The findings revealed that companies with high ESG ratings exhibited lower systematic risk than a market portfolio comprising other companies listed on the Warsaw Stock Exchange.

As part of the second strand of research into socially responsible investing (SRI) in the Polish market, the focus was on the efficiency of Polish SRI funds, which were compared with traditional investment funds and stock market indices in terms of performance. As discussed in Sect. 5.3, the scope of the research is relatively limited due to the small number of SRI funds in Poland.

Despite these objective limitations, SRI funds in Poland are diverse and employ a variety of investment strategies. Many adopt a positive selection approach, focusing primarily on sector strategies. However, others use negative selection based on ethical exclusions (Stańczak-Strumiłło, 2013). The main difficulty in setting up ethical investment funds that allocate assets in Poland is the limited availability of domestic assets that meet SRI criteria and the low level of awareness among market participants of sustainable development. In a study by Wolska and Czerwonka (2013), the performance of the four SRI funds operating in the Polish market at the time was analysed. Three of these funds: Skok Etyczny 1, Skok Etyczny 2 and Climate Change Investor—underperformed relative to the broader market, as represented by the WIG index. In contrast, the PZU Energy, Medicine and Ecology fund achieved positive results, outperforming the market. These findings may explain why the underperforming funds were eventually discontinued due to poor returns and lack of investor interest, while the fourth fund continued to operate.

At around the same time, Lulewicz-Sas and Kilon (2014a) adopted a slightly different perspective in their study. The analysis examined the performance of SRI funds from 2009 to 2013 in comparison to the WIG20 index, to determine the efficiency of SRI investments in the Polish market. The results showed that, for most of the analysed periods, the RESPECT index portfolio did not enable investors to achieve returns above the market average. Only the PZU Energy, Medicine and Ecology fund turned out to be a profitable investment among those analysed, as was found in the research of Wolska and Czerwonka (2013). Interestingly, the risk associated with SRI funds during the period 2009–2013 was significantly lower than that of the overall market. Despite a detailed analysis of the risk and return rates of SRI funds in the context of the WIG, WIG20 and RESPECT indices, the results did not provide clear answers. According to the authors, discrepancies in the results should mainly be interpreted in the context of each fund's individual investment strategy.

Subsequent analyses by the same researchers (Lulewicz-Sas & Kilon, 2014b) also concluded that a comprehensive review of previous studies did not yield clear conclusions about the effectiveness of socially responsible investments in the Polish market. The authors suggest that discrepancies in the findings may be due to differences in investment time horizons, prevailing market conditions during specific periods, and the sectoral composition of the analysed portfolios. Similar conclusions were reached by Jarno (2017), who compared the efficiency of SRI funds with that of hedge funds, the latter of which are primarily guided by financial objectives. His analysis indicates that SRI funds generally produce less satisfactory financial returns than hedge funds.

Jamróz and Żebrowska-Suchodolska (2021) examined the performance of Polish socially responsible investment funds during the pandemic, comparing it to the period before the outbreak. They also compared the results with the performance of the WIG and WIG-ESG indices over the same period. The SRI funds analysed recorded lower returns than the indices in the period immediately before the pandemic. However, during the pandemic, their performance exceeded that of the WIG index. According to the researchers, this may indicate increasing efficiency. Nevertheless, it was not possible to determine whether this upward trend was permanent and driven by structural factors or merely incidental and influenced by pandemic-related conditions.

In a study conducted by Kravchuk (2022), the efficiency of various investment strategies employed by Polish equity funds was analysed. The results suggest that, although these funds offer appealing returns for conservative investors, they are generally not as competitive as stock market indices for those with a higher risk tolerance. These findings are consistent with earlier analyses by Jarno (2017), which showed that hedge funds (also known as speculative funds) generated higher returns for investors with a greater appetite for risk. Kravchuk (2022) also observed that funds focused on ESG standards achieved better results on the European market than their conventional counterparts. There is a growing global trend of interest in investments focused on companies that declare their adherence to ESG principles. Furthermore, ESG funds based in Poland and investing in European instruments performed better than most traditional funds. A comprehensive review of the efficiency, performance and quality of fund management in Polish investment funds between 2017 and 2022 revealed that fund managers employing strategies focused on small- and medium-capitalisation (S&M) funds, as well as ESG strategies targeting European investments, achieved the highest efficiency.

A study by Krawczyńska (2023) analysed the impact of asset price fluctuations on the performance of socially responsible open-end investment funds in the Polish capital market during the period 2020–2021. This analysis was based on the daily quotations of SRI funds that operated continuously throughout the study period. The WIG and WIG-ESG indices were used as benchmarks. Krawczyńska's findings confirmed that market benchmarks significantly influenced the returns of SRI funds in Poland. Notably, the traditional WIG index was found to have a stronger impact on fund performance than its ESG counterpart, the WIG-ESG index.

Analysis of research findings on the effectiveness of investing in portfolios composed of companies from the RESPECT index or WIG-ESG index, as well as in SRI funds, suggests that socially responsible investing on the Polish capital market does not yield superior financial returns compared to traditional investment strategies. According to Dmuchowski et al. (2023), this ambiguity primarily stems from the absence of a clear and consistent definition of responsible investment, coupled with the poor quality of available ESG data and ratings. Nevertheless, numerous studies indicate a positive relationship between ESG indicators and companies' financial performance. Long-term analyses in particular highlight that the benefits of incorporating ESG criteria become more evident over time, contributing to increased firm value. Furthermore, during economic downturns, ESG-focused funds tend to be more resilient to losses than their traditional counterparts. Dmuchowski et al. (2023) argue that, despite the absence of legal obstacles, the Polish economy has significantly lagged behind in adopting ESG criteria, particularly within the financial sector. The authors argue that this delay is unjustified, given Poland's attractiveness as a market for sustainable investments and the opportunities arising from the green transformation. The primary barriers to the development of sustainable finance in Poland are related to education and communication. Therefore, educating all capital market stakeholders is of critical importance.

Last but not least, research into socially responsible investing in the Polish market has focused on the attitudes of investors and broader Polish society towards this form of investment. Unfortunately, the findings in this area thus far have not been encouraging. Polish institutional investors rarely include ESG criteria in their investment strategies, a practice that, according to Doś and Foltyn-Zarychta (2017), indicates a failure to implement SRI principles in reality. Based on document analysis, the researchers estimated the size of the SRI market in Poland in 2016 to be PLN 1.9 billion. This figure is significantly lower than that presented in Chap. 3 of this publication, as reported by Eurosif (2017) in the context of a broader study of the European capital market. The researchers suggest that the limited scale of the Polish SRI market may explain why socially responsible investment practices are implemented and communicated relatively modestly in the country.

In 2022, Dziawgo examined the views of Poles and individual investors on the Warsaw Stock Exchange regarding environmental issues. The study revealed that individual investors in the Polish capital market do not prioritise environmental issues when making investment decisions. While these results cannot be generalised to all investors, it is worth noting that many of the respondents were members of the Association of Individual

Investors. According to Dziawgo (2022), this situation reflects the impact of overlapping crises, including economic, energy and currency issues, high inflation, the pandemic and the war in Ukraine. These challenges may cause environmental protection to cease being a priority for society and the economy. Furthermore, the 'European Green Deal' and the associated 'Polish Green Deal' are controversial. They are considered too ambitious and costly, and the implementation period is too short (by 2050). They could lead to higher living costs, which could result in growing social resistance to environmental initiatives. Therefore, the costs and social attitudes associated with ecological transformation should not be underestimated. Mitigating the negative effects of crises is crucial to maintaining social support for pro-environmental actions. To this end, the promotion of environmental protection measures must be stepped up (Dziawgo, 2022).

In a study conducted by Petelczyc (2022) on a representative group of Polish men and women, individual investors 'attitudes towards ESG aspects were analysed to determine their potential interest in SRI investments. The results indicate that climate change is a significant concern. Many of those surveyed prefer a sustainable approach when thinking about investing in the capital market, although they are not always willing to forego potential profits in favour of pro-environmental and pro-social actions. Interestingly, those who emphasised the importance of social issues were more than twice as likely to make such a sacrifice. Furthermore, women were more likely than men to choose responsible investments, even at the cost of lower profits. There is a positive correlation between investors' attitudes towards climate change and the inclusion of environmental aspects in their investment decisions. Those who considered climate change to be less important were less likely to give up potential profits. These observations align with the findings of international studies (discussed in Chap. 4), which indicate that socially responsible investors often anticipate lower returns and are willing to pay higher fees for managing their SRI investments (Riedl & Smeets, 2017).

In summary, the innovative study by Ziolo et al. (2020) examining the impact of various types of ESG risk on the public and private financial sectors in Poland is worth highlighting. The researchers employed a novel methodology involving fuzzy cognitive maps and engaged eight independent experts to assess a total of 62 ESG factors—21 relating to environmental issues, 25 to social aspects and 16 to governance. The findings revealed that the number and type of ESG factors, as well as the corresponding pillar of sustainable development, varied depending on the financial sector. Consequently, different attitudes towards ESG risk were observed: the public financial sector was more sensitive to environmental factors, whereas the private sector prioritised social considerations. These results offer valuable insights for shaping ESG policies and risk management strategies within public and private financial institutions.

In conclusion, although the Polish market for socially responsible investments is still in its infancy, data analyses indicate a positive growth trend (Remlein, 2017). The main factor hindering the growth of this sector in Poland appears to be the relatively low level of investor awareness of the principles and benefits of responsible investment (Lulewicz-Sas & Kilon, 2014a). Many scholars emphasise the need for broader educational and informational efforts targeting individual and institutional investors, as well as other participants in the capital market. Legal regulations supporting ecological and social investing also play a critical role, and there are still too few of these in Poland. While the Polish SRI market is significantly less developed than those in Western Europe and the United States, the global momentum of the SRI movement, coupled with urgent social and environmental issues and the impact of EU regulations, suggests continued growth in Poland is likely.

7.4 Summary and Conclusions

This chapter is dedicated to analysing the effectiveness of socially responsible investing (SRI) in the in light of empirical research. Although SRI is becoming increasingly popular, the findings regarding its financial performance are inconclusive. Studies of global capital markets reveal mixed correlations—positive, neutral and negative—between applying ESG criteria and financial performance. While many studies highlight the potential for higher returns from SRI, it cannot be conclusively stated that it consistently leads to superior financial outcomes. As the analyses suggest, this ambiguity may motivate some investors to consciously accept lower financial returns in exchange for the non-financial benefits associated with environmental and social engagement.

Similarly, mixed research findings have emerged in the context of the Polish SRI market, which is still in its early stages of development. Studies suggest that socially responsible investing in Poland is not significantly more effective than conventional investment strategies, or the average performance observed in the broader investment market. However, there are some notable positive examples, such as the RESPECT Index, which outperformed other indices on the Warsaw Stock Exchange in certain periods.

The analyses suggest that, although the effectiveness of SRI remains a subject of ongoing debate, a growing body of research and evolving market practices point to the increasing significance of these investments. In this context, there is a clear need for further investor education and a deeper understanding of responsible investment issues, particularly within the Polish market. Despite existing challenges such as limited availability of assets aligned with ESG criteria and low investor awareness, SRI has the potential to become a significant part of financial management in Poland. This is particularly relevant in light of EU regulations mandating non-financial reporting and in response to global challenges such as climate change, social inequalities, military conflicts and trade wars. It is also relevant in the context of the growing development and application of new technologies, including artificial intelligence. Therefore, the future of SRI will depend on further developing analytical tools, increasing investor awareness and establishing responsible regulations, enabling the full utilisation of SRI's potential in Poland and worldwide.

References

Barnett, M. L., & Salomon, R. M. (2006). Beyond dichotomy: The curvilinear relationship between social responsibility and financial performance. *Strategic Management Journal*, *27*(11), 1101–1122.

Bauer, R., Koedijk, K., & Otten, R. (2005). International evidence on ethical mutual fund performance and investment style. *Journal of Banking & Finance*, *29*, 1751–1767.

Bauer, R., Ruof, T., & Smeets, P. (2021). Get Real! individuals prefer more sustainable investments. *The Review of Financial Studies*, *34*(8), 3976–4043. https://doi.org/10.1093/rfs/hhab037

Bolton, P., & Kacperczyk, M. (2021). Do investors care about carbon risk? *Journal of Financial Economics*, *142*(2), 517–549. https://doi.org/10.1016/j.jfineco.2021.05.008

Brooks, C., & Oikonomou, I. (2018). The effects of environmental, social and governance disclosures and performance on firm value: A review of the literature in accounting and finance. *The British Accounting Review*, *50*(1), 1–15. https://doi.org/10.1016/j.bar.2017.11.005

Brzeszczyński, J., & McIntosh, G. (2014). Performance of portfolios composed of british SRI stocks. *Journal of Business Ethics*, *120*, 335–362.

Camilleri, M. A. (2020). The market for socially responsible investing: A review of the developments. *Social Responsibility Journal*, *17*(3), 412–428. https://doi.org/10.1108/SRJ-06-2019-0194

Corporate Knights. (2022). *Global 100: Most sustainable corporations in the world*. Retrieved May 15, 2024, from http://www.corporateknights.com/reports/global-100/
Czerwińska, T. (2009). Społeczna odpowiedzialność polityki inwestycyjnej funduszy emerytalnych. *Wiadomości Ubezpieczeniowe*, *3*, 11–27.
Czerwińska, T. (2012). Efektywność inwestycji społecznie odpowiedzialnych na rynku akcji. *Problemy Zarządzania*, *10*(4/39), 129–140.
Czerwińska, T., & Kaźmierkiewicz, P. (2015). ESG rating in investment risk analysis of companies listed on the public market in poland. *Economic Notes*, *44*(2), 2. https://doi.org/10.1111/ecno.12031
Diltz, J. D. (1995). The private cost of socially responsible investing. *Applied Financial Economics*, *5*, 69–77.
Dmuchowski, P., Dmuchowski, W., Baczewska-Dąbrowska, A. H., & Gworek, B. (2023). Environmental, social, and governance (ESG) model; Impacts and sustainable investment – Global trends and Poland's perspective. *Journal of Environmental Management*, *329*, 117023. https://doi.org/10.1016/j.jenvman.2022.117023
Doś, A., & Foltyn-Zarychta, M. (2017). Socially responsible investment market size in poland: The content analysis. In D. Procházka (Ed.), *New Trends in Finance and Accounting* (pp. 653–663). Springer International Publishing. https://doi.org/10.1007/978-3-319-49559-0_60
Duliniec, A., & Tomaszewski, J. D. (2016). Inwestowanie etyczne – Zasady i efektywność. *Annales Universitatis Mariae Curie-Skłodowska, Sectio H – Oeconomia*, *50*(4). https://doi.org/10.17951/h.2016.50.4.101
Dziawgo, L. (2022). Environmental aspects of investing in the polish stock exchange market according to individual investors. *Financial Internet Quarterly "E-finanse"*, *18*(4), 4. https://doi.org/10.2478/fiqf-2022-0027
Eurosif. (2017). *Report. European SRI study 2016*. Bruksela. Retrieved March 12, 2023, from http://www.eurosif.org
Fama, E. F., & French, K. R. (2007). Disagreement, tastes, and asset prices. *Journal of Financial Economics*, *83*(3), 667–689. https://doi.org/10.1016/j.jfineco.2006.01.003
Feldman, S. J., Soyka, P. A., & Ameer, P. G. (1997). Does improving a firm's environmental management system and environmental performance result in a higher stock price? *Journal of Investing*, *6*, 87–97.
Friede, G., Busch, T., & Bassen, A. (2015). ESG and financial performance: Aggregated evidence from more than 2000 empirical studies. *Journal of Sustainable Finance & Investment*, *5*(4), 210–233. https://doi.org/10.1080/20430795.2015.1118917
Fritz, T. M., & von Schnurbein, G. (2019). Beyond socially responsible investing: Effects of mission-driven portfolio selection. *Sustainability*, *11*(23), 23. https://doi.org/10.3390/su11236812

Gierałtowska, U. (2017). Inwestowanie odpowiedzialne społecznie – Nowy trend na rynku kapitałowym. *Finanse, Rynki Finansowe, Ubezpieczenia*, *6*(90), 23–36. https://doi.org/10.18276/frfu.2017.90-02

Geczy, C. C., Stambaugh, R. F., & Levin, D. (2005). Investing in socially responsible mutual funds. *Social Science Research Network*. https://doi.org/10.2139/ssrn.416380

Guerard Jr, J. B. (1997). Is there a cost to being socially responsible in investing? *Journal of Investing*, *6*, 87–97.

Hartzmark, S. M., & Sussman, A. B. (2019). Do investors value sustainability? A natural experiment examining ranking and fund flows. *The Journal of Finance*, *74*(6), 2789–2837. https://doi.org/10.1111/jofi.12841

Hong, H., & Kacperczyk, M. (2009). The price of sin: The effects of social norms on markets. *Journal of Financial Economics*, *93*(1), 15–36. https://doi.org/10.1016/j.jfineco.2008.09.001

Jamróz, P., & Żebrowska-Suchodolska, D. (2021). Impact of the COVID-19 pandemic on the results of Polish socially responsible funds. *Optimum. Economic Studies*, *106*(4), 4.

Jarno, K. (2017). Socially responsible investment funds in poland: Market diagnosis and performance assessment. *Studia Oeconomica Posnaniensia*, *5*(6). https://doi.org/10.18559/SOEP.2017.6.1

Kim, I., & Venkatachalam, M. (2011). Are Sin Stocks Paying the Price for Accounting Sins? *Journal of Accounting, Auditing & Finance*, *26*(2), 415–442. https://doi.org/10.1177/0148558X11401222

King, A., & Lenox, M. (2002). Exploring the locus of profitable pollution reduction. *Management Science*, *48*(2), 289–299.

Kłysik-Uryszek, A. (2020). Do investors care about CSR? Evidence from polish public listed companies: Annales. *Etyka W Życiu Gospodarczym*, *23*(4), Article 4.

Kotsantonis, S., Pinney, C., & Serafeim, G. (2016). ESG integration in investment management: Myths and realities. *Journal of Applied Corporate Finance*, *28*(2), 10–16. https://doi.org/10.1111/jacf.12169

Kravchuk, I. (2022). Performance of equity fund investment strategies in Poland. *Sustainability*, *14*(20), 20. https://doi.org/10.3390/su1420130783

Krawczyńska-Kaczmarek, M. (2023). Finansowanie w formule Sustainability Linked katalizatorem zrównoważonej transformacji w realnej gospodarce. In W. L. Kotecki (Ed.), *Zielone Finanse W Polsce* (pp. 50–59). Instytut Odpowiedzialnych Finansów.

Lulewicz-Sas, A., & Kilon, J. (2014a). Analysis of the effectiveness of socially responsible investing funds in Poland. *Economics and Management*, *19*(4), 4. https://doi.org/10.5755/j01.em.19.4.8101

Lulewicz-Sas, A., & Kilon, J. (2014b). The effectiveness of SRI funds in Poland. *Procedia – Social and Behavioral Sciences*, *156*, 194–197. https://doi.org/10.1016/j.sbspro.2014.11.170

Mikołajek-Gocejna, M. (2022). Systematic risk of ESG companies listed on the Polish capital market in 2019–2022. *European Research Studies Journal, XXV* (2), 597–615. https://doi.org/10.35808/ersj/2982

Ministry of Finance. (2000). Regulation on the general permission to invest pension fund assets abroad (Dz.U. 2000 No. 15, item 182). *Journal of Laws*, February 18. https://isap.sejm.gov.pl/isap.nsf/DocDetails.xsp?id=WDU20000150182

Moskowitz, M. (1972). Choosing socially responsible stocks. *Business and Society Review*, *1*, 71–75.

MSCI. (2025, February 28). *MSCI KLD 400 social index (USD): Index factsheet.* Retrieved July 15, 2025, https://www.msci.com/documents/10199/af2f3499-c8fe-497c-afde-4f2fc82465bf

Petelczyc, J. (2022). The readiness for ESG among retail investors in central and Eastern Europe: The example of Poland. *Global Business Review*, *23*(6), 6. https://doi.org/10.1177/09721509221114754

Ramchander, S., Schwebach, R. G., & Staking, K. (2012). The informational relevance of corporate social responsibility: Evidence from SD 400 index reconstructions. *Strategic Management Journal*, *33*, 303–314. https://doi.org/10.1002/smj.952

Remlein, M. (2017). Strategie społecznie odpowiedzialnego inwestowania w polityce inwestycyjnej polskich przedsiębiorstw. *Finanse, Rynki Finansowe, Ubezpieczenia*, *88*(1), 541–551.

Revelli, C., & Viviani, J.-L. (2015). Financial performance of socially responsible investing (SRI): What have we learned? A meta-analysis. *Business Ethics: A European Review*, *24*(2), 158–185.

Riedl, A., & Smeets, P. (2017). Why do investors hold socially responsible mutual funds? *The Journal of Finance*, *72*(6), 2505–2550. https://doi.org/10.1111/jofi.12547

Russell, J. W., & Brockman, C. M. (2011). Do shareholders benefit from sound corporate citizenship? *Review of Business Research*, *11*(5), 21–32.

Russo, M. V., & Fouts, P. A. (1997). A resource-based perspective on corporate environmental performance and profitability. *Academy of Management Journal*, *40*, 534–559.

Salaber, J. (2013). Religion and returns in Europe. *European Journal of Political Economy*, *32*, 149–160. https://doi.org/10.1016/j.ejpoleco.2013.07.002

Schroeder, M. (2007). Is there a difference? The performanc characteristics of SRI equity indices. *Journal of Business Finance & Accounting*, *34*(1/2), 331–348.

Stańczak-Strumiłło, K. (2013). Idea społecznej odpowiedzialności inwestycji w polityce inwestycyjnej polskich funduszy inwestycyjnych. *Zarządzanie I Finanse*, *11*(2), 6474–488.

Statman, M. (2000). Socially responsible mutual funds. *Financial Analyst Journal*, *56*(3), 30–39.

Trinks, P. J., & Scholtens, B. (2017). The opportunity cost of negative screening in socially responsible investing. *Journal of Business Ethics, 140*(2), 193–208. https://doi.org/10.1007/s10551-015-2684-3

U.S. Department of Labor. (1974). *Employee retirement income security Act (ERISA)*. Retrieved July 23, 2024, from https://www.dol.gov/general/topic/retirement/erisa

Wolska, M., & Czerwonka, M. (2013). Społecznie odpowiedzialne inwestowanie – Analiza rentowności funduszy SRI w Polsce. *Studia I Prace Kolegium Zarządzania I Finansów, Szkoła Główna Handlowa, 126*, 9–22.

Zioło, M., Spoz, A., Bak, I., Cheba, K., & Filipiak, B. Z. (2020). Environmental, Social and Governance Risk in Public and Private Financial Systems: Fuzzy Cognitive Mapping Comparative Analysis. In *Proceedings of the 2020 2nd International Conference on Management Science and Industrial Engineering* (pp. 31–38). https://doi.org/10.1145/3396743.3396752

CHAPTER 8

Non-Financial Reporting: Current Guidelines and Inherent Challenges

8.1 Introduction

This chapter provides an in-depth analysis of the current guidelines that govern non-financial reporting, as well as the ongoing challenges associated with them. It examines international frameworks, paying particular attention to Environmental, Social and Governance (ESG) criteria, which are crucial for how companies communicate their commitment to sustainable development. Particular focus is given to recent regulatory developments within the European Union, notably the Non-Financial Reporting Directive (NFRD) and its successor, the Corporate Sustainability Reporting Directive (CSRD). These initiatives represent a substantial shift towards more extensive and rigorous disclosure requirements for companies operating within the EU.

In addition, the chapter examines the current state of non-financial reporting in Poland. It outlines the applicable guidelines and regulatory frameworks and presents empirical findings on the reporting practices of Polish companies in this area. It draws attention to the challenges associated with implementing new standards, as well as the benefits of transparency and an integrated approach to reporting that considers both the financial and non-financial aspects of companies' operations. Several challenges are

The original version of the chapter has been revised. A correction to this chapter can be found at https://doi.org/10.1007/978-3-032-11666-6_10

K. Łudzińska, *International ESG Perspectives*,
https://doi.org/10.1007/978-3-032-11666-6_8

also discussed, including the package of simplifications proposed by the European Commission under the name 'Omnibus I'. Overall, the chapter provides a thorough overview of the evolution of non-financial reporting in both the international arena and the Polish context.

8.2 International Guidelines and Key Features of Non-Financial Reporting

8.2.1 *Financial Reporting vs. ESG Reporting*

The contemporary market is placing increasing demands on companies with regard to operational transparency. This requires the disclosure of not only financial information, but also data relating to areas such as environmental protection, human resource management, innovation, development strategies and other non-financial matters. Consequently, non-financial reporting has recently become a vital part of corporate communication with the wider socio-economic environment. It provides valuable insights into management practices and the company's impact on various stakeholders, including employees, the local community and the natural environment. In an era of increasing social awareness and pressure for businesses to be socially and ecologically responsible, investors, consumers and business partners expect transparency in organisations' activities. Moreover, as Świderska (2007) notes, discrepancies between the book value presented in financial reports and the company's actual value suggest that financial statements do not meet stakeholders' informational needs.

Since the concept of Environmental, Social and Governance was first proposed in the 2004 UN report, 'Who Cares Wins: Connecting Financial Markets to a Changing World' (UN, 2004), ESG has become embedded in all regions, industries, and types of companies and organisations. Over time, companies have increasingly allocated resources towards improving their performance in line with ESG criteria (Pérez et al., 2022). Currently, over 90% of companies in the S&P 500 index and around 70% of companies in the Russell 1000 index publish ESG reports (G&A Institute, 2021). A 2020 study by KPMG showed that 80% of global companies publish non-financial reports, including almost 90% of American companies (Threlfall et al., 2020). According to Corporate Register, a total of 31,672 companies worldwide have made over 193,460 non-financial reports available so far (as of 15 March 2025, CorporateRegister.com, 2025). It is worth noting that, until relatively recently, non-financial reporting was voluntary worldwide and not mandated by law. In Europe, this changed with the introduction of the Non-Financial Reporting Directive (NFRD) in 2014, which established the first legal requirements for large organisations within the European Union (European Parliament & Council, 2014). In February 2024, China's three stock exchanges issued ESG reporting guidelines under the auspices of the China Securities Regulatory Commission (CSRC), mandating that companies in the SSE 180 Index, STAR 50 Index, SZSE 100 Index and ChiNext Index, as well as those listed domestically and overseas, disclose their ESG data from 2026 onwards (UNEP, 2025).

In both literature and business practice, non-financial reports are referred to by various terms, including ESG reports, corporate responsibility reports, social reports and sustainability reports. Despite these different labels, they are unified by a common principle: unlike financial reports, which present a company's financial position and economic performance using instruments such as balance sheets, income statements and cash flow statements, non-financial reports focus on a company's actions and outcomes in terms of environmental impact, social responsibility and corporate governance.

Of the many reports that companies prepare and publish, three main categories can be distinguished: financial reports, non-financial reports and integrated reports. Financial reports are the most established of these and are prepared in accordance with national regulatory frameworks, as well as international financial reporting standards. These reports form the basis of corporate reporting worldwide. The leading authority in this area is the IFRS Foundation (International Financial Reporting Standards Foundation), a non-profit organisation dedicated to developing high-quality, understandable and enforceable accounting standards accepted worldwide. In recent years, the IFRS Foundation has also expanded its remit to include the disclosure of sustainability-related information (IFRS Foundation, n.d.-b). In Poland, corporate reporting is governed by the Accounting Act and detailed regulations applicable to specific types of entities (Sejm of the Republic of Poland, 1994). The primary form of periodic disclosure is the annual report, the core component of which is the financial statement. This includes the balance sheet, profit and loss account, cash flow statement and any other documents required by the established legal framework.

Non-financial reports provide information on a company's activities relating to environmental impact, social responsibility and corporate governance over a defined reporting period, usually one year. They present a comprehensive overview of the company's strategy and environmental and social policies, as well as its responsibilities towards key stakeholders. Non-financial reports are intended for a wide range of stakeholders, including not only owners, shareholders and potential investors, but also customers, suppliers and the general public. In most cases, non-financial reports are published electronically and made publicly accessible via company websites.

The third and final type of corporate reporting is the integrated report, which combines financial and non-financial information. It presents key data on an organisation's strategy, governance, performance and future outlook, reflecting the broader economic, social and environmental context in which the company operates (Ministry of Economy of the Republic of Poland, 2013). This format brings together the most essential elements typically disclosed separately, such as the financial report, management report, corporate governance statement and sustainability report, in a single document, thereby offering a more cohesive and comprehensive view of the organisation's activities.

Christensen et al. (2021) provided a thorough summary of the main differences between financial and ESG reporting. According to the authors, the broad scope of issues addressed in ESG reporting often extends beyond companies' core operational activities. Consequently, non-financial reporting differs fundamentally from traditional financial reporting, the latter of which focuses primarily on the financial implications of a company's core business operations. The specific features of ESG reporting are summarised in Table 8.1.

The key features of ESG reporting, as presented in Table 8.1, are associated with heterogeneous reporting practices. The diversity of corporate actions related to ESG aspects poses significant challenges in terms of measurement, comparability and standardisation, including with regard to financial reporting. It is both necessary and timely to develop international accounting standards that incorporate sustainability and ESG criteria, as these are increasingly being demanded by the market.[1]

From a non-financial reporting perspective, it is important to distinguish between ESG reporting and broader non-financial disclosures by companies. The latter are often referred to in the literature as social and

[1] The Integrated Reporting page of the International Financial Reporting Standards (IFRS) Foundation provides informational materials and examples of integrated reports (IFRS Foundation, n.d.-a).

Table 8.1 Characteristics of ESG reporting

No.	*Integral features*	*Characteristics*
1.	Diversity of users and applications	The potential audience for ESG reporting is broader than for financial reporting; even if standards are developed with investors' needs in mind, once ESG information is disclosed, anyone can benefit from it, not just management experts
2.	Diversity of topics	CSR and sustainability encompass a wide range of ESG topics, actions and policies; these topics vary significantly depending on the company, industry and country; as a result, ESG reporting is multidimensional, leading to a wide range of disclosures and reporting formats and making comparisons and standardization difficult (e.g., Liang & Renneboog, 2017b; Amel-Zadeh & Serafeim, 2018)
3.	Purpose function	ESG reporting serves many purposes and responds to a wide range of interests and preferences both inside and outside the company; these interests and preferences can dynamically change, for example, when the company becomes the target of activist campaigns as a result of events such as an accident or a disaster independent of the company (e.g., Bonetti et al., 2023)
4.	Diversity of measurements	Many CSR actions manifest in observable and measurable behaviours or outcomes (e.g., CO_2 emissions, number of trees saved), but they are not necessarily measurable in monetary terms (Kitzmueller & Shimshack, 2012), and due to the lack of uniform ESG reporting standards, it is difficult to apply typical accounting standards to them (e.g., Cohen & Simnett, 2015; Moroney & Trotman, 2016)
5.	Voluntary nature of CSR actions	For most companies, CSR actions and policies are still voluntary and go beyond legal, regulatory and contractual requirements; for example, a company may reduce environmental pollution beyond legal requirements or provide a public good to the local community; as a result, what companies disclose, and report is their choice
6.	Long-term horizon	CSR is often seen as a 'strategic' activity, which foregoes short-term profits in exchange for long-term benefits to the company (e.g., Bénabou & Tirole, 2010); therefore, ESG reporting often has to deal with long-term perspectives, which are difficult to quantify and are intangible in nature (e.g., employee relations)

(continued)

Table 8.1 (continued)

No.	*Integral features*	*Characteristics*
7.	Key role of external effects	CSR often refers to external effects, i.e., the impact of companies on the environment and society, which is a classic example of An example is the emission of CO_2; addressing such external effects is one of the main motivations for the ESG reporting system; moreover, ESG reporting can cover topics and actions that go beyond the traditional boundaries of the company (e.g., when the company imposes restrictions on child labour among partners, in its supply chain)

Source Based on Amel-Zadeh and Serafeim (2018); Bénabou and Tirole (2010); Bonetti et al. (2023); Christensen et al. (2021); Kitzmueller and Shimshack (2012); Liang and Renneboog (2017b); Moroney and Trotman (2016)

environmental disclosures. Non-financial disclosure can be defined as a company providing information to the public concerning its performance, standards or actions within the framework of corporate social responsibility, typically as part of, or in addition to, its annual financial report or in a standalone document (Brooks & Oikonomou, 2018).

In response to demands from investors and other stakeholders, many companies worldwide are disclosing information about their socially and environmentally responsible actions (Tsang et al., 2023). While the number of such disclosures has increased significantly in recent decades, the majority remain voluntary and unaudited (Christensen et al., 2021). This information can have consequences for consumers, various stakeholders and, primarily, capital market participants. Consequently, an increasing number of companies are adopting more professional and responsible disclosure practices. According to a KPMG study of sustainability reporting practices, around 50% of large and medium-sized companies invested in the external verification of their sustainable development information in 2020, representing a 30% increase compared to 2010 (Threlfall et al., 2020). Although ESG disclosure is often equated with reporting (e.g. Brooks & Oikonomou, 2018; Conca et al., 2021), it differs from reporting in several fundamental respects, as presented in Table 8.2. In short, while every non-financial report constitutes a disclosure of company information in the ESG area, not every ESG-related disclosure qualifies as a non-financial report.

Table 8.2 Disclosure versus ESG reporting

ESG disclosure	*ESG reporting*
• Various forms of communication and information transmission, including press releases, interviews, investor presentations, etc.	• Usually in the form of a formal report • Developed in accordance with specific standards and guidelines, which require structure and clarity in presenting information • An organised, formal process that meets specific assumptions and formal requirements regarding, among others, ways of presenting data and information and their analysis
• A flexible process that can encompass various aspects of a company's operations related to ESG factors	• Includes specific information about the company's actions and their results in the environmental, social and corporate governance areas
• Continuously and in response to specific events or needs	• Periodically, for example, once a year
• Flexible selection of communication methods, depending on the needs and capabilities of the organisation, including own websites, social media profiles, external information portals, etc.	• The report is published in a predetermined, agreed-upon manner; the report is most often placed on the official company website and also distributed to interested stakeholders, including investors, regulators, auditors and other participants in the capital market

When it comes to social and environmental reporting, companies can either act proactively, exceeding the minimum expectations of stakeholders, or reactively, responding to social pressures as they arise (Norris & O'Dwyer, 2004). The quantity and quality of ESG disclosure practices can vary significantly depending on the company. Conca et al. (2021) therefore examined the effectiveness of ESG reporting by analysing its impact on the profitability and value of companies listed on European exchanges. Their findings suggest that such practices influence company profitability. Interestingly, they found a positive relationship between profitability and environmental and social disclosure practices, and a negative relationship between market value and corporate governance disclosure practices. These results suggest that greater transparency in disclosing social and environmental information improves company profitability, whereas governance-related disclosures do not have the same effect.

In the context of the evolution of non-financial reporting, a relatively recent trend has emerged: the integration of financial and non-financial information into a single document. Known as 'integrated reporting', this approach is said by its proponents to offer a more comprehensive view of how a company creates value (Landau et al., 2020). Work on international standards for integrated reporting began in August 2010 with the establishment of the International Integrated Reporting Council (IIRC), a global coalition of regulatory bodies, investors, companies, standard-setting entities, accounting professionals, academics and NGOs (International Integrated Reporting Council, n.d.). The IIRC aims to develop a widely accepted conceptual framework for integrated reporting, which it defines as 'a concise communication about how an organisation's strategy, governance, performance and prospects, in the context of its external environment, lead to the creation of value in the short, medium and long term' (International Integrated Reporting Council, n.d.).

In the absence of a uniform standard for non-financial reporting, companies often rely on various widely used guidelines in this area. Figure 8.1 shows the proportion of the most prominent non-financial reporting standards among all the available frameworks recommended by stock exchanges worldwide for their listed companies. One of the most widely used standards is that developed by the pioneering Global Reporting Initiative (GRI), an independent organisation founded in 1997 (GRI, n.d.). The GRI standards are used by companies in over 90 countries to prepare their non-financial

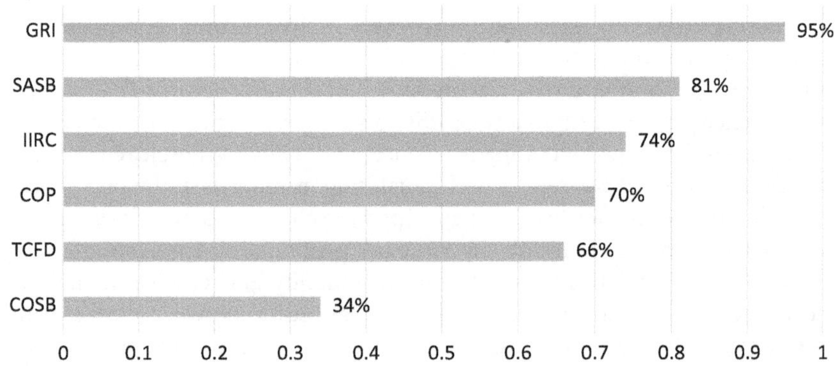

Fig. 8.1 Reporting instruments referenced in stock exchange guidelines documents. *Source* Based on Sustainable Stock Exchange Initiative (2025)

reports. The GRI collaborates with international organisations, including the OECD, the UN Global Compact, the UN Environment Programme (UNEP) and the International Organization for Standardization (ISO), and advises governments, stock exchange boards and legislators in many countries on socially responsible reporting standards. GRI standards are the most widely adopted voluntary guidelines for corporate social responsibility reporting globally. In 2020, 78% of the world's 250 largest companies prepared their sustainability reports in accordance with the GRI framework (Threlfall et al., 2020). GRI standards are periodically updated, typically every few years. The most recent update, the GRI 2021 Standards, replaced the earlier 'G4' standards, which were introduced in 2013 and revised in 2016. The current GRI standards offer a modular system consisting of three series: universal, sectoral and thematic (GRI, 2021).

Non-financial reporting has become an integral part of responsible corporate communication. Such reporting is comprehensive and multi-faceted, going beyond traditional financial information to encompass social, environmental and other aspects that are important to various stakeholders. The benefits of an integrated reporting approach are numerous and significant (IIRC, 2017). By combining financial and non-financial information, integrated reporting provides a more comprehensive view of a company's operations, including its economic, social and environmental performance. This holistic perspective improves understanding of the organisation's impact on its external environment and strengthens the connections between different areas of its operations, facilitating a more effective assessment of their interdependencies. Additionally, integrated reporting provides insight into a company's potential to create value over different time periods, supporting the presentation of its business model and improving access to finance. Thanks to transparency and accountability, this approach fosters trust among stakeholders, mitigates the risk of reputational damage, and encourages a long-term development vision. Furthermore, integrated reporting strengthens relationships with investors and other key stakeholders, thereby increasing market stability and engagement in the reporting process.

In conclusion, despite its growing importance and undeniable benefits, non-financial reporting is not without certain limitations. As Krzysztofek (2018) points out, involving multiple stakeholder groups in the reporting process can lead to complications and conflicting expectations. The lack of standardisation and uniformity of non-financial indicators makes analysing and interpreting data difficult, and non-financial information is not always comparable across companies, which complicates interpretation further.

Moreover, an imbalance in the amount of financial versus non-financial information disclosed may distort the overall perception of a company's operations. Information overload and potential chaos can cause key issues to be overlooked by recipients. The process of creating a non-financial report is often labour-intensive and costly, which can pose a challenge for smaller enterprises. Companies aiming for transparent and accurate non-financial reporting must carefully navigate these challenges to avoid inadvertently misleading stakeholders. For this reason, there is an urgent need to introduce universal, international regulations on non-financial reporting. The European Union has already taken steps in this direction. According to a report by the European Financial Reporting Advisory Group (EFRAG), the introduction of statutory and implementing regulations is necessary to enhance the relevance, comparability and reliability of disclosed environmental, social and governance information (EFRAG, 2021).

8.2.2 Towards International Standards for Sustainability Reporting

The history of non-financial reporting dates back to the 1980s. Until 31 December 2016, it was a voluntary practice for companies in most countries, including those in Europe and Poland. Currently, the disclosure of environmental, social and governance (ESG) information takes various forms internationally. It is mandatory for all capital companies in countries such as the United States, Australia, France, Hong Kong and China, partially mandatory for selected entities in jurisdictions including the European Union, the United Kingdom and mainland China, and voluntary in countries such as Brazil and Singapore (GRI, 2023). In the United States, the Securities and Exchange Commission (SEC) is considering introducing new rules that would require more detailed disclosure of climate-related risks and greenhouse gas emissions. Additional SEC regulations concerning other ESG aspects have also been proposed and are already in the process of being enacted (SEC, 2022). The United Nations has recommended that all large companies be required to publish sustainability reports by 2030 (UNEP, 2013).

In February 2024, the China Securities Regulatory Commission (CSRC) oversaw the publication of ESG reporting guidelines by Chinese securities exchanges. Under the new regulations, companies belonging to the SSE 180, STAR 50, SZSE 100 and ChiNext indices, as well as those listed on domestic and foreign markets, will be required to disclose ESG data from 2026 onwards. The CSRC also encourages other companies to voluntarily publish ESG reports (UNEP, 2025). In December 2024, the Ministry of Finance of the People's Republic of China introduced the 'Corporate Sustainability Disclosure Standards—Basic Standards', establishing general requirements for Chinese enterprises to disclose sustainability information (Briefieng, 2024). These guidelines are largely based on the International Sustainability Standards Board's (ISSB) standards and also require companies to apply the principle of double materiality. This means they must assess the impact of ESG factors on their financial performance, as well as their broader effects on the environment, society and corporate governance.

The publication of these guidelines is a significant step in developing a culture of disclosure in China. It marks the start of the Ministry of Finance of the People's Republic of China's plan to issue general sustainability disclosure standards for enterprises (based on IFRS S1) and climate-related disclosure standards (based on IFRS S2) by 2027. The aim is to lay the groundwork for establishing a national sustainability information disclosure system by 2030 (UNEP, 2025).

The Carbon Disclosure Project (CDP) was one of the first international initiatives for the disclosure of non-financial information, particularly related to climate change. Since 2000, this international non-profit organisation has run the world's largest environmental data disclosure system (CDP, 2025). The system enables enterprises and local government units, including cities and regions, to report the impact of their activities on the climate, water resources and forests in a standardised, comparable format. The CDP promotes and supports environmental transparency to strengthen organisations' responsibility towards the natural environment. Data collected as part of this initiative is one of the most recognised and widely used sources of environmental information in ESG analyses conducted by investors, analysts and researchers worldwide (e.g., Hassan et al., 2013; Li et al., 2018; Matisoff et al., 2013). According to the organisation's data, companies from 130 countries currently report key environmental impact data through CDP, accounting for two-thirds of global market capitalisation (CDP, 2025). Notably, within two years of the initial reporting request, companies disclosing data through the CDP reduce their direct emissions by an average of 7–10%.

The environmental data disclosure questionnaire developed by CDP is aligned with the international sustainability standards and initiatives discussed in Chap. 3. In particular, it supports disclosures in line with the Greenhouse Gas Protocol (GHG Protocol), the Accountability Framework Initiative (AFi) on responsible sourcing and deforestation prevention, and the CEO Water Mandate—a UN initiative that promotes sustainable water resource management within the private sector. Integrating these standards establishes CDP as a reporting tool and a platform that enables the harmonisation of sustainable environmental management practices on a global scale (CDP, 2025).

In response to the growing demand for consistent and reliable reporting on climate risk and related opportunities, the G20 Financial Stability Board established the Task Force on Climate-Related Financial Disclosures (TCFD) in 2015. In 2017, the TCFD presented a climate reporting structure. The TCFD‘s recommendations focus on four key areas: governance, strategy, risk management and metrics and targets (TCFD, 2017). Although the TCFD‘s recommendations are voluntary and stem from a market-led initiative, regulatory bodies actively encourage their adoption by a wide range of market participants. One example of this is the non-binding guidelines on climate-related disclosures that supplement the Non-Financial Reporting Directive (NFRD). These guidelines recognise the TCFD recommendations as authoritative standards for communicating financially material climate information and explicitly incorporate them into their scope (TCFD, 2017).

In March 2022, the International Sustainability Standards Board (ISSB) published draft versions of two standards: IFRS S1 and IFRS S2. Following public consultations, both standards were officially issued in June 2023 in collaboration with the IFRS Foundation. While IFRS S1 outlines general requirements for the disclosure of sustainability-related financial information, IFRS S2 focuses specifically on the disclosure of climate-related information. It is worth noting that these new standards introduce demanding reporting criteria, with a number of consequences for entities subject to them. These include the need to develop a dedicated reporting system and integrate it with existing financial reporting frameworks. Furthermore, the role of auditors and the potential overlap between the new requirements and existing sustainability-related accounting and reporting regulations remain unresolved issues (Indyk, 2022).

On 15 April 2014, the European Parliament adopted Directive 2014/95/EU, commonly known as the Non-Financial Reporting Directive (NFRD), which applies to European Union member states, including

Poland. The Directive introduced a mandatory ESG reporting obligation[2] for 'public interest entities'[3] employing an average of more than 500 people per year, and meeting either of the following financial thresholds: a balance sheet total of at least €20 million at the end of the financial year; or net turnover exceeding €40 million in at least two consecutive financial years (European Parliament & Council, 2014). The directive came into force on 1 January 2017, marking the end of voluntary corporate social responsibility reporting for certain companies. The European Commission estimated that the NFRD initially applied to around 6000 of the largest companies in the EU. In 2019, the directive was supplemented with climate-related disclosure guidelines developed by the Task Force on Climate-related Financial Disclosures (TCFD) (European Commission, 2019a).

These optional guidelines were designed to help organisations subject to the NFRD disclose their environmental impact and the effects of climate change on their operations more effectively. The European Commission encouraged the presentation of climate-related information across the five key reporting areas defined by the NFRD: business model; policies and due diligence; outcomes of these policies; primary risk factors and risk management; and key performance indicators.

On 21 April 2021, the European Commission adopted a proposal for a new directive on corporate sustainability reporting—the Corporate Sustainability Reporting Directive (CSRD)—amending the existing reporting requirements with effect from 1 January 2024. The CSRD introduces mandatory environmental, social and governance (ESG) reporting for all large companies and large capital groups, including large listed companies. This Directive significantly expands the scope of entities subject to non-financial reporting requirements. It also applies to public interest entities such as listed companies, banks and insurance companies, as well as large enterprises with over 500 employees. In subsequent implementation phases, the obligation will extend further. For reports covering the year 2025 (to be published in 2026), it will apply to all remaining large companies under the CSRD, defined as those employing more than 250

[2] In addition to the financial report, companies are required to prepare a separate non-financial report, for which there is no strict format. However, it is recommended that they use international standards such as the GRI Standards, the UN Global Compact or ISO 26,000.

[3] This requirement applies to companies listed on stock exchanges and to entities of public significance, including banks, insurance companies and investment funds. Further details can be found in Sect. 8.2, which covers non-financial reporting in Poland.

people. Finally, for reports covering the year 2026 (to be published in 2027), the requirement will extend to the final group: small and medium-sized listed enterprises with over 10 employees (European Parliament & Council, 2022). Following its publication in the Official Journal of the EU on 16 December 2022, Member States were given 18 months to transpose the Corporate Sustainability Reporting Directive (CSRD) into national law (Ministry of Funds and Regional Policy, 2023). In Poland, the directive was incorporated into the legal framework through an amendment to the Accounting Act, which was adopted on 6 December 2024 (Sejm of the Republic of Poland, 2024). The CSRD replaced the previously applicable Non-Financial Reporting Directive (NFRD). Table 8.3 presents a comparison of the key principles and non-financial reporting requirements set out in both directives.

Since January 2024, the CSRD has mandated large companies to disclose their non-financial performance, with the inaugural ESG reports being published in 2025. The directive establishes a mandatory requirement for Environmental, Social and Governance (ESG) reporting for all substantial companies and capital groups, encompassing listed firms, banking institutions and insurance companies, thereby considerably expanding the ambit of entities obligated to submit non-financial reports. The obligation is being phased in, with the 2025 reports (published in 2026) covering all large companies with more than 250 employees, and the 2026 reports (published in 2027) extending to small and medium-sized listed enterprises with more than 10 employees (European Parliament & Council, 2022).

The European Commission is currently engaged in the development of common, uniform reporting standards for corporate sustainability disclosures. As part of this initiative, on 31 July 2023, it published the inaugural set of 12 European Sustainability Reporting Standards (ESRS), which are to be applied by all companies subject to the Corporate Sustainability Reporting Directive (CSRD) (European Commission, 2023a). The ESRS standards were developed by experts from the European Commission, the European Financial Reporting Advisory Group, EFRAG (EFRAG, n.d.) and the International Sustainability Standards Board (ISSB) (IFRS, 2023a). These organisations collaborated to enhance the interoperability of overlapping disclosure requirements and standards related to environmental protection. Consequently, the guidelines underwent an adaptation process that led to their simplification, with the objective of facilitating their application by entities seeking to comply with both the ISSB and ESRS frameworks. The European Commission, in collaboration with EFRAG and

Table 8.3 Comparison of key principles and reporting requirements under the NFRD and CSRD directives

Instrument	*NFRD*	*CSRD*
Scope	Public companies employing over 500 workers	• From 01.01.2024: companies listed on the stock exchange and large enterprises meeting at least two out of three criteria: balance sheet total min. 20 million EUR; net turnover 40 million EUR, or employment of 250 workers • From 01.01.2027: enterprises employing over 10 workers
Information in the report	• Environmental issues • Social matters and employee situation • Respect for human rights • Anti-corruption measures • Diversity in company boards (in terms of age, gender, education and experience)	Information included in NFRD and: • Company strategy and objectives • Role of management and leadership • Main negative impacts related to the company's operations and its supply chain • Method of identifying reported Information
Reporting standard	None, non-binding guidelines regarding: • Non-financial reporting (2017) and • Climate (2019)	EU standards (European Sustainability Reporting Standards, ESRS) defining the way of reporting threats related to environmental, social and corporate governance areas
Type of document	Report as part of the management report or a separate document	Management report
Report format	Flexible and arbitrary	Digital, machine-readable, considering taxonomy in digital reading
Reporting audit	Not required	Required in the form of ***limited assurance*** (analysis and review of information), and at a later stage—***reasonable assurance*** (detailed analysis of presented information)
Sanctions and enforcement of regulations	None	Enforcement of reporting by relevant national authorities based on the guidelines of the European Securities and Markets Authority (ESMA)

Source Based on Pfaff et al. (2021)

the ISSB, will continue efforts to enhance the interoperability of sustainability reporting standards. In addition to the issuance of guidelines to assist entities in navigating between frameworks, future endeavours will concentrate on the digital tagging of disclosures as a means of further facilitating interoperability. In practice, this includes ensuring that non-financial reports prepared in accordance with the Global Reporting Initiative (GRI) standards, will be compatible with the new ESRS framework (GRI, 2023).

The ESRS standards adopt a modular structure, comprising distinct yet interconnected components (see, Table 8.4). The establishment of uniform reporting requirements represents a significant shift in the practices of disclosing ESG information. A salient development is the implementation of mandatory audits for ESRS-compliant non-financial reports. Furthermore, the provision of false information may result in both financial and criminal liability, including for members of company boards (EFRAG, 2023).

In terms of content, the ESRS constitutes a comprehensive set of standards covering the full spectrum of ESG aspects, with particular emphasis on environmental aspects, especially climate indicators. In the context of the five ESRS standards that pertain to environmental issues, ESRS E1—Climate Change—occupies a position of particular importance (Grzybek, 2023). The primary focus of the initiative is the disclosure of an entity's transition plan towards carbon neutrality. It is imperative to note that these requirements will be binding for all companies, irrespective of whether they have identified these issues as key. Furthermore, the E1 standard places significant emphasis on the reporting of emissions throughout the company's value chain. It is evident that other standards, such as ESRS E2 ('Pollution') and ESRS E3 ('Water and Marine Resources'), similarly emphasise the reporting of policies, objectives and actions pertaining to the control of pollution and the management of water and marine resources. The ESRS E4 standard, which addresses biodiversity and ecosystems, introduces additional requirements related to the setting and disclosure of biodiversity objectives. Conversely, ESRS E5 places emphasis on the effective utilisation of resources and promotes the implementation of circular economy business models. Collectively, these standards constitute a comprehensive framework for environmentally responsible corporate conduct.

While certain aspects pertaining to ESG are universally applicable and of significance to all companies, the relevance of others is subject to variation depending on the industry, the particulars of a given company, and its business context. Consequently, the ESRS reporting standards also indicate

Table 8.4 ESRS standard groups

Cross-cutting standards		
ESRS 1. General principles The ESRS 1 standard does not include specific indicators; instead, it outlines the overarching principles for applying the ESRS framework and for preparing sustainability reports in accordance with its requirements. **ESRS 2. Requirements for disclosing general information, strategy, management and materiality assessment** The ESRS 2 standard includes a set of mandatory indicators (12 required disclosures), related to general information about the reporting entity, strategy, management, as well as the materiality analysis conducted for the purpose of the report (ESRS introduces a double materiality principle in this respect).		
Sector-independent thematic standards *		
Environment (E)	***Society (S)***	***Corporate Governance (G)***
ESRS E1—Climate Change (9) ESRS E2—Pollution (6) ESRS E3—Water and Marine Resources (5) ESRS E4—Biodiversity and Ecosystems (6) ESRS E5—Resource Utilisation and Circular Economy (6)	ESRS S1—Employment (17) ESRS S2—Employees in the value chain (5) ESRS S3—Social environment (5) ESRS S4—Consumers and end users (5)	ESRS G1—Business Practices (6)

* The number of required disclosures is given in brackets
Source Based on European Commission (2023b), EY (2023), KPMG (2023a, 2023b)

which ESG factors to consider important according to the so-called double materiality principle. Double materiality is a concept that provides companies with a framework for determining which actions to include in mandatory non-financial reporting, in accordance with the CSRD directive and ESRS. The principle of double materiality is predicated on two factors: firstly, the significance of the company's impact on society and the environment; and secondly, the financial materiality of these impacts from the company's perspective (see, Fig. 8.2). An ESG-related action is defined as 'double material' if it is significant from the perspective of its impact on

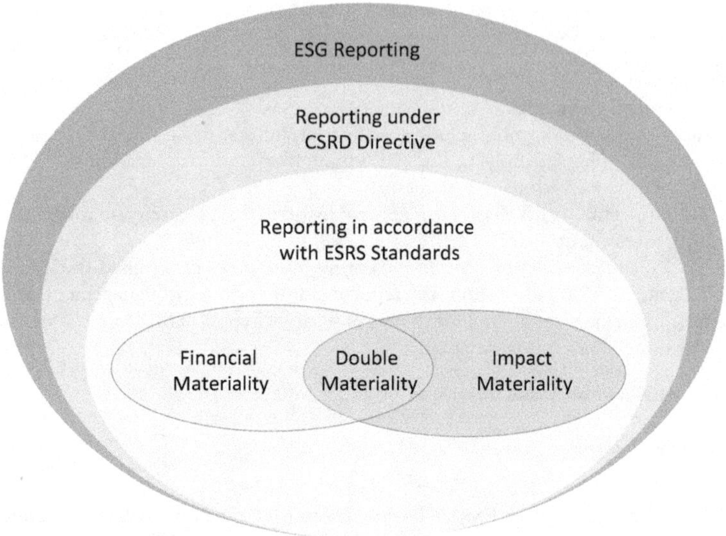

Fig. 8.2 ESG reporting framework under the CSRD directive and ESRS standards. *Source* Inspired by the Polish ESG Association (2024)

society and/or the environment and from a financial perspective, i.e., when it is material from both perspectives simultaneously. The term 'financial significance' is used to denote both actual and potential risks and opportunities that may affect the company's financial condition. Conversely, the concept of impact significance pertains to the tangible or potential adverse ramifications of a company's operations, whether directly or indirectly through its value chain, on the environment and society (EFRAG, 2022).

The most recent legislative act regulating the scope of non-financial reporting in European Union member states, particularly regarding companies' impacts across their value chains, is the Corporate Sustainability Due Diligence Directive (CSDDD), also known as CS3D (European Parliament & Council, 2024). The directive is scheduled to come into force for the first group of entities on 1 January 2027. The Act introduces mandatory due diligence procedures concerning respect for human rights and environmental matters for certain categories of companies, including those that:

- It is imperative that an average of more than 1000 employees is employed, and that global net sales revenues exceeding €450 million are generated.
- In the absence of meeting the aforementioned thresholds, an organisation should employ an average of more than 250 employees and generate net revenues of at least €40 million, provided that it operates in high-impact sectors such as textile production, agriculture, forestry, fishing and extraction of mineral resources.

The CSDDD directive provides a precise definition of companies' responsibility for the potentially negative effects of their activities, thereby facilitating their accountability in the event of causing damage. Individuals adversely affected by the reprehensible actions of corporate entities will be granted enhanced access to legal aid. Moreover, the directive extends the principles of applying due diligence procedures to the entire chain of activities related to companies, obliging them to exercise due diligence throughout their supply chain.

In the context of ESG reporting in the European capital market, including Poland, the provisions of the regulation of the European Parliament and of the Council of 27 November 2019 on sustainability-related disclosures in the financial services sector, commonly known as the Sustainable Finance Disclosure Regulation (SFDR), are also of considerable importance. The SFRD introduces a series of transparency requirements with regard to the communication of sustainability-related information within the financial services sector. It obliges financial market participants to disclose on their websites how they integrate sustainability risks into their investment decision-making processes, as well as how their remuneration policies are aligned with those risks (European Parliament & Council, 2019). At the level of the product, the regulation stipulates that financial service providers must disclose their methodology for considering ESG criteria, as well as their approach to fulfilling the environmental or social characteristics they purport to promote. The regulation aims to eliminate the practice of greenwashing, defined as the false presentation of products as 'green', and seeks to harmonise disclosures so that investors can more easily compare products in terms of their impact on sustainable development.

The provisions of the SFDR regulation were amended and supplemented by the regulation of the European Parliament and the Council (EU) 2020/852 of 18 June 2020 on establishing a framework to facilitate sustainable investments (European Parliament & Council, 2020). This regulation serves to complement and further specify selected aspects of the SFDR regulation. The objective of this supplementary legislation is to ensure that investments financed in the European Union as 'sustainable' contribute to sustainable development goals. In view of the wide range of activities deemed to be socially, environmentally and governance responsible, there was a necessity for a unified classification catalogue. This development subsequently gave rise to the formulation of the aforementioned regulatory framework, which is more commonly referred to as the EU Taxonomy. The EU Taxonomy is a regulatory instrument that establishes comprehensive technical criteria for diverse sectors and categories of economic activity, thereby enabling an evaluation of their adherence to the principles of sustainability. This clarifies which investments can be considered as meeting the environmental, social and governance standards, and which do not meet these criteria. The EU Taxonomy's fundamental objective is to enhance transparency and facilitate comparability of investment practices, thereby enabling investors to make informed decisions that are aligned with sustainable development goals (Maruszkin, 2021). Concurrently, it functions as a mechanism for the redirection of private investments towards more sustainable economic activities, whilst concomitantly promoting transparency and credibility in the financial sector. At present, the EU Taxonomy places the primary emphasis on environmental issues; however, there are also plans to extend it to social and governance aspects. The collaboration between the two regulations, the Sustainable Finance Disclosure Regulation (SFDR) and the EU Taxonomy, is instrumental in enhancing transparency within the domain of sustainable investments within the European Union. This collaboration enables investors to differentiate more accurately between actions that are authentically aligned with the principles of sustainable development and those that may be presented as such but are not, in reality.

Concurrently, the EU Taxonomy constitutes a pivotal element of the European Action Plan for Financing Sustainable Growth (European Commission, 2018) and has been incorporated as a component of the European Green Deal, an initiative designed to achieve climate neutrality by 2050 (European Commission, 2019b). The European Green Deal is a policy agenda aimed at redirecting capital towards sustainable investments. The overarching objective of the Deal is to facilitate sustainable growth, to manage the risks associated with climate change, to reduce the negative environmental impact and to promote transparency in financial and economic activity.

To summarise the overview of key European Union regulations relevant to the non-financial reporting process, it is important to emphasise that these legislative acts are complementary, and their provisions mutually reinforce and supplement one another. The CSRD directive, CSDDD directive and the EU Taxonomy are components of the European Union's comprehensive regulatory framework for sustainable development (Polish ESG Association, 2024). The overarching objective of the aforementioned framework is the promotion of corporate responsibility and sustainable development. The CSRD imposes a detailed reporting obligation on companies regarding their ESG activities, which includes, among other elements, compliance with CSRD requirements and alignment with the criteria of the EU Taxonomy. The CSDDD obliges companies to implement due diligence mechanisms, such as risk management and minimising negative social and environmental impacts, which are often subject to reporting under the CSRD framework. Meanwhile, the EU Taxonomy establishes standards and criteria for identifying sustainable actions, thereby serving as a pivotal reference point for comprehensive reporting within the CSRD framework.

Fig. 8.3 Scope of interaction between EU Regulations in the ESG area. *Note* *Omnibus I update as of 16.04.2025 (European Parliament & Council, 2025b). *Source* Inspired by the Polish ESG Association (2024)

An integrated approach combining CSRD, CSDDD and the EU Taxonomy (Fig. 8.3) enhances the transparency of information provided by companies, thereby enabling more effective ESG risk management and promoting investment in sustainable projects.

8.2.3 Omnibus I: Simplification Package of EU Sustainability Regulations

In response to the mounting discourse surrounding the issue of regulatory overload in the domain of sustainable development, the European Commission has initiated a series of measures aimed at streamlining its legal frameworks. On 26 February 2025, the Commission unveiled a legislative package, designated *Omnibus I*, which signifies the inaugural phase of a more extensive initiative. This simplification package is intended to streamline regulations within the sphere of sustainable development, thereby mitigating the administrative burdens currently experienced by European businesses (European Commission, 2025c). This initiative was announced in response to mounting pressure from business circles and certain member states concerning the complexity and cost of ESG reporting requirements, particularly those stemming from the two directives referenced above: the CSRD and CSDDD directives.

The presentation of the Omnibus I package was situated within a broader context pertaining to the Mario Draghi report on the future competitiveness of the European economy (Draghi, 2024). The report indicates that excessive regulation and bureaucratisation undermine the investment and innovation capabilities of companies in the European Union, especially when compared to competitors from the United States and Asia. The European Commission, having given due consideration to the aforementioned arguments, resolved to undertake a review of prevailing ESG regulations, with the aim of adopting a more balanced approach to the implementation of sustainable development policies.

The Omnibus I package comprises two legislative proposals (European Commission, 2025c). The preliminary proposal anticipates a two-year deferral of the reporting obligation for companies falling under the so-called second and third wave of CSRD implementation. In practice, entities initially expected to commence reporting for the financial years 2025 or 2026 will now be obligated to prepare reports exclusively for the financial years 2027 and 2028. The second key component of the package is the planned reduction in the scope of entities subject to ESG reporting obligations. The European

Commission proposed that this obligation should only apply to large companies with over 1000 employees, recognising that these entities have the greatest impact on the natural environment and society. It is estimated that such a change will exclude approximately 80% of companies that were originally subject to the CSRD regulation (European Commission, 2025b). Concurrently, the proposal entails a reduction in the financial obligations associated with ESG reporting and auditing by stipulating that only limited assurance, as opposed to the prevailing reasonable assurance, will be mandated. This change is expected to engender a reduction in the costs of audit services.

The Omnibus I package also addresses the regulations arising from the CSDDD directive (European Commission, 2025c). The proposed changes include the deferral of the entry into force of due diligence obligations from July 2027 to July 2028, and the narrowing of their scope to cover only direct suppliers, excluding further tiers in the supply chain. Furthermore, the cyclical nature of risk assessment within the chain of activities would be subject to an extension, with the assessment cycle being moved from an annual to a five-yearly basis. In instances where suppliers fail to meet regulatory requirements, the new regulations stipulate a temporary suspension of cooperation, as opposed to the previous practice of complete termination. The proposal also entails considerable restrictions on the information required within the value chain and the CSDDD directive (European Parliament & Council, 2024). In practical terms, companies subject to reporting obligations will not be able to demand from their suppliers and contractors ESG information beyond those specified in voluntary standards developed by the European Commission (so-called ESRS VSME).

From the perspective of Poland, the simplifications related to the Carbon Border Adjustment Mechanism (CBAM) are of particular importance. The CBAM, as discussed in Chap. 3, is one of the key instruments of the European Union's climate policy. This mechanism was included in the Omnibus I deregulation package, presented by the European Commission in March 2025, in response to growing voices from businesses and member states pointing to the excessive complexity and administrative burdens resulting from its application (European Commission, 2025a). Among the proposed changes was the introduction of a new de minimis threshold, under which importers whose annual import of CBAM-covered goods, excluding electricity and hydrogen, does not exceed 50 tonnes will be fully exempt from the obligations imposed by the mechanism. The Commission estimates that this change will apply to approximately 90% of importers, representing around 182,000 economic entities. Concurrently, the existing threshold, which is presently based on the value of the shipment (150 euros), is to be superseded by a more precise limit of 50 tonnes of emissions per year.

It is anticipated that further simplifications will be made to the authorisation procedures for importers, and that the emission calculation methods and rules for the purchase of CBAM certificates will be simplified. A salient benefit of this approach is the capacity to employ default values in scenarios where precise emission data is not available. In this context, it is important to note that from 2027, the European Commission plans to publish annual average CO_2 emission prices in third countries. It is anticipated that this measure will facilitate the reimbursement of carbon costs that have already been incurred outside the EU, thereby ensuring a reduction in CBAM liabilities. A notable element of the package pertains to the deferral of the compulsory acquisition of CBAM certificates from 2026 to 2027, with the objective of mitigating the burden on businesses during the nascent stage of the mechanism's implementation.

The CBAM mechanism and its simplifications are of particular importance for the Polish economy. Notwithstanding the decline in the share of coal in electricity production, Poland remains one of the European Union countries most dependent on this raw material, with 70% of national electricity still being generated from coal (Electricity Market, 2025). The preponderance of coal in Poland's energy portfolio gives rise to a substantial carbon footprint for the national economy, a matter that assumes particular salience within the context of the CBAM. The introduction of simplifications within the Omnibus I package, such as new de minimis thresholds or the simplification of reporting procedures, has the potential to significantly alleviate the burden on Polish enterprises, especially those of a small and medium size, which are particularly exposed to the effects of the high carbon footprint of their products.

Subsequent to the presentation of legislative proposals within the Omnibus I package by the European Commission, the subsequent stage involved their consideration and adoption by the EU's legislative institutions. The culmination of the legislative process was marked by the vote in the European Parliament on 3 April 2025, when the 'Stop the Clock' proposal was adopted by a majority of 531 votes in favour. This decision temporarily suspends the full implementation of the CSRD and CSDDD directives (European Parliament & Council, 2025b).

The vote was conducted under the urgent procedure, which bypassed the standard process of committee work and public consultations. Consequently, on 14 April 2025, the European Parliament and Council (EU) adopted Directive 2025/794, which was subsequently published on 16 April 2025 in the Official Journal of the EU. This directive introduces the Omnibus I simplification package, most notably including the temporary postponement of reporting obligations stemming from the CSRD and CSDDD directives (European Parliament & Council, 2025a). In accordance with the stipulated plan, the 'Stop the Clock' mechanism has been implemented to adjust the deadlines for the submission of certain requirements pertaining to ESG reporting and the due diligence of the CSRD and CSDDD directives, as initially outlined. In practice, this signifies that:

- Large enterprises (second wave) will begin reporting for the financial year 2027 with reports due in 2028 instead of 2026;
- Listed SMEs (third wave) will begin reporting for the financial year 2028, with reports due in 2029 instead of 2027;
- The obligations arising from the CSDDD directive are postponed from 2026 to 2027.

It is anticipated that member states will have transposed the directive into national law by 31 December 2025. The directive was formally implemented on 17 April 2025, the day following its official publication. From a broader standpoint, Omnibus I signals the potential for further ESG policy reforms in the EU, aimed at achieving a balance between environmental and social objectives, on the one hand, and the necessity to support innovation, productivity and the internationalisation of European enterprises, on the other.

Critics of the Omnibus I package argue that the Commission's proposals represent a step backwards for Europe and threaten years of progress in the field of sustainable development and green transformation (Reuters, 2025). Furthermore, a significant number of businesses have already undergone a restructuring of their teams and internal processes, with some nearing full preparedness to implement the obligations arising from the CSRD directive. Indeed, the initial reports have already been produced or are anticipated for publication in the forthcoming months. Companies such as Nestlé, Mars and Unilever have addressed a letter to the President of the European Commission, Ursula von der Leyen, appealing against the postponement

(The Wall Street Journal, 2025). The speakers placed particular emphasis on the notion that investment and competitiveness are contingent on the predictability of the law. They further argued that the 'Omnibus' initiative undermines this stability. It is notable that analogous pleas have been issued by investor organisations responsible for the management of assets. These include the Institutional Investors Group on Climate Change and the UN-supported Principles for Responsible Investment. The prevailing opinion is that the current regulatory framework assists investors in the management of risk, the identification of novel opportunities, and the direction of capital towards a more competitive and sustainable climate-neutral economy (The Wall Street Journal, 2025).

In April 2025, a formal complaint was filed with the European Ombudsman by seven non-governmental organisations, including Client Earth, regarding the Omnibus I package (Abnett, 2025). The subject of the present complaint is the planned amendments to key legal acts in the field of sustainable development, including the CSRD directive, the CSDDD directive and the EU Taxonomy regulation. The organisations accuse the Commission of, among other things, excessively rapid processing of proposals, an inadequate level of social consultation and a lack of consideration for data on the impact of the proposed changes on the environment and society. The authors of the complaint have asserted that the Commission's proposal is predominantly driven by industry interests and disregards scientific evidence and public opinion. Critics have highlighted that the simplification of reporting requirements and due diligence will not only fail to increase competitiveness, but may even result in a weakening of the EU's strategic competitive advantage, which is based on high standards of corporate responsibility. As previously highlighted, regulatory frameworks such as CSRD and CSDDD assume significant importance within the broader context of escalating investor and consumer expectations concerning corporate engagement with sustainable development (Sustainable Views, 2025).

In conclusion, despite the provisions for relief and deferral introduced in the Omnibus I package, non-financial reporting in European Union member states has become a permanent element of responsible business practice, and a means for companies to communicate their impact on society and the natural environment. In the context of mounting expectations and prevailing climate challenges, standards and guidelines for the communication of non-financial information are poised to meet the expectations of both the market and managerial bodies. It is reasonable to hypothesise that companies that recognise not only the regulatory obligation but also the added value of these frameworks are unlikely to abandon them. This approach will certainly be appreciated by the market, business partners, competitors, customers and other stakeholders.

8.3 ESG Reporting in Poland

8.3.1 Status and Local Guidelines for Non-Financial Reporting in Poland

Prior to 2009, a mere three companies in Poland had published non-financial reports in accordance with international GRI standards: British American Tobacco Poland in 2004, Telekomunikacja Polska S.A. in 2006 and Autostrady Eksploatacja in 2009 (Łudzińska, 2013a). Since that time, Poland has undergone a significant metamorphosis, and reports reflecting the non-financial achievements of leading companies have become commonplace. As a member state of the European Union, Poland is subject to the same directives and regulations on disclosure and reporting as all other EU countries. The NFRD directive on the disclosure of non-financial information, and its transposition into local accounting law, has undoubtedly marked a turning point in the development of non-financial reporting in Poland (Wójcik-Jurkiewicz, 2020). Moreover, the advent of novel EU directives on ESG reporting and non-financial information disclosure, EU Taxonomy rules, and the guidelines on corporate sustainability reporting, including ESRS standards discussed in Sect. 8.2, will undoubtedly have tangible implications for Polish companies.

A growing number of companies in Poland are preparing non-financial or integrated reports that present the ESG criteria they deem relevant. These reports facilitate the evaluation of their social and environmental impact, in addition to the quality and strategic orientation of their management practices. The largest and most significant companies, designated as Public Interest Entities (PIEs), have been obligated to prepare non-financial reports in accordance with the NFRD directive since January 2017 (Ministry of Development and Technology, 2023). In accordance with the provisions stipulated in the Accounting Act of 29 September 1994, PIEs in Poland encompass banking institutions, insurance companies, investment funds, issuers of securities admitted to trading, entities intending to apply or applying for admission to trading on one of the regulated markets of the

European Economic Area, as well as national payment institutions and electronic money institutions (Lorenc & Kustra, 2017).

As reported by the Ministry of Development and Technology of the Republic of Poland (2023), over 3500 Polish companies will be obliged to provide information on sustainable development under the CSRD directive from 1 January 2027. This obligation will be implemented in phases, initially applicable to the largest companies that have previously reported under the NFRD directive. The current discretion in choosing reporting standards will also be abolished. In accordance with the provisions of the recently enacted CSRD directive, commercial enterprises operating within Poland are obligated to submit reports in accordance with the European standards (ESRS) that have been formally adopted at the EU level. To date, companies in Poland have reported using various non-financial reporting standards of their own choosing (Fig. 8.4), which have undoubtedly helped them to accrue the necessary experience to implement the new EU reporting standards.

In addition to the NFRD and CSRD directives, the implementation of the European Parliament Regulation EU 2020/852, commonly referred to as the EU Taxonomy (a topic explored in Sect. 8.2), introduces novel non-financial information disclosure obligations for companies operating in Poland. The EU Taxonomy, while not explicitly prohibiting potentially non-ecological investments, promotes measures that are conducive to the protection and renovation of ecosystems (Milewska, 2022). It is imperative that Public Interest Entities, in addition to other companies in Poland, adapt to these guidelines.

The current ESG reporting framework in Poland is thus comprised of a series of standards and regulatory requirements, which are listed below in chronological order:

- 2014: Non-Financial Reporting Directive, NFRD (European Parliament & Council, 2014).
- 2019: Sustainable Finance Disclosures Regulation, SFDR (European Parliament & Council, 2019).
- 2020: EU Taxonomy, a set of detailed criteria for assessing the compatibility of economic activity with the principles of sustainable development (European Parliament & Council, 2020).
- 2022: Corporate Sustainability Reporting Directive, CSRD (European Parliament & Council, 2022).

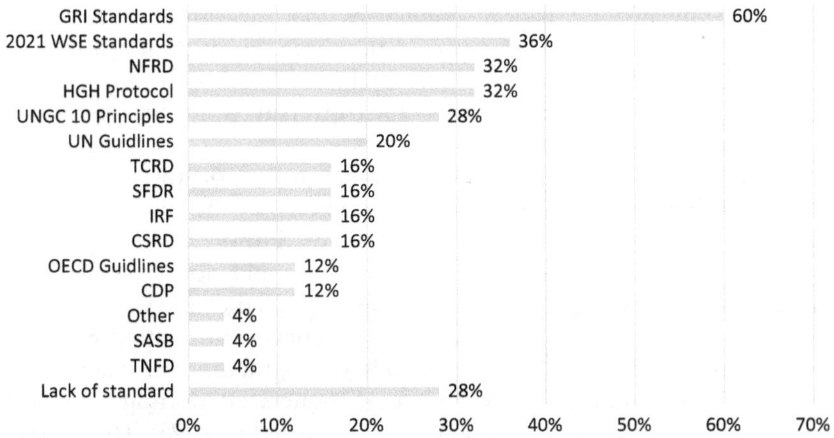

Fig. 8.4 Non-financial reporting standards and frameworks used by companies in Poland. *Source* Based on the Ministry of Development and Technology of the Republic of Poland (2023, p. 55)

- 2023: European Sustainability Reporting Standards, ESRS (EFRAG, 2023) and International Financial Reporting Standards—IFRS S1 and IFRS S2 (IFRS, 2023b, 2023c) as key tools developed by the leading organisation co-creating the non-financial reporting framework in the European Union.
- 2024: Corporate Sustainability Due Diligence Directive, CSDDD (European Parliament & Council, 2024).

Meanwhile, the Accounting Act, which was amended in 2016 and again in 2024, is the key document currently regulating disclosure issues in Poland. The 2016 amendment saw the NFRD directive implemented into the national legal framework, while the 2024 update transposed the CSRD directive. Both of these relate to the disclosure of non-financial information by large Public Interest Entities (PIEs) (European Parliament & Council, 2014; Sejm of the Republic of Poland, 2016, 2024). The NFRD Directive also imposed an obligation to publish diversity information. This aspect was addressed in the Regulation of the Minister of Finance of 25 May 2016 (Ministry of Finance of Poland, Ministry of Finance of the Republic of Poland, 2016), which amended the regulation on continuous and periodic information provided by issuers of securities. In accordance with the stipulated regulation, companies that are listed on the stock exchange and that fulfil at least two of the three specified criteria—that is to say, employment size, balance sheet total, or net turnover—are obligated to disclose information pertaining to their diversity policy with respect to their decision-making bodies.

The NFRD Directive had a considerable impact on the evolution of ESG reporting in Poland, leading to an increase in the number of non-financial information disclosed by companies. However, the significant contributions of local initiatives in this area should not be overlooked, particularly the ESG Reporting Guidelines published by the Warsaw Stock Exchange (WSE, 2021b), and the Non-Financial Information Standard (NIS) developed by the Reporting Standards Foundation in collaboration with the Association of Stock Exchange Issuers (Reporting Standards Foundation, 2021), both of which were published in 2021. The primary objective of the Non-Financial Information Standard (NIS) was to assist companies in fulfilling their reporting obligations arising from the NFRD directive. The NIS focuses on basic guidelines adapted to national and sectoral specifics, thanks to which Polish companies can effectively fulfil the obligations introduced by the NFRD directive and the updated Accounting Act of 2016, which incorporated the directive into the Polish legal system (Reporting Standards Foundation, 2017).

The NIS standard is a complimentary instrument that is available not only to listed companies, but also to other businesses, institutions and organisations. Prior to the introduction of the NIS standard, extensive consultations were conducted with various issuers, state institutions, entities operating within the infrastructure of the Polish capital market and various associations related to the capital market. The objective of the exercise was to adapt the proposed guidelines so as to align them with the prevailing reporting practices specific to the local Polish market.

In May 2021, the Warsaw Stock Exchange, in cooperation with the European Bank for Reconstruction and Development (EBRD) and Steward Redqueen, a consulting firm specialising in sustainable development, published the aforementioned ESG Reporting Guidelines with the aim of further supporting companies in transparently disclosing non-financial information (WSE, 2021b). These guidelines were subsequently updated in October 2023 (WSE, 2023b). In addition, in 2021, the WSE, as a publicly-traded entity, issued its inaugural social report, prepared in accordance with the Global Reporting Initiative (GRI) standards.

The ESG reporting guidelines established by the exchange did not intruduce a novel standard, nor did they supersede prevailing legal regulations in this domain. The objective of the initiative was twofold: firstly, to encourage companies listed on the WSE to disclose information on ESG aspects in a transparent manner; and secondly, to enhance the consistency and comparability of this disclosure (WSE, 2021b). The document, published in 2021, was based on international standards and regulations, including the NFRD directive, the Sustainable Finance Disclosure Regulation (SFDR), the EU Taxonomy, and the recommendations of the Task Force on Climate-related Financial Disclosures (TCFD), all of which were discussed in previous sections. The WSE Guidelines (2021b) functioned as a pragmatic instrument for companies, encompassing both those embarking on their ESG reporting journey and those with more advanced experience. An additional objective of the initiative was to consolidate the position of the Polish capital market and promote the principles of sustainable development within the business sector.

The ESG reporting guidelines of the Warsaw Stock Exchange were developed based on the experiences gained from *The Good Practices of Companies Listed on the WSE* (WSE, 2021a). In accordance with the stipulated guidelines, corporate entities are at liberty to opt for the reporting method that is most congruent with their requirements, provided that it complies with the stipulated legal obligations. A company may elect to pursue three possible courses of action. Firstly, it may prepare an annual activity report that incorporates ESG aspects. Secondly, it may prepare a separate sustainability report. Alternatively, it may prepare an integrated report that presents financial and non-financial information in a single document.

Companies currently subject to the NFRD directive, which remains in force due to the postponement of the CSRD directive's implementation under the Omnibus I package, may publish non-financial reports that either address only the minimum requirements set by the directive or take the form of a more comprehensive sustainability report. In the latter case, it is considered good practice to indicate in the report where the disclosures required by the directive can be found. It is also noteworthy that, according to the NFRD directive, companies have a period of six months from the day of publishing annual reports to publish a sustainability report. However, it is recommended that both reports be published simultaneously, thereby enabling users to gain a comprehensive understanding of the company from both financial and non-financial perspectives.

In order to facilitate the comparison of reports, the Warsaw Stock Exchange guidelines from 2021 and 2023 encourage the disclosure of ESG information in accordance with standards and reporting frameworks that have been widely accepted, including those of the Global Reporting Initiative (GRI), the International Integrated Reporting Council (IIRC) and the International Sustainability Standards Board (ISSB), as discussed in Sect. 8.2. Moreover, the guidelines presented in 2023 provide detailed information related to ESG reporting obligations in line with the new EU CSRD directive and ESRS standards (which are also detailed in Sect. 8.2). In light of the mounting demand from analysts, rating agencies and investors for information on corporate ESG activities, it is imperative that companies listed on the Warsaw Stock Exchange are able to meet these information requirements. The WSE guidelines emphasise that ESG reporting is not a discrete activity, but rather an integral component of the overall management process. It is imperative to acknowledge the merits of integrating ESG components into fundamental business operations, and to recognise the obligation to assume responsibility for a company's societal and environmental impact. These elements are indispensable in the development of a more sustainable business model. The ESG report, developed in accordance with these guidelines, should reflect the company's ongoing commitment to enhancing its practices in this area (WSE, 2021b). The key elements of ESG reporting, as outlined in the guidelines prepared by the Warsaw Stock Exchange, are presented in Table 8.5.

Following the conduction of a materiality analysis and the subsequent implementation of a double materiality analysis in accordance with the CSDR directive, the company is able to initiate the report preparation process. The ESG Reporting Guidelines (WSE, 2021b, 2023b) provide a detailed description of indicators within the main ESG categories: environment (E), society (S) and corporate governance (G), as well as their assigned units of measure. These guidelines show the results of companies within ESG aspects and organise the report structure. Each indicator is assigned a code and should be adapted to the specifics of the company; the WSE guidelines provide detailed information in this regard. The list of basic indicators is presented in Table 8.6.

In an effort to promote the practice of Environmental, Social and Governance reporting, the first national ESG Reporting Tools Ranking was published in 2024. This development signifies a substantial advancement in the direction of professionalisation and digitalisation of sustainable development reporting processes (CSR Info, 2024). The objective of this

Table 8.5 Key elements of ESG reporting according to the Warsaw Stock Exchange Guidelines (2021)

Key element	*Description*
Materiality	Materiality is a key element in the process of preparing a sustainability report. Through materiality analysis, key ESG issues can be identified and their significance properly assessed in the context of the likelihood and scale of their impact on the company's operations. Under the NFRD directive, the concept of materiality includes both financial and environmental and social aspects. According to this approach, the organisation should not only present actual and potential risks and opportunities related to ESG that can significantly affect its results, but also indicate how the company's actions impact the overall context of sustainable development
Objectivity and balance	Information presented in the report should be provided in an unbiased manner, taking into account both positive and negative aspects of operations. It is crucial not to omit or distort significant facts. The company should also precisely define the scope and boundaries of the presented data, indicating, for example, whether they relate to specific segments of operations or to specific dependent units
Strategic and forward-looking perspective	General and routine information does not provide value for analysts and investors. It is important that the ESG issues presented in the report have strategic significance and assist in the decision-making process regarding investments, including identifying key risks and opportunities and ways to manage them. Reporting should also focus on the long-term perspective. Demonstrating how the company's strategy is linked to quantitative ESG indicators and targets allows for a better understanding of its development direction
Clarity and conciseness	The presentation of the company's results should be clear and concise. Conveying excessive or irrelevant data can hinder the reception of the main message of the report, which may cause its users to overlook key information. The use of materiality analysis allows to focus on the most important issues
Comparability and reliability	Investors value numerical data as it allows for comparison of results between companies. Key Performance Indicators (KPIs) should relate to the company's strategy and show effects in the most important ESG areas. It is also important to provide context for the presented data so that the reader

(continued)

Table 8.5 (continued)

Key element	*Description*
	can understand the reasons and background of significant changes and the company's actions
Verifiability	Independent, external verification of ESG data increases their reliability and is an additional asset in the opinion of investors

Source Based on WSE (2021b, pp. 21–23)

Table 8.6 Basic indicators of the *WSE ESG Reporting Guidelines*

Environment (E)	*Society (S)*	*Corporate Governance (G)*
Sustainable Development Management		
E–P1 Greenhouse gas emissions	S–P1 Diversity in supervisory bodies	G–P1 Structure of governing bodies
E–P2 Energy consumption	S–P2 Pay equality indicator	G–P2 Code of ethics
E–P3 Climate-related risks and opportunities	S–P3 Employee turnover	G–P3 Anti-corruption policy
	S–P4 Freedom of association and collective bargaining	G–P4 Whistleblowing mechanism
	S–P5 Human rights policy	
	S–P6 Human rights due diligence procedures	

Source Based on WSE (2021b, p. 26)

initiative is to furnish reporting companies, advisors and auditors with a comprehensive compilation of proven solutions that support compliance with CSRD Directive requirements and ESRS standards. The ranking presents tools that increase the efficiency and quality of reporting processes, contributing to their standardisation and automation. The project was carried out by CSRinfo, a company specialising in ESG education and consulting in Poland, in cooperation with the Polish ESG Association. The ranking, in order of merit, listed the following tools from eighth to first place: SmartHead, Diaphane, IBM Envizi, Envirly, Greenomy, APlanet, Velma ESG, PWC ESG and Management Solution (CSR Info, 2024).

In Spring 2023, KPMG (2023a) published the results of a study conducted in 2022 on the non-financial disclosures of Polish companies in the areas of climate and the environment. The objective of the research was to evaluate the quality and transparency of reporting practices on the Polish market. The analysis encompassed 100 of the largest companies in Poland (by revenue), selected during the initial phase of the study. The research was based on corporate non-financial reports, information published on company websites, press releases and other publicly available sources containing information relevant to the study's objectives. The findings indicated that 45 of the 100 largest companies in Poland did not disclose a standalone non-financial, ESG, or sustainability report for the year 2022. Furthermore, the degree of report preparation exhibited by the remaining 55 companies was found to be inconsistent, thereby indicating that the standards for non-financial reporting in Poland are still in the nascent stages of development. A select group of companies, predominantly from the oil, mining and energy sectors, have demonstrated a notable level of maturity in their ESG reporting. However, it should be noted that these companies represent a minority within the broader corporate landscape. The subsequent group encompassed food companies and trading companies, for example, supermarket chains. In third place ex aequo, there was a tie between trading companies from the furniture, clothing and online trading sectors, as well as food manufacturers. According to the analysis conducted by KPMG (2023a), the prevailing profile of a company that discloses ESG information in Poland is that of a company with Polish capital from the finance sector or the media and information industry, demonstrating a climate-conscious approach, albeit not necessarily extending to other ESG aspects, and listed on the stock exchange. The listing of companies on the stock exchange has been demonstrated to encourage greater transparency and disclosure (see, Łudzińska, 2017). In accordance with the findings of the study, corporate entities listed on the Warsaw Stock Exchange have been found to disclose a greater volume of information pertaining to corporate social responsibility (CSR) in comparison to other enterprises included in the *Rzeczpospolita 500 List* (a ranking of the 500 largest enterprises in Poland).

With regard to the Omnibus I package, the objective of which was to reduce administrative burdens for companies in the field of ESG reporting (see, Sect. 8.2.3), a wide debate was also sparked in Poland. The Polish ESG Association has articulated a critical stance towards the Commission's proposals, emphasising that the changes could potentially lead to market disruption (Polish ESG Association, 2025). Experts have highlighted the issue of companies that have already initiated preparations for reporting according to forthcoming requirements.

In a similar vein, the Instrat Foundation undertook a critical evaluation of the European Commission's proposals encompassed within the Omnibus I package, articulating concerns that the imposition of limitations on ESG reporting might impede Polish companies' capacity to invest in energy efficiency and hinder their access to capital (Instrat, 2025). Experts have emphasised that ESG reporting encourages companies to be more innovative and allows for improved risk management. According to Instrat's analysis, the number of companies subject to reporting obligations in Poland could fall from over 3500 to approximately 500 (Instrat, 2025). Whilst the reduction of obligations may result in a decrease in costs in the short term, it has the potential to hinder companies from gaining visibility among investors and weaken their motivation to pursue climate transformation. The Foundation emphasises the necessity for the establishment of a public, centralised system for the collection of ESG data, observing that the responsibility for this function is predominantly shouldered by non-governmental organisations, such as Instrat.

Polish experts have also posited that, notwithstanding the Omnibus I package's stated objective of simplifying reporting processes, the legislative process may be protracted, and the final version of the changes may deviate considerably from the initial proposal. Consequently, companies are advised to continue preparing for reporting in accordance with the current regulatory framework (Wrembel, 2025). The ESG Committee of the National Chamber of Commerce also articulated its concerns and formulated an opinion on the Omnibus I package, with a particular emphasis on the necessity for support for companies in ESG reporting (National Chamber of Commerce, 2025). The proposals encompass a range of measures, including the establishment of a complimentary, universal instrument for ESG reporting and the elucidation of terminology employed within the ESRS standards.

In anticipation of a potential deferral of the CSRD and CSDDD directives in Poland, the Ministry of Development and Technology has initiated consultations on the EU Taxonomy within the Omnibus I package. The proposed simplifications include, among other measures, the deferral of the obligation to report sustainability-related information for certain companies and the narrowing of the scope of entities subject to this requirement. (Ministry of Development and Technology, 2025).

In conclusion, although the Omnibus I package aims to simplify ESG reporting procedures, many Polish organisations and experts approach it with caution, emphasising the need for further observation of the legislative process and continuation of preparations for reporting in accordance with current regulations.

8.3.2 *ESG Reporting in the Polish Market in Light of Research*

Research on non-financial reporting in Poland can be divided into two distinct periods. The initial period under scrutiny extends up to 2017, preceding the implementation of the NFRD directive, a time when reporting was entirely voluntary. At that time, a significant part of the research focused on the necessity of introducing regulations mandating non-financial reporting and analysed the degree of preparedness of Polish companies for their implementation. The second scope, commencing after 2017, pertains to the period subsequent to the implementation of the NFRD directive, which introduced an unprecedented obligation of non-financial reporting for a select group of the largest companies. The focal point of the discourse encompassed matters pertaining to the degree of preparedness exhibited by Polish companies in regard to the implementation of non-financial reporting in accordance with the recently issued European guidelines. Additionally, the discourse delved into the ramifications these guidelines have exerted on the quality and comparability of such reporting.

Prior to the implementation of the NFRD directive, research on the dynamics and standards of voluntary non-financial reporting was limited, primarily due to the infrequent publication of such documents by companies (Aluchna & Roszkowska-Menkes, 2018a). A study of the entire population of companies listed on the Warsaw Stock Exchange revealed that the number of companies publishing non-financial reports remained at a very low level: 17 companies in 2010 (out of 368 companies then listed), 19 companies in 2011 (out of 409 companies), 21 companies in 2012 (out of 422 companies), 26 companies in 2013 (out of 430 companies) and 27 companies in 2014 (out of 444 companies then listed) (Aluchna & Roszkowska-Menkes, 2018a).

Research conducted by Czerwińska and Kaźmierkiewicz (2015) and Sroka (2018) has indicated a significant paucity of information with regard to the Polish capital market, particularly in relation to ESG reporting. The limited transparency of non-financial information disclosed by issuers has been identified as a significant contributing factor to the prevailing information asymmetry. The majority of companies did not furnish data pertaining to their environmental or social policy. The disclosed information primarily related to corporate governance and was most frequently published by large-capitalisation companies included in the WIG-20 index. Furthermore, Polish companies exhibited a reduced level of data presentation in comparison to their foreign counterparts. In an analysis of capital groups listed on the Warsaw Stock Exchange that published non-financial reports, Sikacz (2016) observed that the majority of these reports focused exclusively on the parent company. This observation gave rise to concerns regarding the extent to which CSR activities carried out by subsidiaries were reflected in group-level disclosures.

Dziawgo (2016) posited that financial statements continue to occupy a central role in the investment decision-making process. The primary challenge, therefore, was to enhance the usefulness of non-financial reports for external stakeholders, particularly investors. The findings of Dziawgo's study indicated that integrated reporting could potentially serve as a solution, as it was well-received by both large institutional and individual investors, suggesting a growing preference for this approach. Nevertheless, questions remained regarding the cost-effective implementation of integrated reporting, as well as the scope and responsibility for its audit and assurance.

As Wiśniewska (2015) concluded in her study of the practices of external verification of non-financial data in social reports, there existed a paucity of clear regulations in Polish companies specifying who was authorised to conduct such verification. However, observations indicated that audits of non-financial information were most commonly conducted by specialised audit, advisory and certification firms, as well as by independent consultants and experts. As part of her analysis, Wiśniewska studied 32 reports submitted in 2013 and 31 reports submitted in 2014 to the Social Reports competition, which was organised by the non-governmental organisation Responsible Business Forum. Her analysis revealed a growing trend among companies to opt for external verification of their social reports. In 2013, 15 out of 32 submitted reports (46.9%) were subject to external verification. In 2014, this figure rose to 61.3%, as 19 out of 31 submitted reports were verified. This represents an increase of 14.4%, indicative of a growing understanding of the value of verifying non-financial data in reports. Concurrently, Wiśniewska (2015) identified three primary groups of entities conducting audits of non-financial reports: the Global Reporting Initiative

(GRI), advisory and audit firms such as Deloitte or PWC, and other specialist advisory firms, e.g. Foundation for AGH or Bureau Veritas Poland. The author's observations revealed a scarcity of entities in Poland specialising in the verification of non-financial data. In view of the rapid increase in the number of social reports and the imminent obligation to disclose non-financial data by large companies, the number of available experts in this field may prove insufficient.

An analysis of CSR-related disclosures in annual reports and other communications by companies listed on the main market of the Warsaw Stock Exchange in 2013 showed that only 18% of the examined social reports had been audited by independent verifiers (Matuszak et al., 2015). Among the companies publishing ESG reports, 70% followed the GRI guidelines. The same study found that 4.6% of firms included in the WIG-Poland index and 70% of those in the RESPECT index issued stand-alone CSR reports, many of which addressed environmental, social and governance aspects. Within the RESPECT Index group, however, only one company published an integrated annual report for 2012. The challenges identified are threefold: the limited scope of non-financial reporting, the lack of widespread independent verification and concerns over the overall quality of the reports.

In their study, Sikacz and Wołczek (2017b) analysed companies from the RESPECT index of the Warsaw Stock Exchange, which, at least in theory, should represent entities demonstrating best practices in sustainability reporting. A thorough examination of the economic, environmental and social dimensions of the companies' social reports revealed that the potential of non-financial communication with stakeholders had not been fully utilised. Disclosures across all three domains remained at a minimal level. The study also highlighted challenges in conducting a comparative analysis of corporate reports due to variations in reporting methodologies. This inconsistency evidently poses a significant challenge for stakeholders seeking to analyse and compare entities based on their non-financial reports.

In a subsequent study, Sikacz and Wołczek (2018) arrived at conclusions that were analogous to those previously mentioned. The study examined the transparency of environmental, social and governance (ESG) information disclosure by companies included in three social responsibility indices: the Polish RESPECT Index, which is listed on the Warsaw Stock Exchange, and the Austrian VÖNIX and CEERIUS indices, which are listed on the Vienna Stock Exchange. It was established that companies included in these indices encountered negligible challenges in disclosing information relevant to corporate governance. However, these companies encountered significant challenges in ensuring transparency with regard to the environmental dimension. In the ESG information transparency ranking, companies from the VÖNIX Index achieved the highest results, while those from the RESPECT index performed relatively the worst. The study also revealed a decline in the transparency of environmental, social and governance information disclosure among companies from social responsibility indices.

Aluchna et al. (2018) conducted an analysis of the reporting practices of leading companies listed on the Warsaw Stock Exchange and included in the WIG20 index. The study revealed significant diversity in reporting approaches among the companies examined, particularly in terms of reporting period, report format, length and the standards applied. The primary conclusion drawn from their research was that, despite global trends and the extensive development of ESG reporting on a global scale, non-financial reporting among Polish companies remained at a nascent stage of development. Remlein (2018) adopted a slightly different perspective, analysing the valuation methods and scope of information on socially responsible investments presented in the financial statements of companies included in the RESPECT Index. The investigation revealed that, despite investments being presented in accordance with Polish accounting legislation and International Financial Reporting Standards (IFRS), the balance sheets in question lacked information regarding socially responsible investments. The management commentaries were predominantly descriptive in nature, which limited the ability to perform meaningful comparisons across companies. According to Remlein (2018), financial reporting in Poland did not keep pace with business practice, indicating a need to adopt consistent, uniform standards for reporting ESG aspects.

Conversely, Badura-Mojza's (2017) conclusions, derived from studies conducted prior to the implementation of the NFRD directive, exhibited a more optimistic outlook. The present study's analytical framework encompassed the social reports of companies listed on the primary market of the Warsaw Stock Exchange, and included in the WIG30 index. Her analyses revealed that companies included in the WIG30 index increasingly chose dedicated reports and published information on their websites to present socially and environmentally responsible actions. Furthermore, she identified an emerging trend towards integrated reporting among leading Polish companies.

The advent of the impending NFRD directive has prompted researchers in Poland to undertake an examination of the associated reporting requirements, even in advance of its implementation. Szadziewska's (2015) analysis examined the transparency and comparability of non-financial disclosure in the context of regulatory changes within the European Union. In a similar vein, Fijałkowska's (2016) study examined the challenges associated with non-financial reporting in accordance with the new NFRD directive. Consequently, Zyznyrska-Dworczak (2016) conducted a study on the evolution of non-financial reporting and the feasibility of its external verification. These studies reflect the strong interest of Polish scholars in the issue of non-financial reporting, particularly in the context of emerging EU regulations and their impact on the transparency and comparability of disclosed information. The introduction of the NFRD directive and the first social and integrated reports, which appeared for the year 2017, marked a shift in the research perspective on ESG reporting in Poland.

One of the first studies in Poland to assess the quality of non-financial reporting based on the guidelines of the newly implemented NFRD directive was conducted in 2017 by Wójcik-Jurkiewicz and Sadowska (2018). The findings suggest that Polish companies listed on the stock exchange, particularly public interest entities (PIEs), encountered challenges in aligning their practices with the provisions stipulated in the Accounting Act of 15 December 2016. This legislative response by Poland to the NFRD directive underscores the complexity of regulatory compliance for these entities. The study concluded that while a significant proportion of companies based their reports on recognised standards such as GRI or local NIS, more than 50% either used their own reporting frameworks or did not specify any standards at all. This underscores the intricacy and heterogeneity in the methodologies employed by Polish companies with regard to non-financial reporting.

In a 2022 study, Aluchna, Roszkowska-Menkes and Kamiński analysed the impact of the NFRD directive on the ESG performance of Polish companies listed on the Warsaw Stock Exchange, using data from the Refinitiv database. The study revealed an increase in efforts within the environmental and social dimensions following the implementation of the directive; however, no significant improvement was observed in the area of management and corporate governance. The authors emphasise that companies require time to adapt to new regulatory requirements and that the full effects of implementing the NFRD directive may only become apparent over time. The findings of Aluchna et al. (2022) provide evidence that lends support to the hypothesis that mandatory legal frameworks in countries with a historically low level of voluntary non-financial disclosure can play a promising role. Papa et al. (2023) also evaluated the effects of implementing the NFRD directive. However, their focus was more narrowly on the improvement of diversity-related disclosures in Polish-listed companies. The present study analysed whether diversity information from 2018 was statistically different from that of 2016 (i.e., in the periods before and after the introduction of the NFRD directive). The findings suggest that the quality of the diversity information disclosed improved following the implementation of the directive, despite no alterations being made to the nature of the disclosures themselves.

In their seminal study, Matuszak and Różyńska (Matuszak & Różańska, 2021) sought to identify and analyse the disparities in the manner in which non-financial information is presented by companies listed on the Warsaw Stock Exchange. This analysis was conducted in the period preceding the implementation of the NFRD directive. The analysis encompassed 134 companies, utilising a multifaceted approach that incorporated content analysis of their management reports and the application of a transparency index to evaluate the extent of transparency in non-financial disclosures. An exploration was conducted into practices in disclosing information over two years—in 2015, prior to the introduction of the directive, and in 2017, when it was already in force. The research indicated a significant increase in compliance with EU standards for non-financial reporting transparency, especially in the areas of human rights and anti-corruption.

In light of earlier research by Matuszak and Różańska (2017), which analysed the social reporting practices of companies subject to the NFRD directive and found that the majority did not comply with the new requirements, the more recent analysis indicates a significant improvement in this area. The introduction of the NFRD directive guaranteed that all the companies studied considered reporting related to sustainable development. The most significant improvements were observed among companies that had previously demonstrated a low level of transparency. The research findings also demonstrated greater consistency in non-financial disclosures across different sectors and evidenced the effectiveness of the directive during its initial years of implementation, particularly with regard to the increase in the number of reporting companies and the broadened scope of disclosed information. The directive effectively encouraged companies to increase their level of transparency compared to the period when reporting was voluntary. The 2021 study by Matuszak and Różańska thus confirms the hypothesis that companies are more likely to adapt to social expectations when those expectations are embedded in legal regulations. Consequently, the findings lend support to the legitimacy theory of corporate disclosures and its alignment with stakeholder theory, thereby highlighting the importance of institutionalising social expectations through mandatory regulations governing the disclosure of non-financial information in the ESG domain.

In addition, Konarzewska (2020) analysed the content of non-financial reports of companies listed on the Warsaw Stock Exchange, with a particular focus on those included in the WIG-ESG index. The findings of the study revealed significant discrepancies in the scope and presentation of the reported data, which made it difficult to compare results across companies. Consequently, Konarzewska contends that endeavours to enhance the quality of non-financial reporting in Poland are imperative. In particular, she emphasises the importance of applying international non-financial reporting standards and ensuring the independent verification of these reports by qualified auditors.

In response to these recommendations, some researchers have examined whether Polish enterprises are prepared to report in accordance with international non-financial reporting frameworks beyond national regulations. In 2022, Indyk examined the preparedness of Polish companies for reporting on climate challenges in the context of sustainable development in accordance with the International Financial Reporting Standards (IFRS) S1 and S2. The study analysed the compliance of the new standards with Polish legal regulations, non-mandatory sustainability guidelines, and the findings of empirical research. The empirical component was based on data from 177 companies listed on the Warsaw Stock Exchange, using company responses to selected ESG sections of the *2021 Code of Good Practice* survey conducted by the Warsaw Stock Exchange as the primary data source. The study yielded several noteworthy conclusions. Despite the integration of ESG aspects into corporate operations becoming increasingly prevalent (with 60% of companies in the sample classified as advanced in this regard), the full implementation of reporting in accordance with IFRS S1 and IFRS S2 necessitates a more profound integration of ESG considerations into the overall activities and strategic management of enterprises. A mere 60 companies (34%) indicated that they had incorporated ESG aspects into their strategic framework, while a comparatively limited number of 32 companies (18%) disclosed strategic data, including goals and achievements related to ESG. Thirty companies (17%) assessed their environmental impact as insignificant, either due to the nature of their operations or because they were not subject to non-financial reporting requirements. As Indyk (2022) observes, the mounting significance of ESG criteria necessitates a fundamental restructuring of reporting methodologies, particularly with respect to sustainability aspects, for a considerable number of companies.

Tylec (2022) provided a summary of the existing and planned legal frameworks for non-financial reporting in Poland. A review of the literature indicates that, although ESG reporting is not a new concept, its significance is growing and is likely to continue increasing in the future. The mounting interest and social pressure on companies to act responsibly in environmental and social terms is concomitant with their efforts to present accurate information on these issues. While some actions are initiated by companies, a growing number are mandated by law. Non-financial information is becoming increasingly important for a variety of stakeholders, who are increasingly recognising the importance of environmental, social and governance aspects. It has therefore become evident that the presentation of ESG data, although partly motivated by marketing considerations, is becoming a necessity and is subject to growing regulatory oversight. This assertion is further substantiated by the recent regulations established at the EU level, which have been integrated into the Polish legal framework. A thorough examination of prevailing regulations and the proposed amendments under the CSRD directive suggests that the European Commission has recently implemented substantial enhancements to the ESG reporting requirements. This trend is anticipated to persist.

Research conducted by the Warsaw Stock Exchange in 2022 (WSE, 2022) indicates that the introduction of mandatory non-financial reporting for certain companies has resulted in the market-expected changes in this area. As Dietl (2023) points out, almost 200 publicly listed companies regularly publish reports on sustainability indicators. Furthermore, these companies are obligated to submit statements in accordance with the comply or explain model, as outlined in the Good Practices for Companies Listed on the Stock Exchange (WSE, 2021a). In these statements, companies address ESG-related topics, including climate change, sustainable development and employee-related issues such as gender equality, workers' rights and relations with local communities. In mid-2022, the

Warsaw Stock Exchange conducted a study among professional market participants, including stock analysts, investment advisors and investment fund managers, on the impact of ESG factors on investment decisions. This marked the fifth time the Exchange had conducted such a study. The findings of the present study corroborate the significance of reporting in the domain of sustainable development (WSE, 2022b). A study on the WIG-ESG index and its impact on analysts' recommendations found that information about the index's composition was of moderate significance. A mere 6% of analysts incorporated descriptions of the WIG-ESG index composition into their reports, while an additional 22% indicated their intention to include such information within the subsequent two years. Nevertheless, respondents asserted that information regarding a company's inclusion in the WIG-ESG index could serve as a valuable source of insight when making investment decisions. It is also worth noting that 16% of respondents reported relying on direct contact with companies during their analyses. However, none of the participants indicated that they used the services of specialised rating agencies that assess companies based on ESG factors.

This prompts the question of whether investors in Poland genuinely recognise and value the recent advancements in non-financial reporting. The research findings suggest that, as of yet, investors in Poland do not fully recognise or appreciate these improvements. Dziawgo's (2021) study examined how Polish individual investors assess the usefulness of individual elements of financial statements. The investor's perception of the usefulness of these elements is indicated by the findings. The majority of usefulness ratings fell within the 1–20% range, with the income statement (16%) and the balance sheet (12%) receiving the highest usefulness ratings at the 91–100% level. Conversely, information pertaining to corporate social responsibility (CSR) was evaluated as the least useful, with 21% of respondents categorising it as completely useless, and 43% assigning it a usefulness rating of 1–10.

In the contemporary business environment, characterised by the mounting significance of the sustainability concept and the economic turbulence precipitated by the pandemic and the war in Ukraine, non-financial factors are undergoing a paradigm shift in their role in evaluating corporate financial health, operational risk and future development prospects (Rogowski & Lipski, 2022). An assessment based solely on data and information presented in the financial statements may lead to misleading conclusions and, consequently, to suboptimal investment decisions. In the realm of available non-financial information sources, the non-financial report assumes a pivotal role in the assessment of securities value by capital market participants (Kłobukowska, 2020).

Concurrently, non-financial reporting underscores the expanding role of a diverse range of stakeholders in business operations, extending beyond the owners and shareholders. Contemporary challenges, both environmental (e.g. air pollution, greenhouse gas emissions and climate change) and social (e.g. social inequalities, poor working conditions and child labour), are reshaping the way businesses perceive their responsibilities, prompting a broader understanding of the needs and expectations of diverse stakeholders. It is imperative to emphasise that ESG reporting constitutes a component of a comprehensive sustainable development strategy, necessitating a proactive approach and the implementation of substantial changes in business operations, including those of companies in Poland. The advent of the new EU reporting standards as instruments of institutional enforcement will undoubtedly accelerate this transformation, not only among the largest market leaders, but ultimately also among small and medium-sized enterprises.

8.4 Summary and Conclusions

This chapter presents a detailed analysis of non-financial reporting, taking into account its growing importance in the context of global and European regulations. The study examines key international reporting frameworks, such as the Global Reporting Initiative (GRI) and International Financial Reporting Standards (IFRS), as well as the new European Sustainability Reporting Standards (ESRS). The objective of the ESRS is to standardise ESG reporting practices across European Union member states. The chapter also traces the evolution of non-financial reporting regulations, focusing on the implementation of the NFRD and CSRD directives, which significantly expand disclosure obligations for companies operating also in the Polish market. These developments are discussed in the context of the new and widely debated EU simplification package, *Omnibus I.*

Non-financial reporting in Poland is still in the development phase, but it is gaining increasing importance. An analysis of previous studies reveals a growing number of Polish companies publishing non-financial reports, in line with international standards. This can be considered a response to increasing regulatory requirements and market expectations.

The introduction of the NFRD and CSRD directives was a pivotal element in the development of non-financial reporting, obliging leading companies to disclose detailed non-financial information. The new regulations promote standardisation and comparability of data, which is crucial at both the national and international levels. Nevertheless, the diversity of reporting practices persists, impeding the capacity for effective comparisons between companies. The standardisation efforts initiated by recent EU regulations and endorsed by international organisations seek to mitigate these discrepancies and enhance the consistency and transparency of non-financial disclosures.

The implementation of new, mandatory reporting guidelines poses several challenges, including the need to adapt to evolving requirements, to integrate financial and non-financial reporting, and to establish appropriate verification and audit mechanisms. However, organisations that successfully adopt non-financial reporting practices may benefit from increased stakeholder trust and an enhanced competitive position in the market.

In conclusion, it is evident that non-financial reporting has become an essential component of responsible management and market communication. The effective implementation of ESG guidelines and the submission of related reports by companies serve not only to enhance transparency and risk management capabilities, but also to contribute to the creation of long-term value.

References

Abnett, K. (2025, April 18). *EU Commission faces complaint over easing of sustainability rules*. Reuters. Retrieved April 18, 2025, from https://www.reuters.com/sustainability/climate-energy/eu-commission-faces-complaint-over-easing-sustainability-rules-2025-04-17/

Aluchna, M., Kytsyuk, I., & Roszkowska-Menkes, M. (2018). Raportowanie społecznej odpowiedzialności biznesu. Przypadek społek z WIG20. *Zeszyt Naukowy Kolegium Zarządzania I Finansów SGH Warszawa*, *170*, 9–27.

Aluchna, M., & Roszkowska-Menkes, M. (2018a). Early adopters of integrated reporting. The practical evidence from warsaw stock exchange companies. In W. S. Idowu & M. Del Baldo (Eds.), *Integrated reporting: Antecedents perspectives/ outlooks for organisations and stakeholders*. Springer.

Aluchna, M., Roszkowska-Menkes, M., & Kamiński, B. (2022). From talk to action: The effects of the non-financial reporting directive on ESG performance. *Meditari Accountancy Research*, *31*(7). https://doi.org/10.1108/MEDAR-122021-1530 (Article 7).

Amel-Zadeh, A., & Serafeim, G. (2018). Why and how investors use esg information: Evidence from a global survey. *Financial Analysts Journal, 74*(3), 87–103. https://doi.org/10.2469/faj.v74.n3.2
Badura-Mojza, A. (2017). Zmiany w raportowaniu CSR w Polsce — Studium przypadku. *Zarządzanie Finansami I Rachunkowość, 5*(3), 5–17.
Bénabou, R., & Tirole, J. (2010). Individual and corporate social responsibility. *Economica, 77*(305), 1–19. https://doi.org/10.1111/j.1468-0335.2009.00843.x
Bonetti, P., Cho, C. H., & Michelon, G. (2023). Environmental disclosure and the cost of capital: evidence from the fukushima nuclear disaster. *European Accounting Review, 0*(0), 1–29. https://doi.org/10.1080/09638180.2023.2203410
Brooks, C., & Oikonomou, I. (2018). The effects of environmental, social and governance disclosures and performance on firm value: A review of the literature in accounting and finance. *The British Accounting Review, 50*(1), 1–15. https://doi.org/10.1016/j.bar.2017.11.005
Briefieng, C. (2024, 23 December). *China Unveils Its First Set of Basic Standards for Corporate Sustainability (ESG) Disclosure.* Retrieved January 25, 2024, from https://www.china-briefing.com/news/china-unveils-basic-standards-for-corporate-sustainability-esg-disclosure/
CDP. (2025). *Turning transparency to action.* Retrieved March 10, 2025, from https://www.cdp.net/en
Christensen, H. B., Hail, L., & Leuz, C. (2021). Mandatory CSR and sustainability reporting: Economic analysis and literature review. *Review of Accounting Studies, 26*(3), 1176–1248. https://doi.org/10.1007/s11142-021-09609-5
Cohen, J. R., & Simnett, R. (2015). CSR and assurance services: A research agenda. *AUDITING: A Journal of Practice & Theory, 34*(1), 59–74. https://doi.org/10.2308/ajpt-50876
Conca, L., Manta, F., Morrone, D., & Toma, P. (2021). The impact of direct environmental, social, and governance reporting: Empirical evidence in European-listed companies in the agri-food sector. *Business Strategy and the Environment, 30*(2), 1080–1093. https://doi.org/10.1002/bse.2672
CorporateRegister.com. (2025). *The global online directory of corporate responsibility (CR) reports.* Retrieved March 16, 2025, from https://www.corporateregister.com/
CSR Info. (2024). *Ranking narzędzi raportowania ESG 2024.* Retrieved January 15, 2025, from https://www.csrinfo.org/ranking-narzedzi-raportowania-esg-2024
Czerwińska, T., & Kaźmierkiewicz, P. (2015). ESG rating in investment risk analysis of companies listed on the public market in poland. *Economic Notes, 44*(2), 211–248. https://doi.org/10.1111/ecno.12031

Dietl, M. (2023). Taksonomia unijna: Jakie jest podejście inwestorów do kwestii raportowania ESG i jaki jest wpływ raportowania na wycenę spółek. W. L. Kotecki & P. (120–121). Instytut Odpowiedzialnych Finansów.

Draghi, M. (2024). *The future of european competitiveness: A competitiveness strategy for Europe (Part A)*. European Commission. https://commission.europa.eu/document/download/97e481fd-2dc3-412d-be4c-f152a8232961_en

Dziawgo, D. (2016). Znaczenie raportowania pozafinansowego w opinii indywidualnych inwestorów;w. *Prace Naukowe Uniwersytetu Ekonomicznego We Wrocławiu*, *436*, 105–114.

Dziawgo, L. (2021). Energy sectors on capital market—financing the process "towards sustainability". *European Research Studies Journal*, *24*(2B), 938–955.

EFRAG. (2021). Proposals for a relevant and dynamic EU sustainability reporting standard-setting [PDF]. Retrieved from https://www.efrag.org/Assets/Download?assetUrl=%2Fsites%2Fwebpublishing%2FSiteAssets%2FEFRAG%2520PTF-NFRS_MAIN_REPORT.pdf

EFRAG. (2022, November 2022). *Draft European Sustainability Reporting Standards. ESRS 1 General Requirem*ents. Retrieved from https://www.efrag.org/sites/default/files/sites/webpublishing/SiteAssets/ED_ESRS_1.pdf

EFRAG. (2023). *The first set of ESRS—the journey from PTF to delegated act*. Retrieved August 4, 2023, from https://www.efrag.org/lab6

EFRAG. (n.d.). *European financial reporting advisory group*. Retrieved August 2, 2024, from https://www.efrag.org/

Electricity Market. (2025, March 1). *Produkcja energii elektrycznej w Polsce—luty 2025*. Retrieved April 18, 2025, from https://www.rynekelektryczny.pl/produkcja-energii-elektrycznej-w-polsce/

European Commission. (2018). Action plan: Financing sustainable growth. Retrieved from https://finance.ec.europa.eu/publications/renewed-sustainable-finance-strategy-and-implementation-action-plan-financing-sustainable-growth_en

European Commission. (2019a). *Commission guidelines on non-financial reporting: Supplement on reporting climate-related information* (2019/C 209/01). Retrieved from https://eur-lex.europa.eu/legal-content/EN/TXT/?uri=CELEX:52019XC0620(01)

European Commission. (2019b). *The European Green Deal* (COM(2019) 640 final). Retrieved from https://eur-lex.europa.eu/legal-content/EN/TXT/?uri=CELEX%3A52019DC0640

European Commission. (2023a). *Daily News 31/07/2023*. Retrieved August 2, 2024, from https://ec.europa.eu/commission/presscorner/detail/en/MEX_23_4044

European Commission. (2023b). Delegated Regulation (EU) 2023/2772 supplementing Directive 2013/34/EU as regards sustainability reporting standards.

Official Journal of the European Union, Retrieved August 24, 2024, from https://finance.ec.europa.eu/system/files/2023-10/231017-proposal-sustainability-reporting-standards_en.pdf

European Commission. (2025a, 28 March). *Carbon Border Adjustment Mechanism*. Taxation and Customs Union. Retrieved April 16, 2025, from https://taxation-customs.ec.europa.eu/carbon-border-adjustment-mechanism_en

European Commission. (2025b, February 26). *Commission simplifies rules on sustainability and EU investments, delivering over €6 billion in administrative relief*. Retrieved March 1, 2025, from https://ec.europa.eu/commission/presscorner/detail/en/ip_25_614

European Commission. (2025c, February 26). *Omnibus I*. Retrieved March 1, 2025, from https://commission.europa.eu/publications/omnibus-i_en

European Parliament & Council. (2014). Directive 2014/95/EU amending Directive 2013/34/EU as regards disclosure of non-financial and diversity information by certain large undertakings and groups. *Official Journal of the European Union, 330*, 1–9. https://eur-lex.europa.eu/eli/dir/2014/95/oj/eng

European Parliament & Council. (2019). *Regulation (EU) 2019/2088 of 27 November 2019 on sustainability-related disclosures in the financial services sector*. Retrieved from https://eur-lex.europa.eu/legal-content/EN/TXT/PDF/?uri=CELEX:32019R2088

European Parliament & Council. (2020). Regulation (EU) 2020/852 on the establishment of a framework to facilitate sustainable investment and amending Regulation (EU) 2019/2088. *Official Journal of the European Union, 198*, 13–43. https://eur-lex.europa.eu/eli/reg/2020/852/oj/eng

European Parliament & Council. (2022). Directive (EU) 2022/2464 amending Regulation (EU) No 537/2014, Directive 2004/109/EC, Directive 2006/43/EC and Directive 2013/34/EU, as regards corporate sustainability reporting. *Official Journal of the European Union, 322*, 15–80. https://eur-lex.europa.eu/eli/dir/2022/2464/oj/eng

European Parliament & Council. (2024). Directive (EU) 2024/1760 of 13 June 2024 on corporate sustainability due diligence and amending Directive (EU) 2019/1937 and Regulation (EU) 2023/2859. *Official Journal of the European Union, 1760*, 1–40. Retrieved from https://eur-lex.europa.eu/eli/dir/2024/1760/oj

European Parliament & Council. (2025a). Directive (EU) 2025/794 of 14 April 2025 amending Directive (EU) 2022/2464 and Directive (EU) 2024/1760 as regards the dates for the application of certain sustainability reporting and due diligence requirements (Text with EEA relevance). *Official Journal of the European Union*, 16 April 2025. https://eur-lex.europa.eu/eli/dir/2025/794/oj

European Parliament & Council. (2025b). *Sustainability and due diligence: MEPs agree to delay application of new rules* [Press release]. Retrieved April 3, 2025, from https://www.europarl.europa.eu/news/en/press-room/20250331IPR27557/sustainability-and-due-diligence-meps-agree-to-delay-application-of-new-rules

EY. (2023). *European Sustainability Reporting Standards (ESRS)*. Retrieved August 4, 2024, from https://www.ey.com/en_gl/ifrs-technical-resources/european-sustainabilityreporting-standards-esrs-adopted-by-ec

Fijałkowska, J. (2016). Raportowanie informacji niefinansowych zgodnie z nową dyrektywą UE 20142014/95/EU jako wyzwanie dla przedsiębiorstw. *Prace Naukowe Uniwersytetu Ekonomicznego We Wrocławiu*, *436*, 115–122.

G&A Institute. (2021). *Sustainability reporting in focus*. Governance & Accountability Institute. Retrieved June 20, 2023, from https://www.ga-institute.com/2021-sustainability-reporting-in-focus.html.

GRI. (2021). *A Short Introduction to the GRI Standards*. Retrieved August 2, 2024, from https://www.globalreporting.org/media/wtafl4tw/a-short-introduction-to-the-gri-standards.pdf

GRI. (2023). *European Commission signals ESRS alignment with GRI*. Retrieved August 4, 2024, from https://www.globalreporting.org/news/news-center/european-commissionsignals-esrs-alignment-with-gri/

GRI. (n.d.). *GRI – Global Reporting Initiative*. Retrieved May 8, 2023, from https://www.globalreporting.org/

Grzybek, M. (2023). *Raportowanie ESG – czym są ESRS i w jaki sposób rozpocząć ich wdrażanie?* KPMG. Retrieved August 5, 2024, from https://kpmg.com/pl/pl/blogs/home/posts/2023/01/raportowanie-esg-czym-sa-esrs-i-w-jaki-sposob-rozpoczac-ichwdrazanie.html

Hassan, A., Wright, A., & Struthers, J. (2013). Carbon Disclosure Project (CDP) scores and the level of disclosure on climate change related activities: An empirical investigation of the FTSE 100 companies. *International Journal of Sustainable Economy*, *5*(1), 36–52. https://doi.org/10.1504/IJSE.2013.050598

IFRS. (2023a). About the international sustainability standards board. Retrieved August 2, 2024, from https://www.ifrs.org/groups/international-sustainability-standards-board/

IFRS. (2023b). IFRS S1 general requirements. Retrieved July 21, 2024, from https://www.ifrs.org/issued-standards/ifrs-sustainability-standards-navigator/ifrs-s1-general-requirements/

IFRS. (2023c). IFRS S2 climate-related disclosures. Retrieved July 21, 2024, from https://www.ifrs.org/issued-standards/ifrs-sustainability-standards-navigator/ifrs-s2-climate-related-disclosures/

IFRS Foundation. (n.d.-a). *IFRS – International Financial Reporting Standards*. Retrieved July 21, 2024, from https://www.ifrs.org/

IFRS Foundation. (n.d.-b). *Integrated reporting examples database*. Retrieved March 16, 2025, from https://examples.integratedreporting.org/

IIRC. (2017). *Creating value benefits to investors*. Retrieved from https://www.integratedreporting.org/wp-content/uploads/2017/11/CreatingValue_Benefits_to_InvestorsIIRC.pdf

Indyk, M. (2022). Are the companies prepared for sustainability reporting under the ED IFRS S1 and S2? evidence from poland. *Audit Financiar*, *20*(168), 168.

Instrat. (2025, February 26). *Ograniczenie raportowania ESG nie jest dobrym rozwiązaniem dla polskich firm. Pierwsze wnioski po publikacji unijnego Omnibusa*. Retrieved April 5, 2025, from https://instrat.pl/2025/02/26/

International Integrated Reporting Council. (n.d.). *Integrated reporting—home*. Retrieved May 12, 2023, from https://www.integratedreporting.org/

Kitzmueller, M., & Shimshack, J. (2012). Economic perspectives on corporate social responsibility. *Journal of Economic Literature*, *50*(1), 51–84. https://doi.org/10.1257/jel.50.1.51

Kłobukowska, J. (2020). Raportowanie zintegrowane w procesie budowania wartości dla inwestorów na rynku kapitałowym. *Pieniądze i Więź*. Retrieved August 21, 2024, from https://www.p-i-w.edu.pl/piw/article/view/4

Konarzewska, U. (2020). Raportowanie społecznej odpowiedzialności biznesu na polskim rynku kapitałowym. *Marketing I Rynek*, *XXVII*(9), 24–33. https://doi.org/10.33226/1231-7853.2020.9.3

KPMG. (2023a). *Benchmark klimatyczno-środowiskowy. Analiza raportowania zrównoważonego rozwoju*. Retrieved August 20, 2024, from https://kpmg.com/pl/pl/home/insights/2023/06/benchmark-klimatyczno-srodowiskowy-analiza-raportowania-zrownowazonegorozwoju.html

KPMG. (2023b). *Raportowanie ESG – czym są ESRS i w jaki sposób rozpocząć ich wdrażanie?* Retrieved August 20, 2024, from https://kpmg.com/pl/pl/blogs/home/posts/2023/01/raportowanie-esg-czym-sa-esrs-i-wjaki-sposob-rozpoczac-ich-wdrazanie.html

Krzysztofek, A. (2018). Zintegrowane raportowanie na przykładzie spółek Respect Index. *Zarządzanie I Finanse*, *2*, 133–154.

Landau, A., Rochell, J., Klein, C., & Zwergel, B. (2020). Integrated reporting of environmental, social, and governance and financial data: Does the market value integrated reports? *Business Strategy and the Environment*, *29*(4), 1750–1763. https://doi.org/10.1002/bse.2467

Li, D., Huang, M., Ren, S., Chen, X., & Ning, L. (2018). Environmental legitimacy, green innovation, and corporate carbon disclosure: evidence from cdp china 100. *Journal of Business Ethics*, *150*(4), 1089–1104. https://doi.org/10.1007/s10551-016-3187-6

Liang, H., & Renneboog, L. (2017b). On the foundations of corporate social responsibility. *The Journal of Finance*, *72*(2), 853–910. https://doi.org/10.1111/jofi.12487

Lorenc, S., & Kustra, A. (2017). Raportowanie danych niefinansowych w świetle aktualnych zmian ustawy o rachunkowości. *Prace Naukowe Uniwersytetu Ekonomicznego We Wrocławiu, 488*, 99–113.

Łudzińska, K. (2013a). Indeksy zrównoważonego rozwoju a wycena przedsiębiorstw przez rynki kapitałowe. *W A. Szablewski (Red.), Zmienność Rynków a Wartość Przedsiębiorstw*, 239–249. Poltext. 5

Łudzińska, K. (2017). Społeczna odpowiedzialność a wartość przedsiębiorstw na rynku kapitałowym. *Problemy Zarządzania, 15*(1/66), 207–220.

Maruszkin, R. (2021). Czym jest Taksonomia? O nowym prawie UE dotyczącym klasyfikowania działalności gospodarczej jako zrównoważonej środowiskowo. *Biuletyn Euro Info, 7*. PARP. Retrieved July 29, 2023, from https://www.parp.gov.pl/component/content/article/75026:czym-jest-taksonomia-o-nowym-prawie-ue-dotyczacymklasyfikowania-dzialalnosci-gospodarczej-jako-zrownowazonej-srodowiskowo

Matisoff, D. C., Noonan, D. S., & O'Brien, J. J. (2013). Convergence in Environmental Reporting: Assessing the Carbon Disclosure Project. *Business Strategy and the Environment, 22*(5), 285–305. https://doi.org/10.1002/bse.1741

Matuszak, Ł., & Różańska, E. (2017). CSR disclosure in polish-listed companies in the light of directive 2014/95/eu requirements: empirical evidence. *Sustainability, 9*(12), 2304. https://doi.org/10.3390/su9122304

Matuszak, Ł., & Różańska, E. (2021). Towards 2014/95/EU directive com. pliance: The case of Poland. *Sustainability Accounting, Management and Policy Journal, 12*(5), 1052–1076. https://doi.org/10.1108/SAMPJ-02-2020-0042

Matuszak, Ł., Różańska, E., & Macuda, M. (2015). The concept of CSR in accounting theory and practice in Poland: An empirical study. *Zeszyty Teoretyczne Rachunkowości, 84*.

Milewska, A. (2022). Green bonds as an opportunity to rationalise local-government finances/Zielone obligacje jako szansa racjonalizacji finansów samorządowych. *Economic and Regional Studies, 15*(3), 323–333. https://doi.org/10.2478/ers2022-0022

Ministry of Development and Technology of the Republic of Poland. (2023). *Realizacja celów zrównoważonego rozwoju w Polsce. Raport 2023 w ramach programu monitoringu realizacji Agendy 2030*. Retrieved July 14, 2024, from https://www.gov.pl/web/rozwoj-technologia/monitoring-realizacji-agendy-2030

Ministry of Development and Technology of the Republic of Poland. (2025). *Komisja Europejska przedstawiła pierwszy pakiet uproszczeń „Omnibus"—weź udział w konsultacjach ws. Taksonomii UE*. Retrieved April 5, 2025, from https://www.gov.pl/web/rozwoj-technologia/komisja-europejska-przedstawila-pierwszy-pakiet-uproszczen-omnibus–wez-udzial-w-konsultacjach-ws-taksonomii-ue

Ministry of Economy of the Republic of Poland. (2013). *Raportowanie danych pozafinansowych. Przewodnik dla przedsiębiorstw*. Retrieved October 12, 2022, from https://docplayer.pl/1060184-Raportowanie-danychpozafinansowych-przewodnik-dla-przedsiebiorstw.html

Ministry of Finance of the Republic of Poland. (2016). *Regulation of 25 May 2016 amending the regulation on current and periodic information submitted by issuers of securities and on the conditions under which information required under the law of a non-member state is recognized as equivalent* (Journal of Laws 2016, item 860). Retrieved July 29, 2024, from https://isap.sejm.gov.pl/isap.nsf/DocDetails.xsp?id=WDU20160000860

Ministry of Funds and Regional Policy of the Republic of Poland. (2023). *Raportowanie niefinansowe – kluczowy element CSR/RBC*. Retrieved August 3, 2023, from https://www.gov.pl/web/fundusze-regiony/raportowanie-spoleczne

Moroney, R., & Trotman, K. T. (2016). Differences in auditors' materiality assessments when auditing financial statements and sustainability reports. *Contemporary Accounting Research*, *33*(2), 551–575. https://doi.org/10.1111/19113846.12162

National Chamber of Commerce. (2025). *Stanowisko Komitetu KIG ds. ESG w sprawie Pakietu Uproszczeniowego Omnibus*. Krajowa Izba Gospodarcza. Retrieved April 5, 2024, from https://kig.pl/opinia-2/stanowisko-komitetu-kig-ds-esg-w-sprawie-pakietu-uproszczeniowego-omnibus/

Norris, G., & O'Dwyer, B. (2004). Motivating socially responsible decision making: The operation of management controls in a socially responsive organisation. *British Accounting Review*, *36*, 173–196.

Papa, M., Wieczorek-Kosmala, M., & Syty, K. (2023). Does non-financial reporting regulation increase diversity and equal opportunity disclosures? Evidence from Poland. *Zeszyty Teoretyczne Rachunkowości*, *47*(2), 141–160.

Pérez, L., Hunt, V., Samandari, H., Nuttall, R., & Biniek, K. (2022). Does ESG really matter—and why? *McKinsey Quarterly*. Retrieved August 21, 2024, from https://www.mckinsey.com/~/media/mckinsey/businessfunctions/sustainability/ourinsights/doesesgreallymatterandwhy/does-esg-really-matter-and-why-vf.pdf

Pfaff, N., Utermarck, S., Carabia, A., & Altun, O. (2021). *The sustainability disclosure regime of the European Union*. International Capital Market Association. Retrieved from https://www.icmagroup.org/assets/documents/Sustainable-finance/The-Sustainability-Disclosure-Regime-of-the-European-Union-ICMA-September-2021-220921.pdf

Polish ESG Association. (2024). *Przewodnik po ESG dla firm z sektora MŚP*. Retrieved from https://polskiestowarzyszenieesg.pl/wp-content/uploads/Przewodnik-ESG-dla-MSP.pdf

Polish ESG Association. (2025, February 28). *Co zmieni Omnibus? Komentarze ekspertów*. Retrieved April 5, 2025, from https://polskiestowarzyszenieesg.pl/2025/02/28/co-zmieni-omnibus-komentarze-ekspertow/

Remlein, M. (2018). Socially responsible investments in financial statements of Polish public companies. *European Financial and Accounting Journal*, *13*(3), 37–54. https://doi.org/10.18267/j.efaj.213

Reuters. (2025, February 26). *What's inside the EU's 'Simplification Omnibus' on sustainability rules*. https://www.reuters.com/sustainability/whats-inside-eus-simplification-omnibus-sustainability-rules-2025-02-26

Reporting Standards Foundation. (2017). *Standard informacji niefinansowych*. Retrieved August 12, 2023, from https://standardy.org.pl/sin/

Rogowski, W., & Lipski, M. (2022). Znaczenie informacji niefinansowej w świetle wymogów zrównoważonego rozwoju oraz turbulentnego otoczenia. *Kwartalnik Nauk O Przedsiębiorstwie*, *64*(2), 33–44. https://doi.org/10.33119/KNoP.2022.64.2.3

SEC. (2022, 25 May). *Response to climate and ESG risks and opportunities*. SEC press release, Retrieved from https://www.sec.gov/news/statement/peirce-statement-esg-052522

Sejm of the Republic of Poland. (1994). *Ustawa z dnia 29 września 1994 r. o rachunkowości* (Dz.U. 1994 Nr 121, poz. 591 z późn. zm.). https://isap.sejm.gov.pl/isap.nsf/DocDetails.xsp?id=wdu19941210591

Sejm of the Republic of Poland. (2016). *Ustawa z dnia 15 grudnia 2016 r. o zmianie ustawy o rachunkowości* (Journal of Laws 2017, item 61). Retrieved September 2, 2024, from https://isap.sejm.gov.pl/isap.nsf/DocDetails.xsp?id=WDU20170000061

Sejm of the Republic of Poland. (2024). *Act of December 6, 2024, amending the Accounting Act, the Act on Statutory Auditors, Audit Firms, and Public Oversight, and certain other acts*. Journal of Laws, 2024, item 1863. https://isap.sejm.gov.pl/isap.nsf/DocDetails.xsp?id=WDU20240001863

Sikacz, H. (2016). Raportowanie informacji pozafinansowych grup kapitałowych. *Finanse, Rynki Finansowe, Ubezpieczenia*, *4*(82/1), 239–250. https://doi.org/10.18276/frfu.2016.4.82/1-20

Sikacz, H., & Wołczek, P. (2017b). Analiza raportów informacji niefinansowych spółek z RESPECT Index. *Marketing I Rynek*, *11*(CD), 540–552.

Sikacz, H., & Wołczek, P. (2018). Transparentność ujawnianych danych ESG przedsiębiorstw z indeksów giełdowych spółek społecznie odpowiedzialnych z Europy Środkowo-Wschodniej. *Prace Naukowe Uniwersytetu Ekonomicznego We Wrocławiu*, *516*, 64–75.

Sroka, R. (2018). ESG transparency on the polish capital market. Annales. *Etyka W Życiu Gospodarczym*, *21*(2), 55–72.

Sustainable Stock Exchange Initiative. (2025). *ESG Disclosure Guidance Database*. Retrieved March 9, 2025, from https://sseinitiative.org/esg-guidance-database/

Świderska, G. (2007). *Wyzwania Dla Ekspertów Rachunkowości Wobec Nowych Koncepcji Raportowania, Rachunkowość, Wczoraj, Dziś I Jutro*. Stowarzyszenie Księgowych w Polsce.

Szadziewska, A. (2015). Przejrzystość i porównywalność informacji niefinansowych w sprawozdawczości spółek w świetle zmian regulacji unijnych. *Prace Naukowe Uniwersytetu Ekonomicznego We Wrocławiu, 396*, 141–149.

TCFD. (2017). *TCFD recommendations*. Retrieved May 26, 2023, from https://www.fsb-tcfd.org/recommendations/

The Wall Street Journal. (2025, February 12). *Europe is looking to roll back climate accounting rules*. Retrieved from https://www.wsj.com/articles/europe-is-looking-to-roll-back-climate-accounting-rules-32c72856

Threlfall, R., King, A., Shulman, J., & Bartels, W. (2020). *The time has come. The KPMG Survey of Sustainability Reporting 2020*. KPMG International. Retrieved May 8, 2022, from https://assets.kpmg/content/dam/kpmg/xx/pdf/2020/11/the-time-hascome.pdf

Tsang, A., Frost, T., & Cao, H. (2023). Environmental, Social, and Governance (ESG) disclosure: A literature review. *The British Accounting Review*, *55*(1), (Article 1). https://doi.org/10.1016/j.bar.2022.101149

Tylec, A. (2022). ESG reporting framework in Poland – The current and perspectives. *Zeszyty Naukowe. Organizacja I Zarządzanie/Politechnika Śląska, 157*, https://doi.org/10.29119/1641-3466.2022.157.39

UN. (2004). *Who cares wins. Connecting Financial Markets to a Changing World*. Retrieved January 9, 2025, from https://documents1.worldbank.org/curated/fr/444801491483640669/pdf/113850-BRI-IFC-Breif-whocares-PUBLIC.pdf

UNEP. (2013). Frequently asked questions on corporate sustainability reporting. Tackling the big questions around the global corporate sustainability reporting agenda. Retrieved April 9, 2024, from https://wedocs.unep.org/bitstream/handle/20.500.11822/26171/FAQ_Corporate_Sustainability.pdf?sequence=1&isAllowed=y

UNEP. (2025, January 7). *China embarks on a journey of esg disclosure: 2024 progress and focus for 2025*. Retrieved January 25, 2025, from https://www.unepfi.org/industries/banking/china-embarks-on-a-journey-of-esg-disclosure/

Views, S. (2025, April 18). *Seven NGOs file complaint with European Ombudsman against Commission's 'omnibus' proposal*. Retrieved April 18, 2025, from https://www.sustainableviews.com/ngos-launch-complaint-against-eu-omnibus-on-sustainability-reporting-and-due-diligence-rules-60e167a3/

Wiśniewska, J. (2015). Weryfikacja danych pozafinansowych w raportach CSR polskich spółek. *Prace Naukowe Uniwersytetu Ekonomicznego We Wrocławiu, 396*, 159–168.

Wójcik-Jurkiewicz, M. (2020). Raportowanie niefinansowe banków z perspektywy społecznie odpowiedzialnej – przykłady z WIG-ESG. *Zeszyty Teoretyczne Rachunkowości*, *108*(164), 207–228.

Wójcik-Jurkiewicz, M., & Sadowska, B. (2018). Non-financial reporting standards and evaluation of their use illustrated with example of Polish listed companies. *European Journal of Service Management*, *27*(3/2), 539–545.

Wrembel, M. (2025, March 10). *Raportowanie ESG: czy firmy zyskają na zmianach? Pakiet Omnibus może je opóźnić*. Business Insider Polska. Retrieved April 5, 2025, from https://businessinsider.com.pl/prawo/opinie/raportowanie-esg-czy-firmy-zyskaja-na-zmianach-pakiet-omnibus/nrhz81k

WSE. (2021a). *Dobre Praktyki Spółek Notowanych na GPW 2021*. Retrieved September 2, 2024, from https://www.gpw.pl/dobre-praktyki2021

WSE. (2021b). *Wytyczne do raportowania ESG. Przewodnik dla spółek notowanych na GPW*. Retrieved September 2, 2024, from https://www.gpw.pl/pub/GPW/ESG/Wytyczne_do_raportowania_ESG.pdf

WSE. (2022). *Komunikat prasowy z dn. 22.07.2022. Inwestorzy stawiają na ESG*. Retrieved July 23, 2023, from https://www.gpw.pl/aktualnosc?cmn_id=112787&title=Inwestorzy+stawiaj%C4%85+na+ESG

WSE. (2022b). *Wpływ czynników ESG na decyzje inwestycyjne [PDF]*. Retrieved from https://www.gpw.pl/pub/GPW/files/PDF/Raport_badanie_ESG_2022.pdf

WSE. (2023b). *Wytyczne do raportowania ESG Przewodnik dla spółek. Październik 2023*. Retrieved November 14, 2023, from https://www.gpw.pl/pub/GPW/ESG/Wytyczne_do_raportowania_ESG.pdf

Zyznyrska-Dworczak, B. (2016). Rozwój sprawozdawczości niefinansowe a możliwości jej zewnętrznej weryfikacji. *Studia Ekonomiczne. Zeszyty Naukowe Uniwersytetu Ekonomicznego W Katowicach*, *285*, 218–227.

CHAPTER 9

Final Conclusions and Recommendations

Both management theory and practice are in the midst of a transition away from the traditional model based solely on economic efficiency. Attention is now being directed towards integrating environmental, social and corporate governance (ESG) aspects. In this approach, sustainability is not only perceived as a response to urgent ecological and social challenges, but also as a strategic necessity. However, it is widely recognised that actions solely focused on minimising harm are no longer sufficient. It is equally important to transition from sustainable development strategies to more ambitious goals, such as biodiversity, bioregeneration and the restoration of degraded ecological and social systems. However, achieving these goals requires a fundamental change in the current paradigm, which prioritises economic efficiency over the long-term environmental and social consequences. Therefore, including non-financial factors in the analysis of corporate performance is becoming an essential requirement, not merely an option.

Against this backdrop, a new management paradigm is emerging—one in which the traditional focus on maximising profit gives way to the concept of creating value for all stakeholders in economic, social and environmental terms. Despite the growing criticism of the ESG concept, including concerns about its efficiency and potential effect on financial performance, there is a broad scientific consensus regarding the scale and urgency of the challenges facing the modern economy. These challenges include climate change, loss of biodiversity and deepening social inequalities. Recent research indicates

K. Łudzińska, *International ESG Perspectives*,
https://doi.org/10.1007/978-3-032-11666-6_9

that business activity has contributed the most to greenhouse gas emissions in recent decades. According to an analysis by Callahan and Mankin (2025), published in Nature, the 111 largest companies worldwide generated climate damages totalling 28 trillion US dollars. Over half of this amount came from just ten companies in the fossil fuel sector, including Saudi Aramco, Gazprom and Chevron. The authors estimate that Chevron alone is responsible for a global temperature increase of 0.025 °C. These findings confirm the need to revise the current economic model and integrate environmental and social responsibility as permanent elements of business management.

However, companies are not solely responsible for the current state of affairs. Consumers are equally responsible, as their daily purchasing decisions support the very entities identified in Callahan and Mankin's (2025) study. In the context of the free market, which is governed by supply and demand, economic development is inextricably linked to the growing expectations and needs of stakeholders. Since Adam Smith's time, it has been recognised that the market is not free from limitations and failures, one of which is disregarding social and environmental costs. In this context, management that considers all three dimensions of ESG seems a rational and pragmatic response to the need to integrate economic, social and environmental goals.

The conclusions drawn from the numerous studies discussed in this monograph support this hypothesis. The consideration of ESG aspects, as well as the pursuit of sustainable development goals, is becoming increasingly integrated into the core activities of modern markets and organisations. By combining financial goals with social, environmental and governance aspects, businesses become economically viable and socially necessary. Organisations are directing their activities towards ESG areas, not only in response to gradually introduced legislative regulations, but also within their own areas of expertise. This enables them to promote development, demonstrate their achievements, improve management methods and tools, and encourage innovation, with the ultimate goal of maximising economic, social and environmental value in a socially inclusive and environmentally sustainable manner over the long term.

This study provides an overview of the actions and initiatives related to the integration of ESG factors, with a particular focus on the Polish market. Poland is now considered a mature economy and is one of the key member states of the European Union. While the ESG market and non-financial reporting practices in Poland are still in their infancy, they are highly significant for the European financial market. Significant developments in this area include the launch of the RESPECT Index on the Warsaw Stock Exchange—the first ESG index in Central and Eastern Europe—and the introduction of mandatory non-financial reporting guidelines in the form of the EU NFRD directive, followed by the CSRD directive.

In light of the analyses and research findings presented, it is worth emphasising that, although the SRI investment market in Poland is not yet deeply rooted, it has shown significant development since 2009, as evidenced by the launch of the RESPECT Index. The introduction of various local initiatives, such as the Warsaw Stock Exchange's non-financial reporting guidelines and the WIG-ESG index, has further driven its growth. Recent research indicates that the number of companies publishing ESG reports is steadily increasing.

At the same time, the main challenges to the further development of ESG integration in Polish companies, and of ESG investments more broadly, appear to be a low level of awareness of both the challenges of sustainable development and the ESG concept itself. Many market participants do not recognise the full benefits of incorporating ESG factors into organisational activities or socially responsible investing, and are often unfamiliar with the available tools and practices in this area.

Nevertheless, research conducted in Poland indicates an increasing number of initiatives focusing on the theory and practice of ESG actions and investments. These initiatives offer valuable recommendations and highlight potential development pathways for the Polish market in this area. This momentum has its roots in external and internal factors, including European and national regulations and local and international sustainability reporting guidelines. Furthermore, ESG regulations introduced by European institutions are prompting Polish companies to undergo transformational processes and address various barriers and challenges.

As a member state of the European Union and one of its largest markets, Poland is well-positioned to benefit from the ongoing shift towards sustainable development and socially responsible investment. The CSRD directive and mandatory ESRS non-financial reporting standards provide a clear impetus for further development of the ESG market in Poland.

In recent years, the importance of non-financial reporting has grown substantially, establishing itself as a vital component of responsible corporate communication. Companies worldwide, including those in Poland, are increasingly required to disclose information that goes beyond traditional financial metrics. This reporting covers issues related to environmental protection, social responsibility and corporate governance. Many also choose to report such information voluntarily. As expectations from investors, consumers and regulators rise, transparency of non-financial activities has become essential, not just welcomed.

Non-financial reporting provides key information on management practices and the effect that companies' activities have on various stakeholder groups, such as employees, local communities and the natural environment. Despite the numerous challenges involved, such as the lack of uniform standards and the difficulty of measuring and comparing non-financial data, the importance of these reports is constantly growing. Research shows that companies that effectively integrate ESG reporting with traditional financial statements gain market trust, stability and long-term value.

The introduction of uniform international reporting standards, such as the GRI, the IFRS and the new European ESRS, is a step towards standardising non-financial reporting practices. This is a lengthy and complex process that has been developed over many years and is still being refined, as evidenced by the provisions of the EU *Omnibus I* simplification package, which is discussed in Chap. 8. In Poland, as in other EU member states, the implementation of the NFRD and CSRD directives defined the scope and standards of non-financial reporting, initially obliging the largest companies to meet the new requirements. In light of these changes, non-financial reporting is evolving from an additional obligation into a vital strategic management tool that promotes sustainable development and corporate responsibility.

The modern approach to incorporating ESG criteria is becoming increasingly integrated into core business activities, the business model and the company's mission, vision and strategy. Such changes do not happen overnight or within a single year. They represent a process of iterative trial and error, from which conclusions are drawn and improvements implemented. This approach is based on the well-established Deming Cycle model (also known as the PDCA Cycle, or plan-do-check-act), which is a systematic method of achieving continuous process improvement (e.g. Koiesar, 1994; Moen & Norman, 2009; Isniah et al., 2020).

The PDCA Cycle Model (plan–do–check–act), also known as the Deming wheel, inspired the development of a conceptual process model for integrating environmental, social and governance (ESG) aspects into management practices. This model summarises the analyses presented in this study. The PDCA Cycle Model originated in quality management and was inspired by the Japanese work ethic. It is widely used in operational management, but its principles are universal (e.g. Walton, 1988; Anderson, Rungtusanatham & Schroeder, 1994). The Deming Cycle model promotes a culture of continuous improvement by emphasising the need to systematically review plans and actions and evaluate achieved results in order to identify areas requiring improvement. This approach aims not only to achieve the best possible results, but also to ensure the highest possible quality of processes and products by constantly adapting them to changing conditions and needs.

This process is continuous and requires ongoing improvement in line with the principles of Kaizen, a Japanese philosophy and management method focused on continuous, incremental progress (Imai, 1986; Singh & Singh, 2009; Carnerud, Jäca & Bäckström, 2018). Kaizen is based on the idea of systematically improving organisational processes through regular, small changes that do not disrupt the organisation's current functioning. A key element of this method is involving all employees, regardless of their position in the organisational hierarchy, in improvement activities. This inclusive approach enables operational efficiency and quality to be gradually and systematically enhanced. In practice, Kaizen emphasises teamwork and the continuous analysis and improvement of existing processes, offering an alternative to large-scale, one-off organisational reforms.

In this context, the conceptual model of a process approach to ESG, presented in Fig. 9.1, highlights the importance of continuous improvment in sustainability practices and strategies. The model's main objective is to clarify the links between different organisational activities and the organisation's interactions with its internal and external ecosystems in relation to ESG dimensions. The model focuses on the outcomes of actions evaluated through the lens of ESG criteria, taking into account the need for constant improvement to ensure the most effective and impactful results possible. At the same time, the model assumes that these actions are grounded in high standards of management, collaboration, environmental stewardship and work ethics, with active stakeholder involvement. Only under these conditions can economic, social and environmental outcomes be maximised and the evolving ESG concept be effectively aligned with organisational practice and stakeholder expectations and needs.

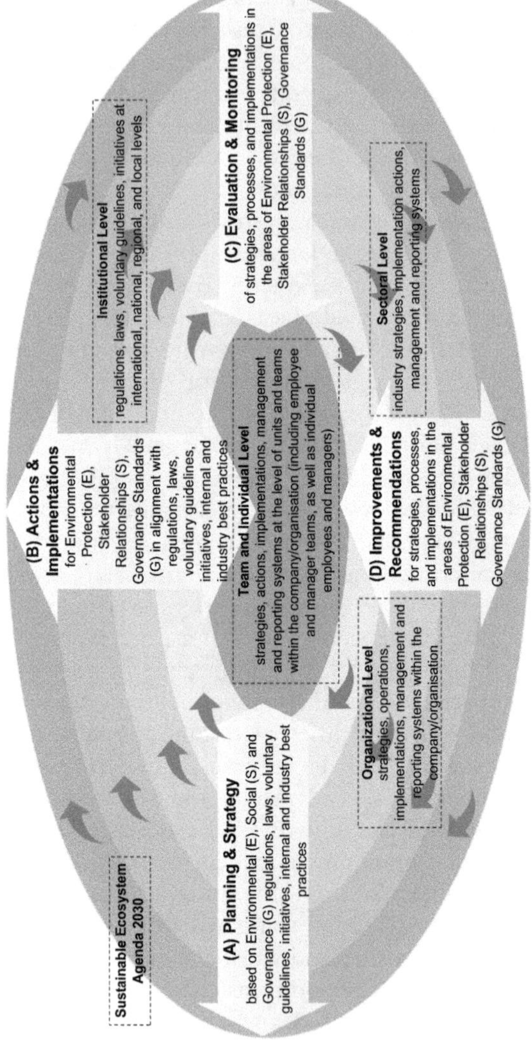

Fig. 9.1 Conceptual model of the process-oriented approach to ESG

The process consists of four main stages (see, Fig. 9.1) and begins with the planning and strategy phase (stage A), during which environmental (E), social (S) and governance (G) regulations, standards and voluntary guidelines are formulated, as well as internal and industry-specific initiatives. The next stage involves actions and implementations that incorporate environmental protection, stakeholder relationships and governance standards in alignment with relevant regulations, voluntary guidelines and initiatives, as well as internal and industry best practices. The third stage (C) is the evaluation and monitoring phase, involving the review and assessment of the implemented strategies, actions and processes related to environmental protection (E), stakeholder relationship management (S) and governance standards (G). The final stage (D) completes the cycle by providing recommendations to improve existing strategies, processes and implementations related to environmental protection (E), stakeholder needs and expectations (S), and management practices (G). Based on the conclusions drawn, improvements can be implemented by planning and developing subsequent actions and strategies, revising existing ones or formulating new proposals, such as regulations, guidelines or future initiatives and activities.

The process-oriented ESG model (Fig. 9.1) encompasses five ecosystem spheres, in which ESG aspects are embedded. The first sphere, viewed from the outside, is sustainable development goals and the 2030 Agenda. Next is the institutional and regulatory environment, at both the international (e.g. within the European Union) and national levels, where various ESG regulations, directives, local laws, voluntary guidelines and international and national initiatives are developed. Next is the sectoral or industry level, where ESG guidelines and regulations account for differences between sectors, which are not treated uniformly due to their specificity and diversity. The subsequent level comprises organisations themselves, along with their internal guidelines and practices for integrating ESG aspects into strategy and operations. The innermost level of the model comprises the teams and individuals within these organisations because ultimately, it is people who create organisations and make all decisions regarding current and future actions, plans and strategies.

Therefore, the ESG process can be implemented at various levels, including individual organisations, value chains, clusters, communities, countries and supranational bodies. At the supranational level, this process may involve introducing sustainable development regulations such as EU directives like the NFRD, CSRD and CSDDD, which have been transposed into national laws. Following an intensive implementation period, particularly for the CSRD, it became apparent that these directives were facing criticism from certain stakeholders. This was particularly the case for companies that were initially required to undertake complex, time-consuming and resource-intensive ESG reporting. These concerns were acknowledged, contributing to a broader review of ESG-related EU regulations. Consequently, an expert-driven debate emerged, resulting in the proposal of the *Omnibus I* simplification package. Its provisions are now set for implementation, with outcomes to be closely monitored. This monitoring will inform future evaluations and guide improvements at both the macro (institutional and regulatory) and micro (individual organisation) levels.

The process approach effectively captures observable practices at international and national levels, as well as those of individual organisations, within the ESG domain. Unlike a project, which has a clearly defined beginning and end, the process approach to ESG is open-ended. While it is possible to identify when the concept of ESG first emerged and when it began to be implemented within a given institution, country or organisation, it is unclear whether and when the consideration of ESG aspects will ever definitively end. Currently, ESG criteria are the only widely accepted framework for evaluating corporate performance in environmental, social and governance areas. Although this framework has its limitations (as discussed in Chap. 2), it remains a useful tool that can continue to evolve and improve.

The theoretical basis of the process-oriented ESG model is rooted in Open Systems Theory (OST), which is a subset of General Systems Theory (GST). GST, often referred to simply as 'systems theory', aims to develop universally applicable concepts, principles and frameworks across a wide range of disciplines (von Bertalanffy, 1975). A core principle of GST is that systems should be understood as integrated wholes rather than merely as the sum of their parts. This reflects the phenomenon of synergy, whereby the whole is greater than the sum of its parts (Whitchurch & Constantine, 2009). Furthermore, since no system exists in isolation, the model integrates the principles of OST, which assumes that systems maintain dynamic equilibrium by exchanging matter, energy and information with their environment (von Bertalanffy, 1950). This approach also promotes synergy, whereby the whole is greater than the sum of its parts. In line with this theory and the acknowledgement that no system operates in isolation, the conceptual model of the process approach to ESG emphasises dynamic equilibrium, which is maintained through continuous resource and information exchange with the environment.

According to systems theory, the five spheres in which ESG aspects are considered function as interpenetrating systems. The largest system, which encompasses all the smaller systems operating within it, is the entire ecosystem of sustainable development and the 2030 Agenda. Each smaller system interacts with every other system included in it. While regulations introduced at the EU and national levels influence the actions of organisations and their stakeholders, these organisations and stakeholders also affect the development of international regulations, national laws and sectoral guidelines.

Although this study aims to present the described phenomena and resulting analyses objectively based on many years of the author's research, it is not without limitations. The most significant of these limitations stem from the subjective selection of source literature and expert reports, as well as from the inherently dynamic nature of the ESG field. The field is constantly changing, often turbulently, driven largely by the unstable geopolitical situation, growing criticism of the ESG concept—especially in the US, as discussed in Chap. 1—and ongoing revisions to ESG regulations, such as those introduced through the *Omnibus I* simplification package. Given these dynamics, it is highly likely that the ESG landscape will continue to evolve, underscoring the need for ongoing research and regular updates to the literature.

Furthermore, the conceptual model of a process-based approach to ESG, presented in Fig. 9.1, is still in the theoretical stage and has not yet been tested in practice. However, applying this model to the actual activities of organisations and shaping their processes could provide valuable insights, particularly when analysing activities across different sectors and within the three dimensions of ESG, both collectively and individually. Such empirical testing would refine the model and contribute to the analysis of relationships between environmental, social and corporate governance aspects within and across different ecosystems.

Based on the conclusions drawn from the theoretical and empirical analyses presented, key recommendations for business practice have been formulated, particularly with regard to the Polish market. Notably, it is recommended that the Warsaw Stock Exchange or other index providers prioritise developing a dedicated ESG index tailored to the Polish context. The experience of the WIG-ESG index shows that the methodology—particularly the selection criteria—is crucial. Inclusion should not be limited to companies already listed in selective base indices (such as WIG20 or WIG40 in the case of WIG-ESG), but should also extend to companies from a broad market index that demonstrate strong environmental, social and governance performance. Preparing a company for inclusion in an ESG index prompts a thorough review of existing management practices and methods. This process engages managers and employees at various levels of the organisation, thereby improving communication and fostering team integration. Consequently, the quality and scope of ESG reporting tends to improve, since inclusion in the index necessitates preparing a report that aligns with sustainability guidelines.

It would be beneficial for all companies in Poland, not just the largest ones, to start incorporating ESG considerations into their operations and publishing non-financial reports in line with recognised guidelines, such as the European ESRS standards, the international GRI standards, or the Warsaw Stock Exchange's non-financial reporting guidelines. This would provide valuable experience and better prepare these companies for the implementation of the CSRD and CSDDD directives, as well as future legislative and reporting requirements. Furthermore, ESG reporting strengthens relationships with stakeholders and builds trust among investors, customers and business partners. Transparency regarding environmental, social and management strategies demonstrates a company's commitment to responsible practices, which can increase its competitiveness in the market. A regular reporting process can also help to identify potential risks and opportunities, which may lead to long-term economic benefits.

The results of the analysed studies on ESG suggest that certain aspects have a greater impact on company performance than others. The use of comparable ESG criteria is particularly important as it helps to eliminate information asymmetry (Cappucci, 2018) and minimise reputational and regulatory risk (Humphrey et al., 2012). ESG assessments increase environmental awareness among managers and encourage the development of higher quality and greater quantity of green innovations within companies (Tan & Zhu, 2022). They also contribute to more effective risk management (Rodriguez-Fernandez, 2016; Wang & Sarkis, 2017; Brooks & Oikonomou, 2018). Therefore, businesses should place particular emphasis on integrating these management aspects into their daily operations to uphold high standards and contribute effectively to achieving sustainable development goals and the 2030 Agenda.

When summarising this monograph, it is important to highlight two key trends that will likely shape the theory and practice of ESG integration at the organisational level and within the broader context of market dynamics in the coming years, particularly in the financial sector. The first of these trends is the growing importance of artificial intelligence (AI) in supporting data analysis, automating decision-making processes and facilitating non-financial reporting. The second is the increasingly vocal crisis surrounding the concept of ESG, encompassing doubts about its effectiveness and criticism of its politicised and elitist nature.

The ability of artificial intelligence to analyse large data sets and learn continuously makes it an indispensable tool for supporting management processes in every company today. AI is increasingly seen as a key factor in improving organisational efficiency, streamlining decision-making processes and reducing operational costs (Iansiti & Lakhani, 2020). AI has become a subject of strategic interest for companies that implement it and actively shape AI research and applications (Davenport & Ronanki, 2018). AI has become a key tool in helping companies to achieve their ESG goals by improving decision-making, enhancing operational efficiency and promoting more sustainable resource use (Burnaev et al., 2023; Mori, 2023).

A growing body of research emphasises the important role of AI in promoting sustainable development. Various AI algorithms are being applied across industries to support the adoption of genuinely sustainable practices (Kar, Choudhary & Singh, 2022). Thanks to its data analysis capabilities, intelligent optimisation algorithms and efficient decision support systems, AI technology shows considerable potential in this area (Luqman et al., 2024). Furthermore, AI facilitates the shift from high-emission energy sources to cleaner alternatives, thereby playing a pivotal role in mitigating greenhouse gas emissions and attaining global climate objectives (Wang et al., 2024). AI also has the potential to improve ESG reporting by enabling more transparent and cognitively useful disclosure of information (Leitner-Hanetseder & Lehner, 2022).

While AI applications have the potential to significantly enhance productivity and operational efficiency, they may also have mixed implications for the social dimension of ESG, particularly in relation to the labour market (Furman & Seamans, 2019). Du and Xie (2021) identify several key ethical challenges related to the development and implementation of AI, including algorithmic bias, ethical design, consumer privacy, cybersecurity, individual autonomy and well-being, and unemployment. They emphasise the need for companies to engage actively in corporate social responsibility (CSR) to guide the development of ethical AI. They also highlight the risk of replacing workers with advanced AI systems, arguing that this issue should be considered in ESG discussions.

Despite the growing link between sustainable development priorities and technological progress in the field of AI, research into the relationship between AI and the ESG concept is limited. In particular, knowledge of the relationship between AI implementation at an organisational level and the ESG results achieved by companies is insufficient. The existing literature primarily focuses on the macroeconomic effects of AI adoption and its impact on sustainable development (Kar, Choudhary & Singh, 2022) and the role of AI in enhancing operational efficiency via digital transformation (Holmström, 2022; Iansiti & Lakhani, 2020). However, little is known about the impact of AI implementation on the achievement of ESG goals at company level.

Understanding the relationship between AI technologies and corporate ESG performance is crucial for assessing how digital innovations can support—or potentially undermine—responsible and sustainable business practices. Closing this research gap will undoubtedly provide valuable insights for institutions, regulators, managers, owners, shareholders and other stakeholders interested in integrating AI with the ESG agenda strategically. Consequently, future research in the ESG field is likely to focus heavily on this intersection.

At the same time, a second significant trend has emerged: a growing crisis of confidence in the concept of ESG. Although more than two decades have passed since its inception and it initially appeared to have secured a lasting position in corporate strategy, legislative frameworks and market practices, its success has proven to be more fragile than anticipated. The apparent consensus surrounding ESG was largely built on the alignment of a relatively narrow group of stakeholders, including regulators, select business leaders, certain academics and sustainability 'evangelists', particularly from non-governmental organisations, as evidenced by the studies analysed in this monograph. These stakeholders' efforts were primarily directed towards establishing a unified approach to the ESG concept, developing assessment criteria for corporate actions in environmental, social and governance dimensions, and standardising progress reporting. However, this often came at the expense of focusing on organisations' actual positive impact: protecting the natural environment, reducing social inequalities and creating genuine opportunities for long-term sustainable development.

Therefore, it is essential to draw on the everyday experiences of organisations and develop forms of cooperation that extend beyond a narrow circle of specialists and experts. This requires engaging with a wide range of stakeholders, including company employees, consumers, market participants and ordinary citizens. Only by meaningfully involving these groups in a dialogue about the values, goals and future direction of ESG development can the concept gain genuine social legitimacy and become firmly embedded in business and economic practice.

Importantly, the effective integration of ESG aspects requires openness and a willingness to engage in dialogue, cooperate and co-create goals and frameworks for action, at both the institutional (international and national) level and within the sectoral, organisational and social dimensions. The ESG concept can only continue to evolve through inclusive and participatory mechanisms developed in line with the principle of continuous, processual improvement. In this way, the current crisis need not mark the end of the ESG concept, but rather a new beginning.

In an era of unprecedented technological advancement and rapid shifts in the economic, political and social landscape, predicting the evolution of corporate actions, standards and regulations related to sustainable development and ESG remains challenging. Nonetheless, ethical, ecological and social values are likely to retain their importance and continue to shape organisational strategies and practices in the years to come.

References

Anderson, J. C., Rungtusanatham, M., & Schroeder, R. G. (1994). A theory of quality management underlying the deming management method. *Academy of Management Review*, *19*(3), 472–509. https://doi.org/10.5465/amr.1994.9412271808

Brooks, C., & Oikonomou, I. (2018). The effects of environmental, social and governance disclosures and performance on firm value: A review of the literature in accounting and finance. *The British Accounting Review*, *50*(1), 1–15. https://doi.org/10.1016/j.bar.2017.11.005

Burnaev, E., Mironov, E., Shpilman, A., Mironenko, M., & Katalevsky, D. (2023). Practical AI Cases for Solving ESG Challenges. *Sustainability*, *15* (17), Article 17. https://doi.org/10.3390/su151712731

Callahan, C. W., & Mankin, J. S. (2025). Carbon majors and the scientific case for climate liability. *Nature*, *640*(8060), 893–901. https://doi.org/10.1038/s41586-025-08751-3

Cappucci, M. (2018). The ESG Integration Paradox. *Journal of Applied Corporate Finance*, *30*(2), 22–28. https://doi.org/10.1111/jacf.12296

Carnerud, D., Jaca, C., & Bäckström, I. (2018). Kaizen and continuous improvement–trends and patterns over 30 years. *The TQM Journal, 30*(4), 371–390.

Davenport, T. H., & Ronanki, R. (2018). Artificial intelligence for the real world. *Harvard Business Review, 96*(1), 108–116.

Du, S., & Xie, C. (2021). Paradoxes of artificial intelligence in consumer markets: Ethical challenges and opportunities. *Journal of Business Research, 129*, 961–974. https://doi.org/10.1016/j.jbusres.2020.08.024

Furman, J., & Seamans, R. (2019). AI and the Economy. *Innovation Policy and the Economy, 19*, 161–191. https://doi.org/10.1086/699936

Holmström, J. (2022). From AI to digital transformation: The AI readiness framework. *Business Horizons, 65*(3), 329–339. https://doi.org/10.1016/j.bushor.2021.03.006

Humphrey, J. E., Lee, D. D., & Shen, Y. (2012). Does it cost to be sustainable? *Journal of Corporate Finance, 18*(3), 626–639. https://doi.org/10.1016/j.jcorpfin.2012.03.002

Iansiti, M., & Lakhani, K. (2020). *Competing in the age of AI: Strategy and leadership when algorithms and networks run the world.* Harvard Business Review Press.

Imai, M. (1986). *Kaizen: The Key to Japan's Competitive Success.* McGraw-Hill Education.

Isniah, S., Purba, H. H., & Debora, F. (2020). Plan do check action (PDCA) method: Literature review and research issues. *Jurnal Sistem Dan Manajemen Industri, 4*(1), 72–81.

Kar, A. K., Choudhary, S. K., & Singh, V. K. (2022). How can artificial intelligence impact sustainability: A systematic literature review. *Journal of Cleaner Production, 376*, 134120. https://doi.org/10.1016/j.jclepro.2022.134120

Koiesar, P. J. (1994). What Deming Told the Japanese in 1950. *Quality Management Journal, 2*(1), 9–24. https://doi.org/10.1080/10686967.1994.11918672

Leitner-Hanetseder, S., & Lehner, O. M. (2022). AI-powered information and Big Data: Current regulations and ways forward in IFRS reporting. *Journal of Applied Accounting Research, 24*(2), 282–298. https://doi.org/10.1108/JAAR-01-2022-0022

Luqman, A., Zhang, Q., Talwar, S., Bhatia, M., & Dhir, A. (2024). Artificial intelligence and corporate carbon neutrality: A qualitative exploration. *Business Strategy and the Environment, 33*(5), 3986–4003. https://doi.org/10.1002/bse.3689

Moen, R., & Norman, C. (2009, September 17). The history of the PDCA cycle. Proceedings of the 7th ANQ Congress, Tokyo 2009. Retrieved February 15, 2025, from https://www.scribd.com/document/665922598/Moen-Norman-2009-PDCA

Mori, M. (2023). AI as a Catalyst for ESG Investing. In Z. Hu, Z. Ye, & M. He (Eds.), *Advances in Artificial Systems for Medicine and Education VI* (pp. 15–24). Springer Nature Switzerland. https://doi.org/10.1007/978-3-031-244681_2

Rodriguez-Fernandez, M. (2016). Social Responsibility and Financial Performance: The Role of Good Corporate Governance. *BRQ Business Research Quarterly, 19*(2), 137–151. https://doi.org/10.1016/j.brq.2015.08.001

Singh, J., & I Singh, H. (2009). Kaizen philosophy: A review of literature. *IUP Journal of Operations Management, 8*(2), 51.

Tan, Y., & Zhu, Z. (2022). The effect of ESG rating events on corporate green innovation in China: The mediating role of financial constraints and managers' environmental awareness. *Technology in Society, 68*, 101906. https://doi.org/10.1016/j.techsoc.2022.101906

von Bertalanffy, L. (1950). The theory of open systems in physics and biology. *Science, 111*(2872), 23–29. https://doi.org/10.1126/science.111.2872.23

von Bertalanffy, L. (1975). General system theory. In B. D. Ruben & J. Y. Kim (Eds.), *General systems theory and human communication* (pp. 6–20). Hayden.

Walton, M. (1988). *The Deming management method: The bestselling classic for quality management.* Penguin.

Wang, Q., Zhang, F., Li, R., & Sun, J. (2024). Does artificial intelligence promote energy transition and curb carbon emissions? The role of trade openness. *Journal of Cleaner Production, 447*, 141298. https://doi.org/10.1016/j.jclepro.2024.141298

Wang, Z., & Sarkis, J. (2017). Corporate social responsibility governance, outcomes, and financial performance. *Journal of Cleaner Production, 162*, 1607–1616. https://doi.org/10.1016/j.jclepro.2017.06.142

Whitchurch, G. G., & Constantine, L. L. (2009). Systems theory. In P. Boss, W. J. Doherty, R. LaRossa, W. R. Schumm, & S. K. Steinmetz (Eds.), *Sourcebook of family theories and methods* (pp. [specific pages if known]). Springer. https://doi.org/10.1007/978-0-387-85764-0_14

Correction to: Non-Financial Reporting: Current Guidelines and Inherent Challenges

Correction to: Chapter 8 in: K. Łudzińska, *International ESG Perspectives*, https://doi.org/10.1007/978-3-032-11666-6_8

Table 8.4 (p. 215): The content in the second column of Table 8.4 was inadvertently published with incorrect details (duplicate of the first column). The table has now been corrected.

Table 8.4 ESRS standard groups

Cross-cutting standards
ESRS 1. General principles The ESRS 1 standard does not include specific indicators; instead, it outlines the overarching principles for applying the ESRS framework and for preparing sustainability reports in accordance with its requirements.

(continued)

The updated version of this chapter can be found at https://doi.org/10.1007/978-3-032-11666-6_8

K. Łudzińska, *International ESG Perspectives*, https://doi.org/10.1007/978-3-032-11666-6_10

Table 8.4 (continued)

Cross-cutting standards		
ESRS 2. Requirements for disclosing general information, strategy, management and materiality assessment The ESRS 2 standard includes a set of mandatory indicators (12 required disclosures), related to general information about the reporting entity, strategy, management, as well as the materiality analysis conducted for the purpose of the report (ESRS introduces a double materiality principle in this respect).		
Sector-independent thematic standards*		
Environment (E)	***Society (S)***	***Corporate Governance (G)***
ESRS E1—Climate Change (9) ESRS E2—Pollution (6) ESRS E3—Water and Marine Resources (5) ESRS E4—Biodiversity and Ecosystems (6) ESRS E5—Resource Utilisation and Circular Economy (6)	ESRS S1—Employment (17) ESRS S2—Employees in the value chain (5) ESRS S3—Social environment (5) ESRS S4—Consumers and end users (5)	ESRS G1—Business Practices (6)

* The number of required disclosures is given in brackets

Source Based on European Commission (2023b), EY (2023), KPMG (2023a, 2023b)

Index

K. Łudzińska, *International ESG Perspectives*,
https://doi.org/10.1007/978-3-032-11666-6

FSC
www.fsc.org
MIX
Papier | Fördert
gute Waldnutzung
FSC® C083411

Kolibri 360 GmbH
Ferdinand-Jühlke-Straße 7
99095 Erfurt, Deutschland
produktsicherheit@kolibri360.de